IMAGES
of America

THE ADIRONDACKS 1830–1930

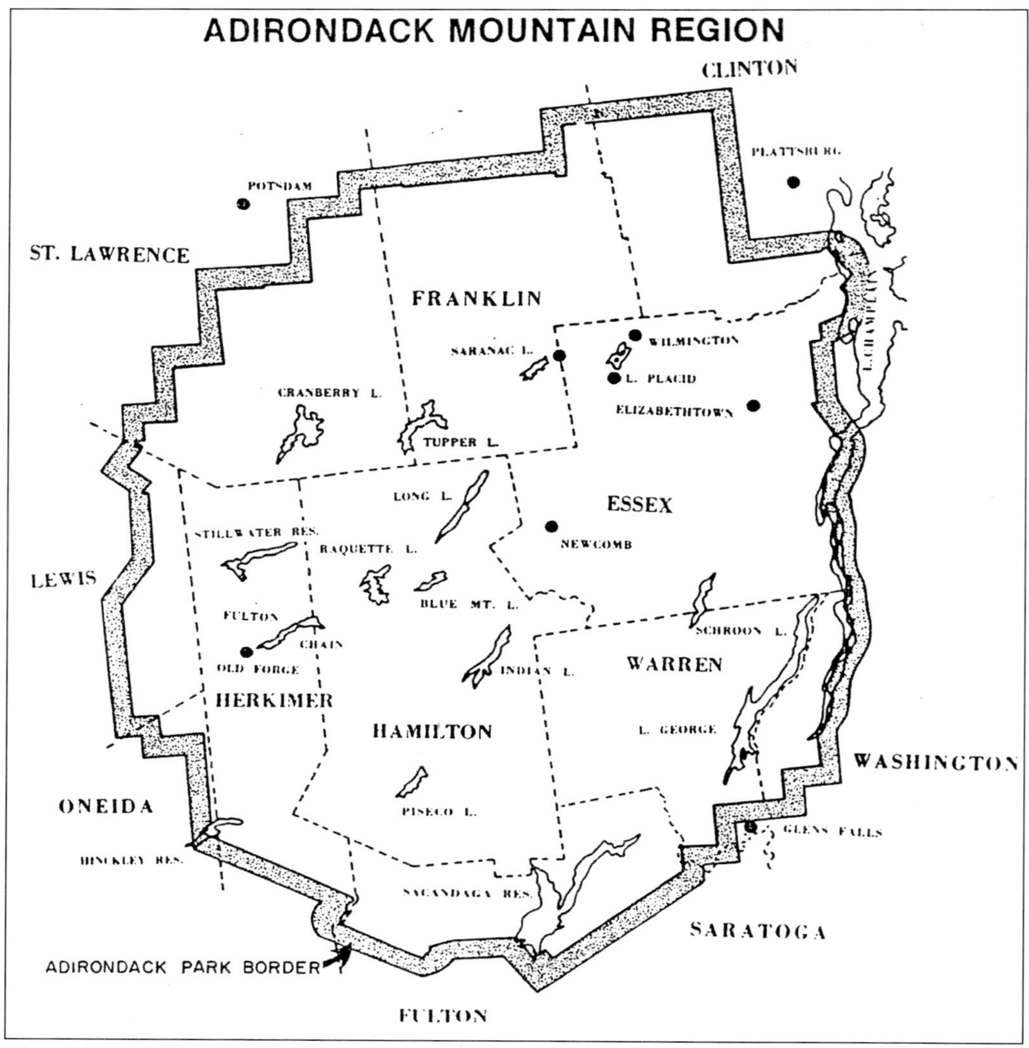

The Adirondack mountain region includes all or part of 12 New York State counties.

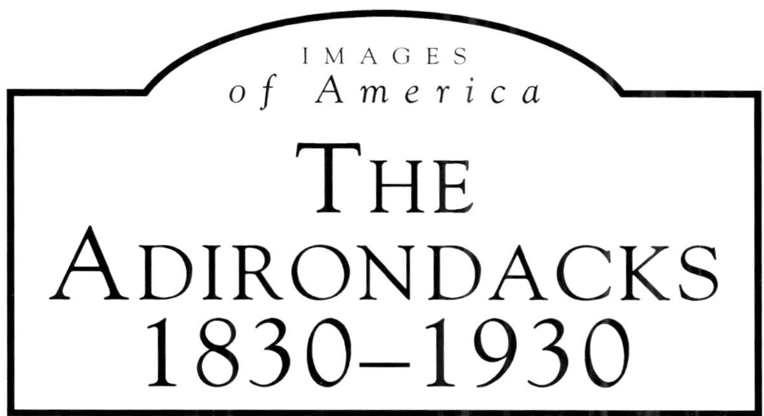

Donald R. Williams

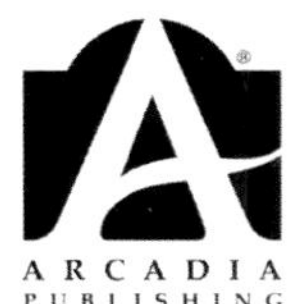

ISBN 978-0-7385-1094-1

Published by Arcadia Publishing
Charleston, South Carolina

Printed in the United States of America

Library of Congress Catalog Card Number: 2002108540

For all general information contact Arcadia Publishing at:
Telephone 843-853-2070
Fax 843-853-0044
E-mail sales@arcadiapublishing.com
For customer service and orders:
Toll-Free 1-888-313-2665

Visit us on the Internet at www.arcadiapublishing.com

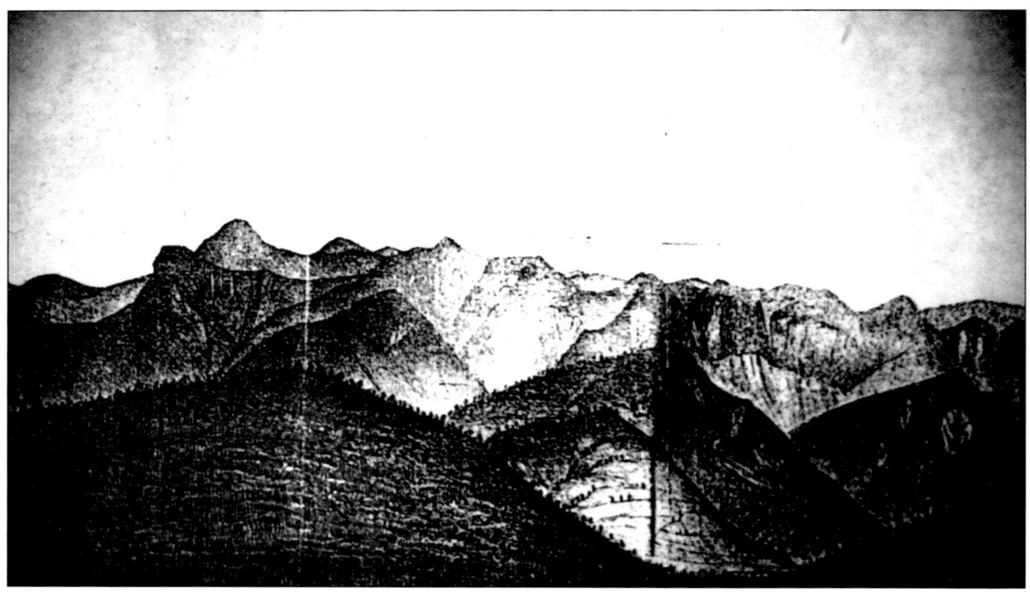

In the summer of 1837, Ebenezer Emmons of Williams College, the New York State geologist-in-chief, made his historic ascent of Mount Marcy, the top of the Adirondacks. He was exploring the natural resources of the wilderness when he made the climb and named the mountains Adirondack Group. Artist Charles Cromwell Ingham joined the group to make sketches of the views and features of the land, which later became Bufford lithographs. The Bufford's lithograph shown here, which may have been drawn by Emmons, became the first sketch of the Adirondack mountain range and was included in New York State Assembly Document No. 200, 1838, the report of Emmons's expedition entitled "Visit to the Mountains of Essex."

Contents

Acknowledgments

All of the photographs in *The Adirondacks: 1830–1930* came from a 50-year collection of Adirondackia. It is only through the sharing of our family, friends, and Adirondack historians, and from those sales, flea markets, auctions, and antiques stores where vintage photographs and documents rise up that we have these connections to the Adirondack past. A sincere thank-you goes out to those who kindly provided me with firsthand stories and rare pictures so I might make them a part of the printed history of New York's great Adirondack country.

—Donald R. Williams

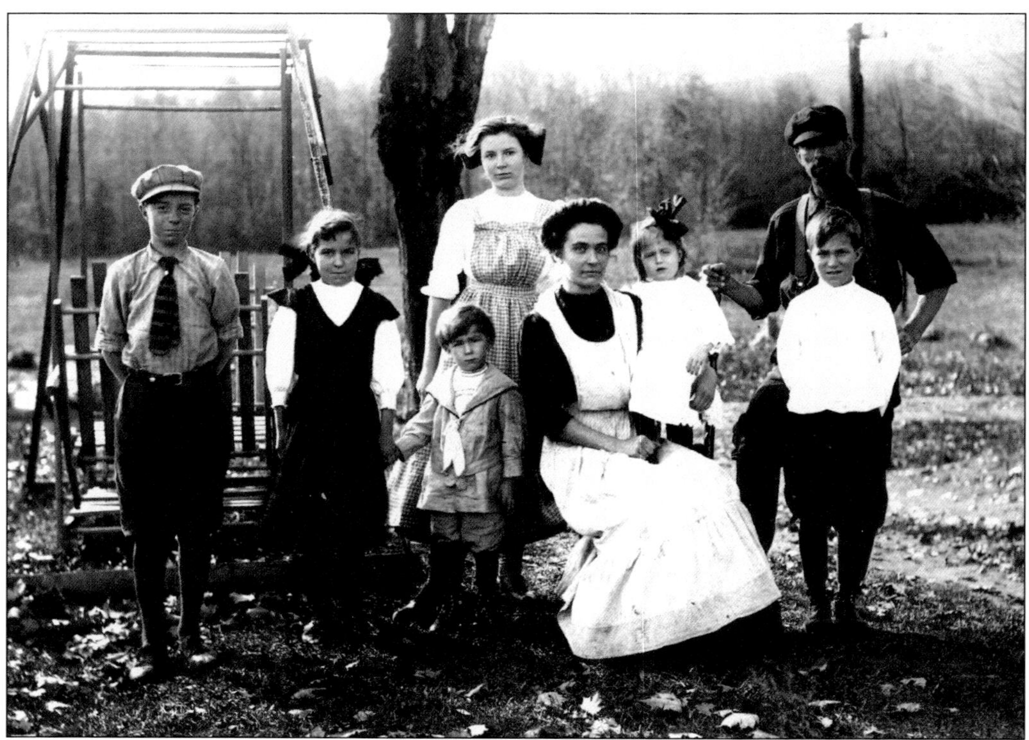

The author is a seventh-generation Adirondacker. His great-great-great-great-grandparents Isaiah and Hannah Whitman came to the southern Adirondacks in the 1790s to open Hamilton County's first tannery. This Whitman family photograph shows the author's grandfather John H. Whitman (right), a well-known Adirondack guide, and his mother, Laura, on grandmother Stella's lap. With them, from left to right, are Arthur, Olive, William, Viola, and Arnold.

INTRODUCTION

The Adirondack region covers the northeastern quarter of New York State, about six million acres of forested mountains and freshwater lakes. The Adirondack Park, which is made up of public and private lands, is the size of Yellowstone, Yosemite, Grand Canyon, Glacier, and Great Smokey Mountain National Parks combined. The Forest Preserve, lands owned by the people of New York State, covers some 2.7 million acres.

The Adirondacks were created by some three billion years of birth and rebirth of geological history. The eventual creation of the forested mountains interspersed with natural and glacial lakes provided a special environment for living creatures. Moose and elk, wolves and fishers, along with 50 or more different species, known and unknown, roamed the endless forest. More than 50 kinds of fish multiplied boundlessly where nourishment flourished in the clean rivers, streams, and lakes. Trees fell and new trees grew. Eagles, osprey, falcons, and more than 200 other creatures of the air claimed their chosen lands in the vast wilderness. Reptiles and amphibians moved about the moist and shaded forest floor.

Some say that early man entered the Adirondack region c. 70,000 years ago. Native Americans were known to make seasonal visits to the remote Adirondack country. Evidence of their hunting and fishing trips has been found in the Champlain Valley, near Seventh Lake, and along streambeds. Shale beds provide evidence of their tools, including arrowheads. Eventually, the trappers, both Native American and European settlers, came to get the big Adirondack beaver hides to trade in the European markets.

The dense wilderness of the Adirondacks became its greatest protection in those early years. Mapmakers recorded the remoteness and vague knowledge of the Adirondack wilds. Early maps called it Couchsachrage Country or beaver-hunting grounds. A 1775 British Colony map noted, "by reason of mountain swamps and drowned lands, [the wilds] are impassable and uninhabited." Guy Johnson's map of 1771 stated, "The boundary of New York, not being closed this part of the Country, shall belong to the Mohawk Indians." William Ritche's state map number seven calls the mountains "uninhabited." Nelson Green in his Mohawk Valley books warned farmers that the Adirondacks were "clothed with dreary forests with a soil that forbids cultivation." John Eddy's 1818 map of New York State summarizes the early thinking: "A wild barren tract extends hereabouts, the property of the State, covered with almost impenetrable bogs, marshes and ponds, and uplands with rocks and evergreens."

Samuel de Champlain became one of the first white men to make his mark on the Adirondacks. In a 1609 skirmish with the Mohawk Indians on the shores of his namesake lake, he opened a wound that set the Iroquois against the French forever. The battle for the furs of the Adirondacks had begun. Prof. Ebenezer Emmons made his exploration of the Adirondacks in 1837 and named the mountains Adirondack. Verplanck Colvin started his 35-year survey of the Adirondack wilderness in 1865. The Reverend John Todd passed through the Adirondacks in 1841 and recorded his findings, too.

The lands of the Adirondacks became the subject of great purchases as speculators saw opportunities to make a fortune. The Jessup brothers acquired lands in today's Hamilton, Essex, and Warren Counties in what was called the Jessup's Purchase or the Totten and Crossfield

Purchase. (Totten and Crossfield, shipwrights, simply lent their names to the purchase.) It took some political maneuvering to make a purchase that was likely to be approved by the Native Americans and the Crown. Alexander Macomb pulled off a four-million-acre purchase of Adirondack lands in 1792. Other names appear in Adirondack land deals, including Palmer's Purchase, Benson Tract, Nobleborough, John Brown Tract, Roaring Brook Tract, and Moose River Tract. Some 11 other lesser purchases were added to the land deals.

Pioneers were found scattered throughout the mountains in the early days, including Sir William Johnson and others who had established fishing lodges in the Adirondacks before the Revolution. William Gilliland had his place in the eastern Adirondacks. Charles Frederick Herreshoff tried the Brown's Tract. In the 1790s, William Wells and Isaiah Whitman came to the southern Adirondacks from Long Island. By the start of the 19th century, serious settlers were finding the Adirondacks in numbers. Andrew Morehouse attempted a settlement in the 1840s. The MacIntrye Iron Mine brought in many of the early settlers. Artists, writers, and sports enthusiasts were attracted to the picturesque mountains. The wealthy found the mountains to be an ideal vacation spot and built their "great camps"—massive camp complexes, most with a huge main building made of logs surrounded by 20 to 70 support buildings. Paul Smith built his first hotel in 1848 and launched the hotel era in the Adirondacks. Eventually, the Adirondack guides evolved to make it possible to open up the entire Adirondack region of New York State.

Three special years should be noted in the saving of the Adirondacks. In 1885, the Forest Preserve was created by the New York State Legislature to keep the state-owned lands as wild forestlands. In 1890, a blue line was drawn on a map to outline the boundary of a proposed Adirondack park, and in 1892, Adirondack Park was legally established. In 1894, the Adirondacks were given their constitutional protection in Article I, Section XIV by the people of New York State: "The lands of the State now owned or hereafter acquired constituting the Forest Preserve as now fixed by law, shall be forever kept as wild forestlands. They shall not be leased, sold, or exchanged, or be taken by any corporation, public or private, nor shall the timber thereon be sold, removed, or destroyed."

The Adirondack region, now under a regional zoning plan maintained by the Adirondack Park Agency, is growing. Settlements, hamlets, and villages have grown throughout the Adirondacks, and many summer tourists are becoming permanent residents. The permanent population is reportedly about 130,000. Thousands of visitors find the Adirondacks each year, and the forested mountains and sparkling lakes are still there to inspire the artists, stimulate the writers, invite the visitors, satisfy the sports enthusiasts, reduce stress, and heal the sick. Enjoy the trip back through the Adirondack years 1830 to 1930, shown here and in the next book, *The Adirondacks: 1831–1990*, and plan to make your own Adirondack history by finding your own Adirondack experience.

One

Water, Mountains, and Woods

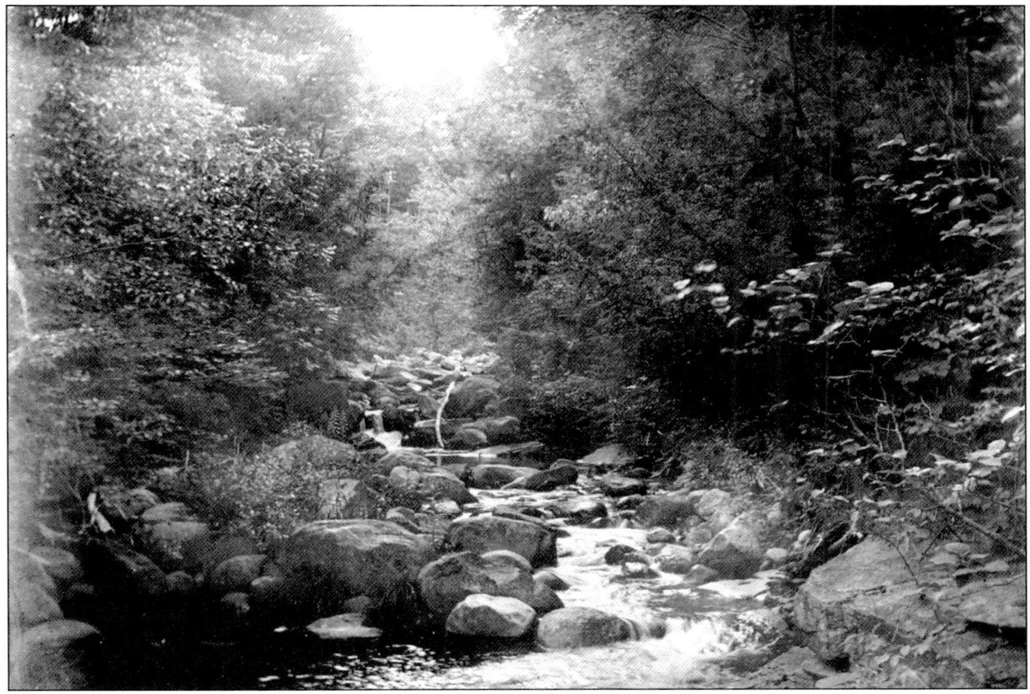

There are reportedly some 30,000 miles of streams and rivers in the Adirondacks. Most are spring fed or outlets of Adirondack lakes. These streams and rivers send their waters to the St. Lawrence, Lake Champlain, Black River, Mohawk River, and the Hudson River basins. Fishermen and those seeking relief from the heat of summer enjoy the recreation provided by the cooling waters. Children find hours of entertainment wading and playing in the Adirondack creeks (pronounced "cricks" in the Adirondacks).

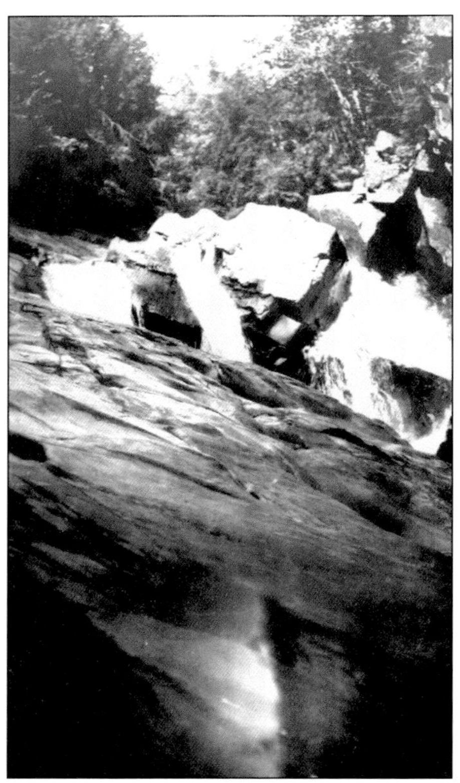

One of the southern Adirondacks' most popular tramps is the short hike to Auger Falls on the Sacandaga River above Wells. On some of the old maps, it was named Olger Falls, and once it was the site of a power dam. The rushing waters of the Sacandaga River have cut a deep crevice and ground out some potholes at the site. Picnickers, fishermen, and photographers can be found at the falls during the hiking season. Snowshoes or skis can be used for a winter hike to see the falls with their icy coverings.

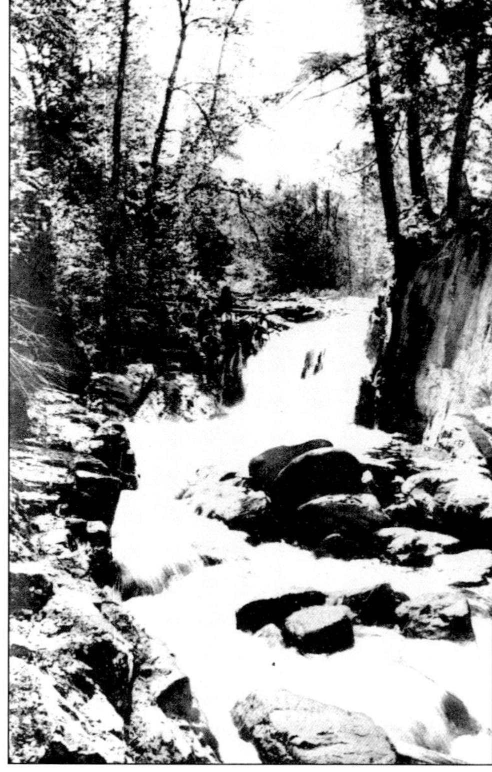

Christine Falls on the Sacandaga River near Speculator was the site of an early power station, which generated electricity from the rushing waters. When electric companies merged and became bigger and bigger, the site was abandoned. In recent years, with the need for more power, the station has been rebuilt, and its power is being added to the existing supply.

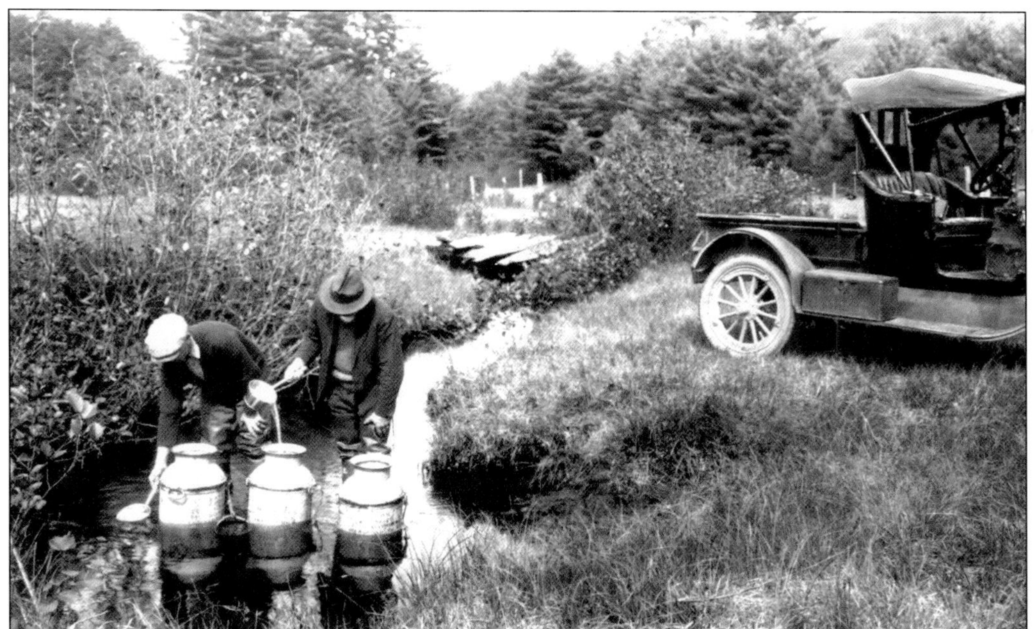

The Adirondacks are noted for their top fishing streams and lakes. Fish stocking was carried out by the New York Conservation Commission in the early 1900s, and it continues to this day. In this conservation department photograph from 1925, the technicians are adding stream water to the 200 fingerlings in each can to equalize the temperatures before releasing them into their Adirondack home.

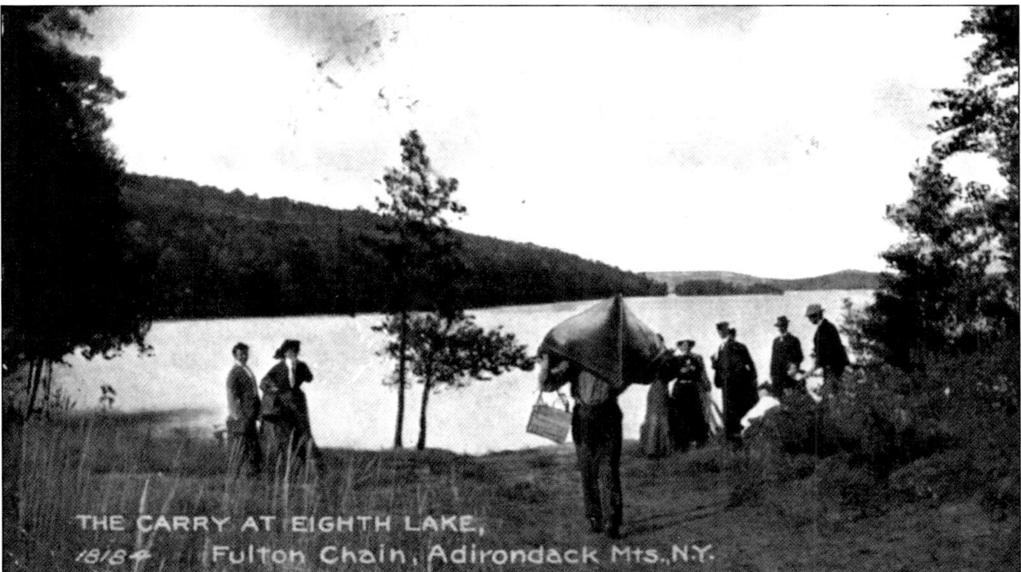

Portages required to get from one waterway to another are known as carries. Guides often had to carry their guide boats and supplies from a lake to a stream or between lakes. The carry between Eighth and Seventh Lakes on the Fulton Chain is just over a mile in length. In this 1907 photograph, note the well-dressed "sports"—as city folk who came to the Adirondacks to camp, hike, hunt, and fish were called—watching the guide carry the load.

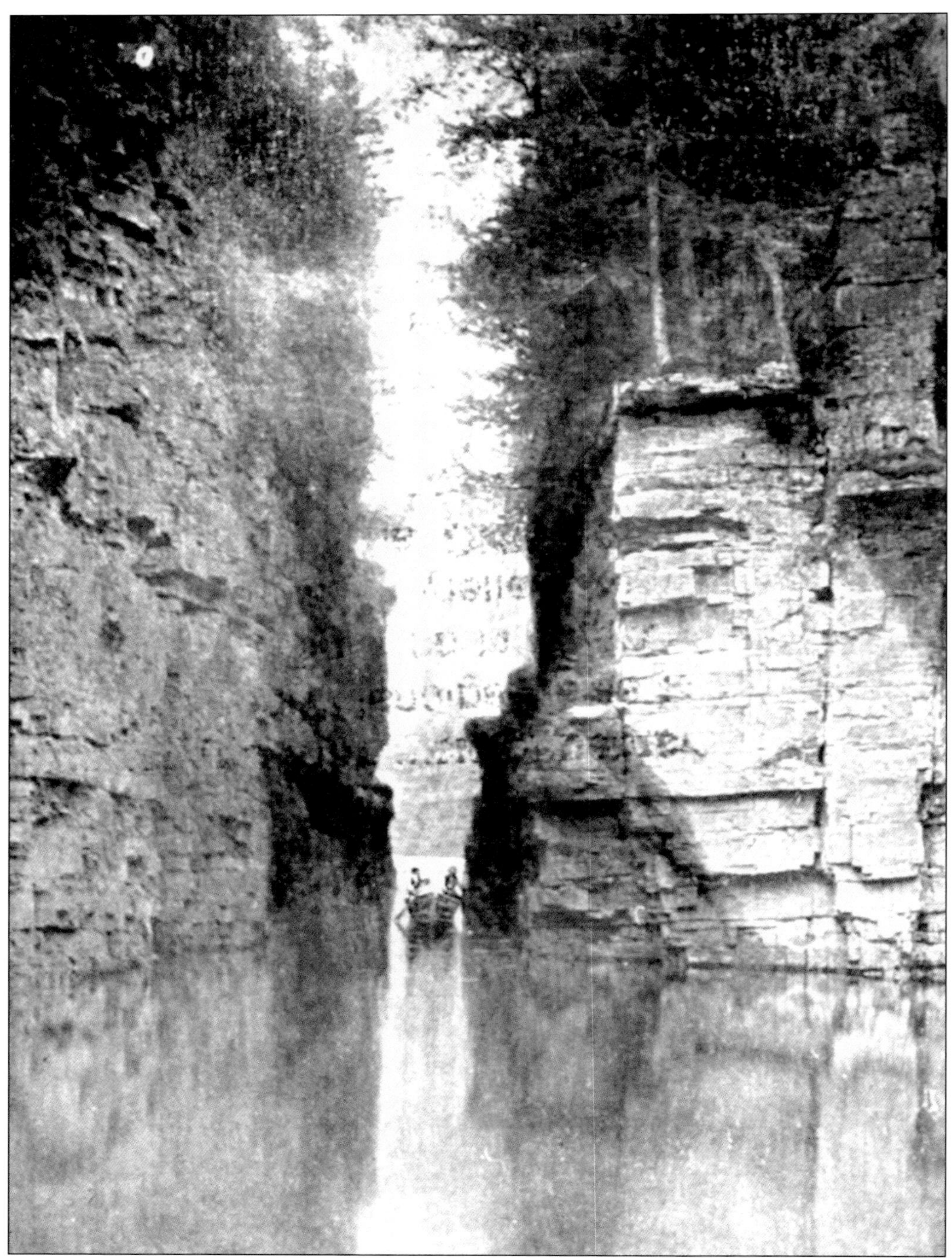

Ausable Chasm is known as the Grand Canyon of the East. Adirondack photographer S.R. Stoddard of Glens Falls produced this postcard of the chasm. One of the original large wooden boats (no longer in use) is shown coming through the Lower Gallery. Wooden boats once took passengers through the flume to view the geological wonders of Ausable Chasm. Rafts are used today.

Ausable Chasm, one of nature's awe-inspiring wonders, has been attracting people to the Adirondack region for more than 130 years. The tour through a two-mile gorge, cut by the Ausable River on its way to Lake Champlain, leads visitors past several natural rock formations. The chasm also can be viewed from 150 feet above the river.

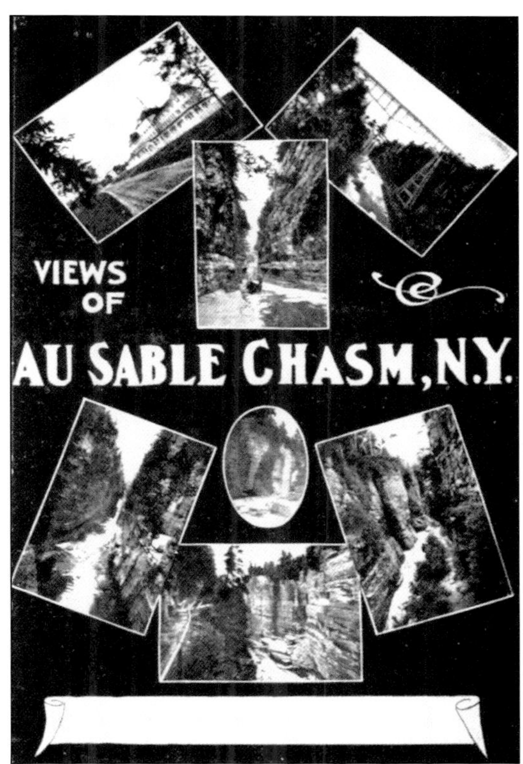

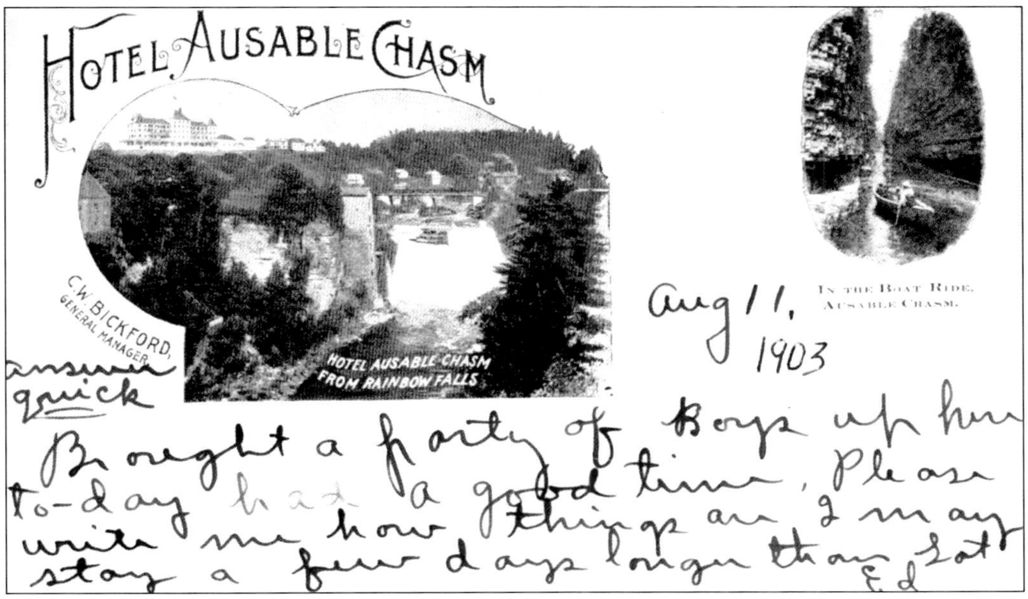

Pioneer landowner William Gilliland visited Ausable Chasm in 1765 and speculated that the "prodigious cleft" was caused by an earthquake. The chasm has remained virtually unchanged since those days because of a power dam that keeps the river in check most of the time and helps to avoid natural river erosion. However, unusual floods have wreaked havoc on occasion, altering the walkways.

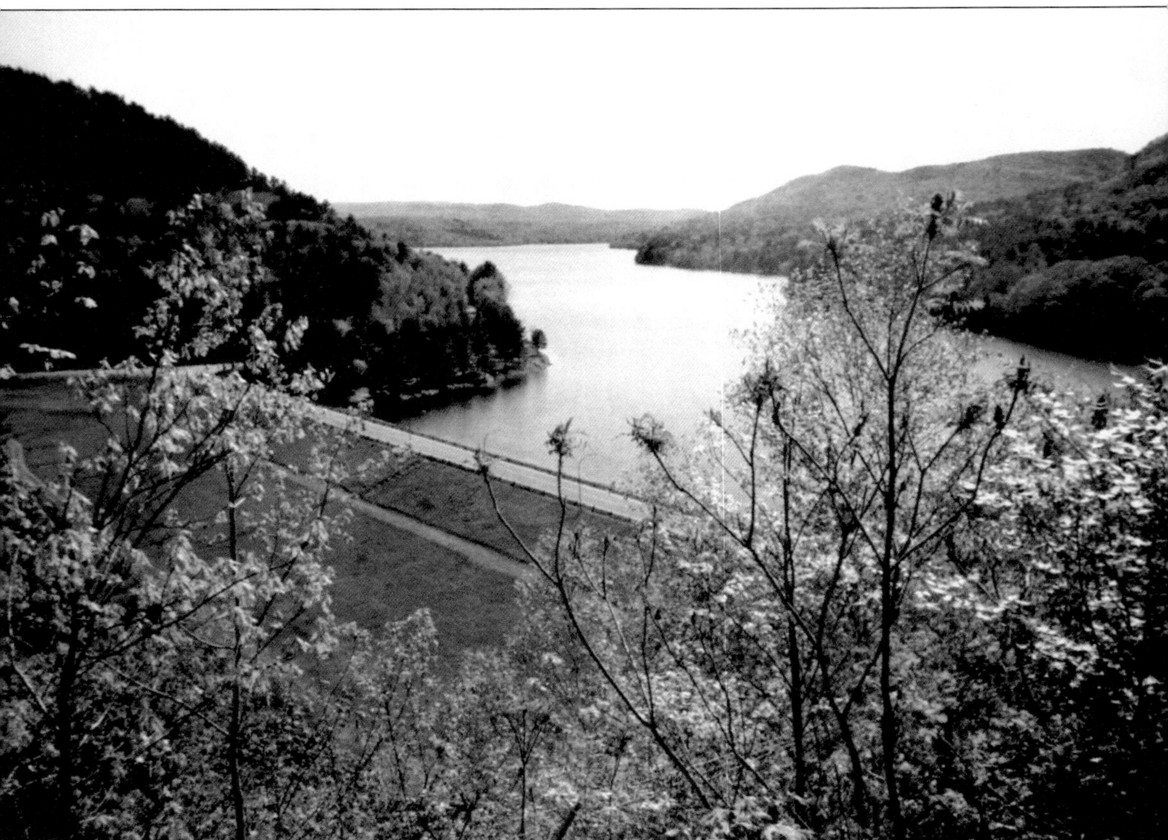

Damming the Adirondacks was a popular activity for many years in New York's mountain region in order to raise lake levels and impound water for power, flood control, and canals. More than 900 Adirondack bodies of water are maintained by dams. However, flooding of forestlands became controversial in later years and dam building ceased. Several proposed dams were not constructed when the state's citizens objected to the flooding of Adirondack lands. When the Sacandaga Reservoir, now the 42-square-mile Great Sacandaga Lake, was proposed in the early 1900s to control the flooding at Albany and downriver and to supply needed power, many opposed it. Sportsmen lost hunting and fishing grounds, some 12 settlements were abandoned, and 22 cemeteries had to be moved. Today, the Great Sacandaga still controls flooding, provides power, and has developed into a popular recreational attraction.

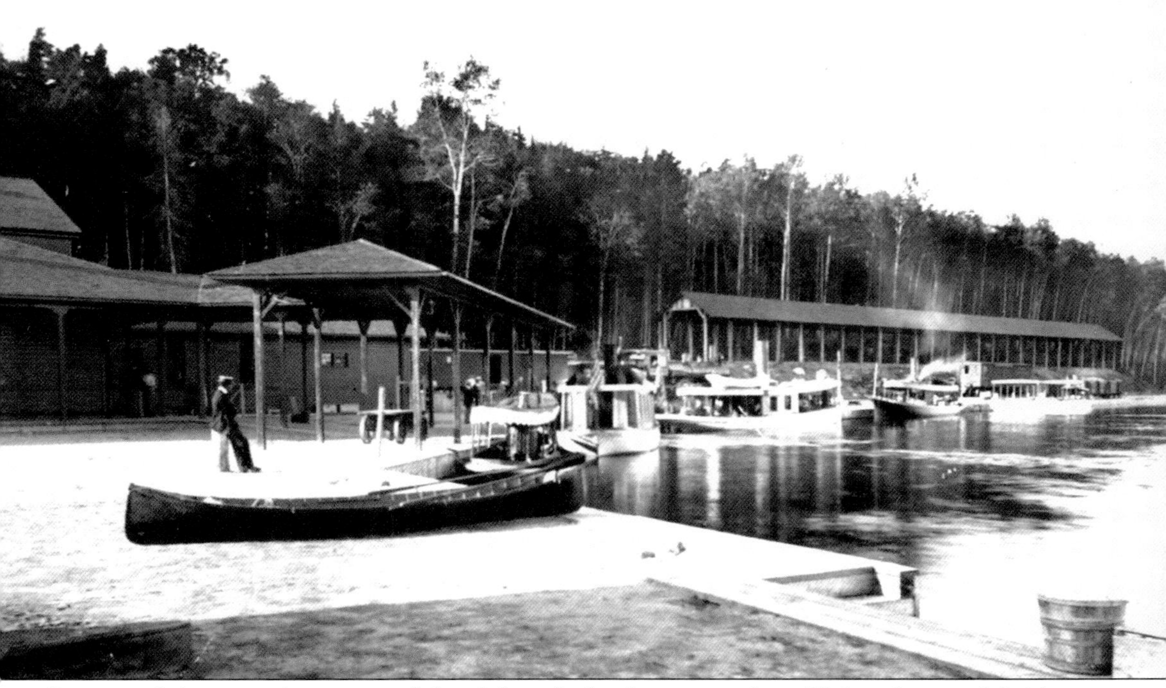

Raquette Lake is in the center of the Adirondacks. It is more than 70 feet deep and fed by clear, cold mountain springs. It has almost a 100-mile shoreline, most of which is surrounded by state-owned land. The settlement at Raquette Lake originated in 1835 and has attracted hundreds ever since. The wealthy Durant family settled in Raquette Lake country, bringing railroads and steamboats with them. A rail line brought visitors to the local station, and the steamboats traversed the lake. The steamboats in this 1910 photograph include the *Sagamore*, the *Killoquah*, and the *Lorna Doone*.

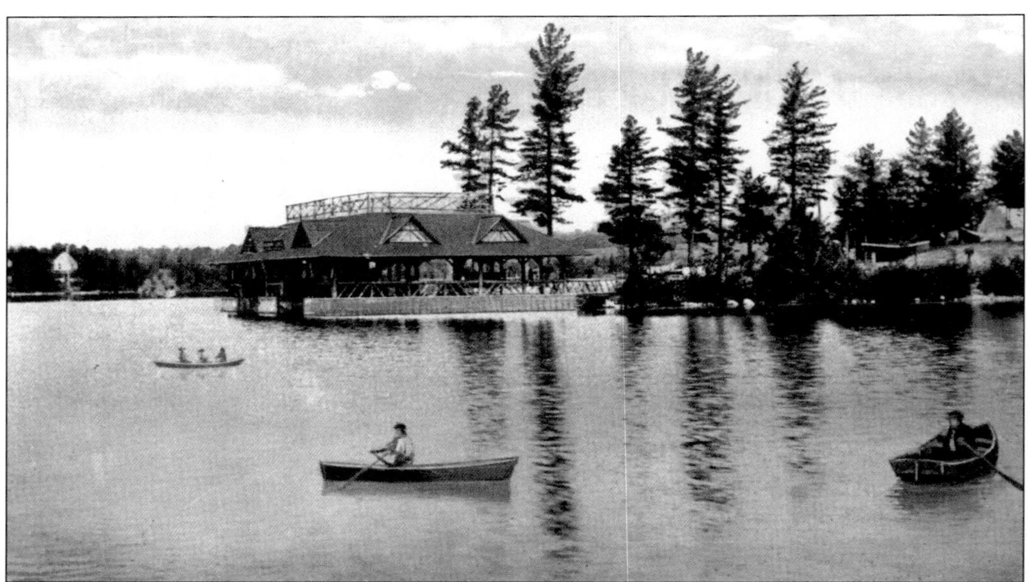

A man by the name of Simonson came from Long Island during the first decade of the 1900s and built this boathouse on a point of East Caroga Lake. He had a star and a cross put on the roof that he could light up each night with a generator—a surprising decoration in a day when most people were still using kerosene lamps. This postcard is postmarked from Knight's store and post office at East Caroga in 1914.

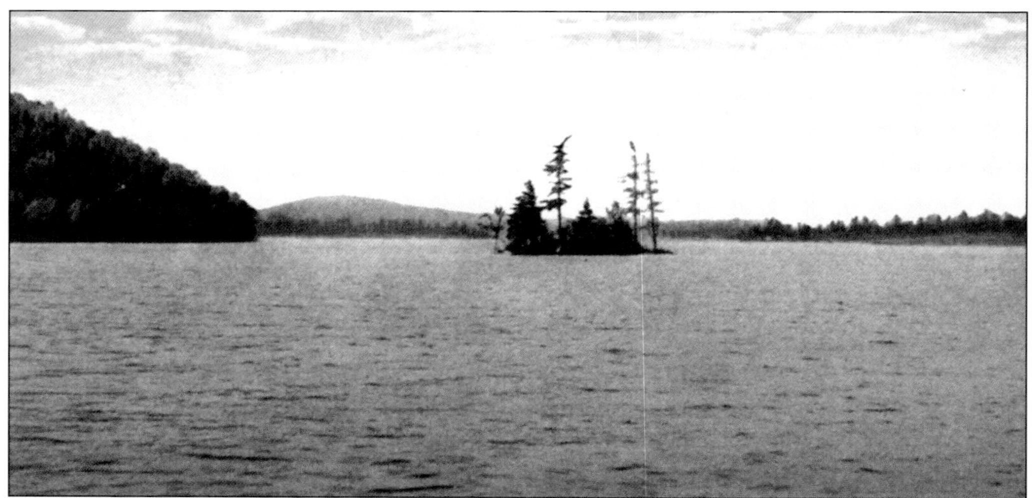

An island in the middle of Canada Lake is named after one of the Adirondacks' first guides, Nicholas Stoner. Oral tradition tells of Nick Stoner swimming underwater to the island, a reckless stunt. Stoner's biographer, Jeptha Simms, also shared a story of Stoner guiding two hunters and capsizing the guide boat near the island. After they spent the night on the island, it became known as Stoner Island.

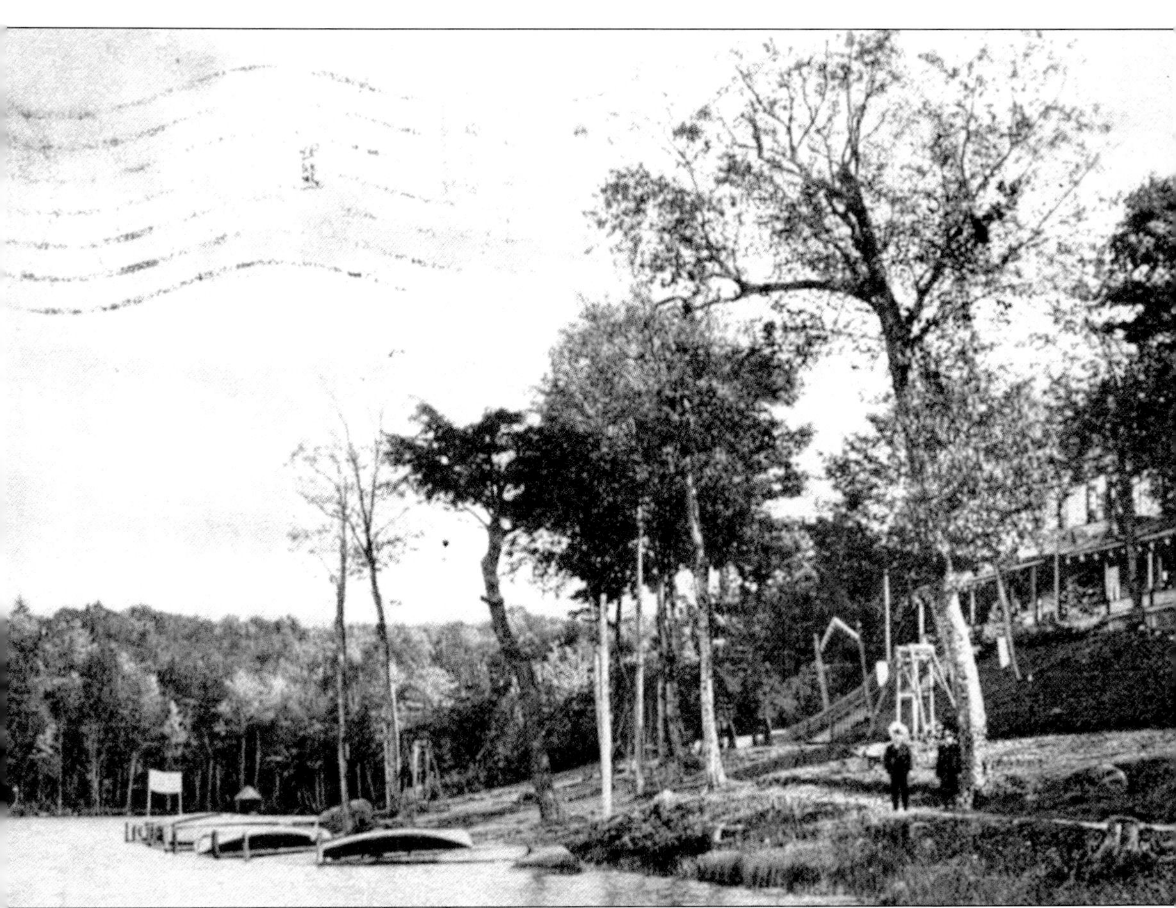

Mountain Lake typifies the summer places found adjacent to populated areas common throughout the Adirondacks. City residents migrated to the lakes and woodlands to escape the summer heat and to find rest and relaxation. Hotels located on the lakeshore, and cabin and cottage colonies sprouted up here and there. An electric railway once ran from the city of Gloversville to Mountain Lake. The railway had a tragic train wreck on July 4, 1902. The wreck was caused by a heavier car, No. 5, overtaking an open car, No. 1, and crashing into the rear of it. It was 10:00 p.m., and passengers were trapped and died in the darkness. A total of 13 people died, and scores more were injured. The line was sold, and it ran for another 15 years after the wreck.

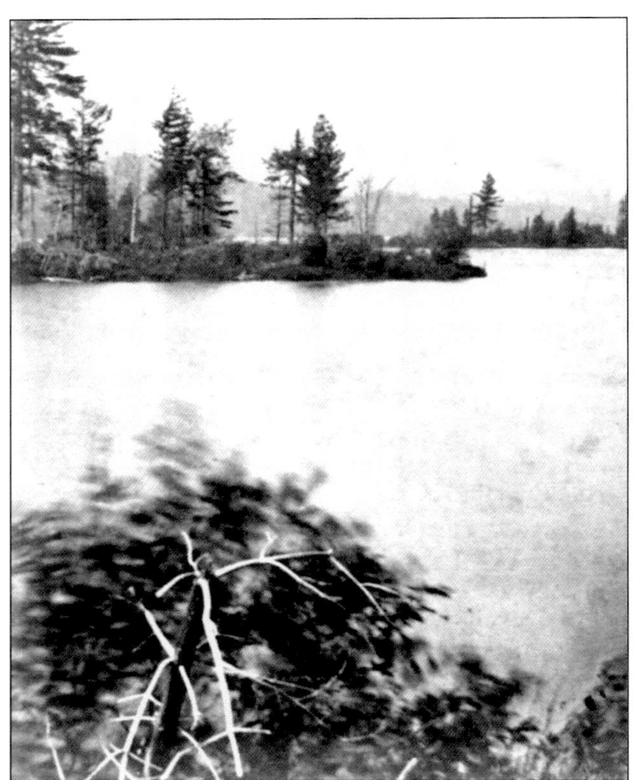

The history of the St. Regis Lakes area goes back to Paul Smith's arrival on the scene in the 1850s. His hotel became world famous, and he made $1 million in the St. Regis region. Upper and Lower St. Regis Lakes, along with Spitfire Lake, form a popular canoe route, which can also be extended to include seven adjoining ponds. The lakes were and are surrounded with the camps of well-known families, including those of New York Herald Tribune editor Whitelaw Reid and diabetes pioneer Graham Lusk, and Topridge, Marjorie Merriweather Post's estate.

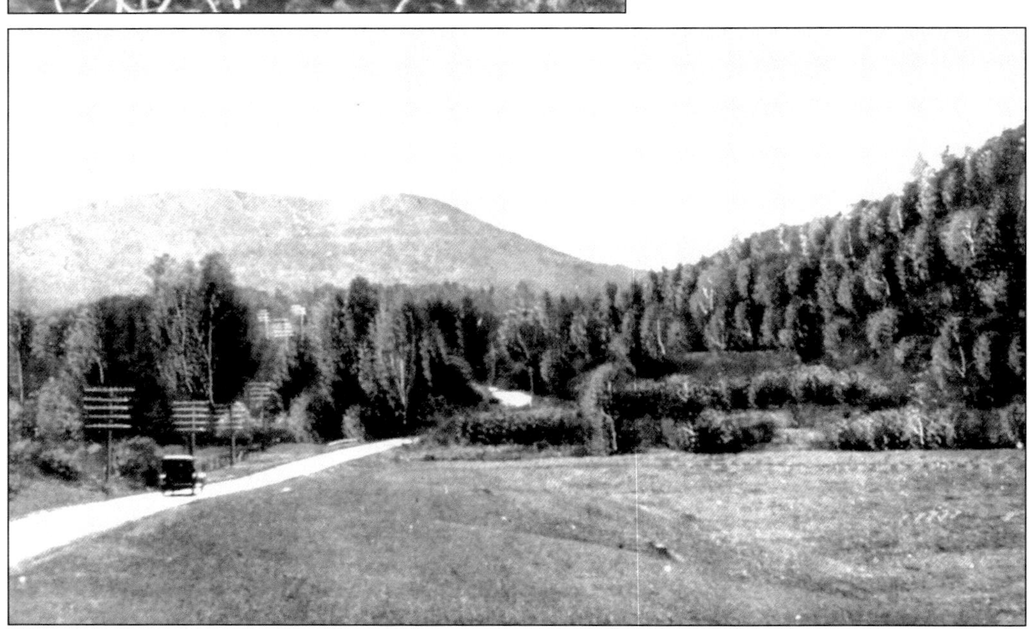

St. Regis, possibly a name that came from Jean Francois Regis, who was canonized in 1737, has been used and reused in Paul Smith country. The name has been attached to St. Regis Mountain, Upper and Lower St. Regis Rivers, St. Regis Pond, Upper and Lower St. Regis Lakes, Regis Church, St. Regis Falls, and the small settlement of St. Regis.

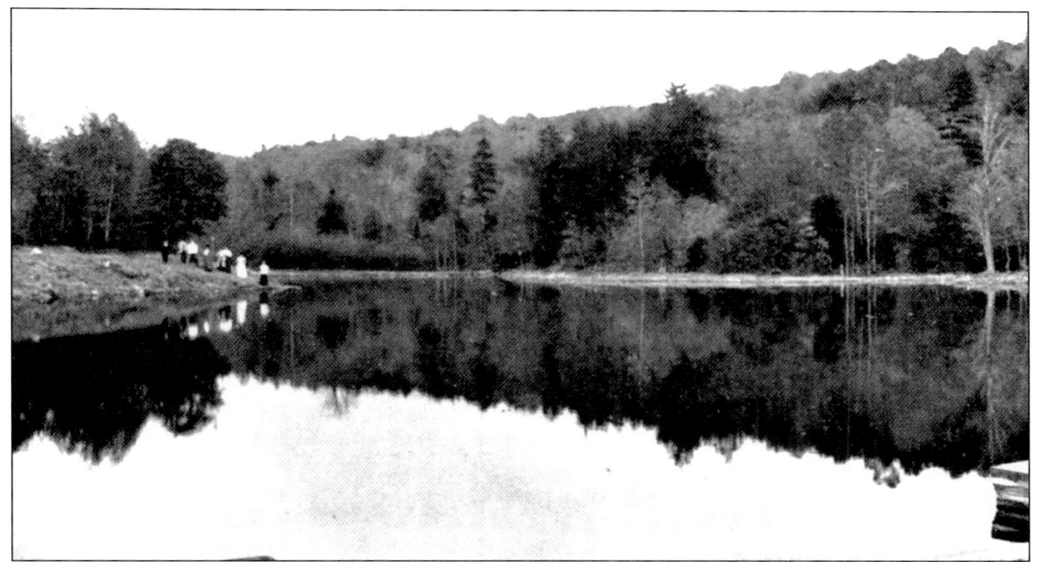

Water for public consumption is plentiful in the Adirondacks, and most communities have an established reservoir to serve their citizens. The grounds of the reservoir properties became parklike by including acreage for tree plantations. Shown in this 1908 photograph is a group of visitors enjoying a trip to the Northville Reservoir.

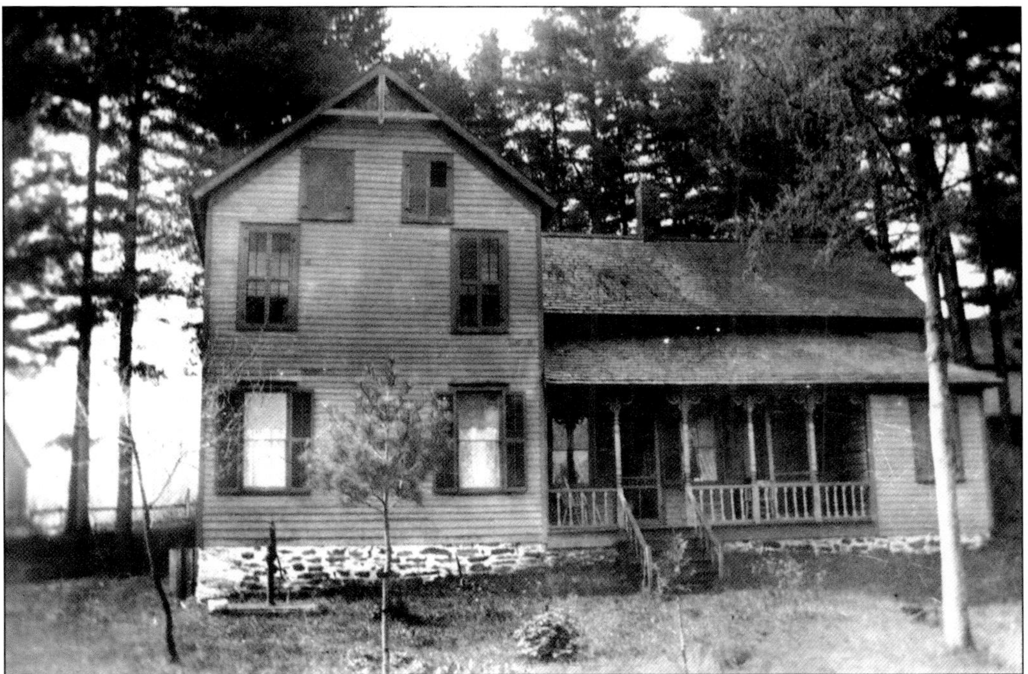

The Whitman family home in the hamlet of Wells served four generations before a surprise flood of the Sacandaga River and man-made Lake Algonquin overran their banks in December 1949. Family heirlooms were washed downriver only to be destroyed or confiscated by scavengers. Quilts and other knit goods from the 1800s made by town weaver Emma Whitman were lost in the flood.

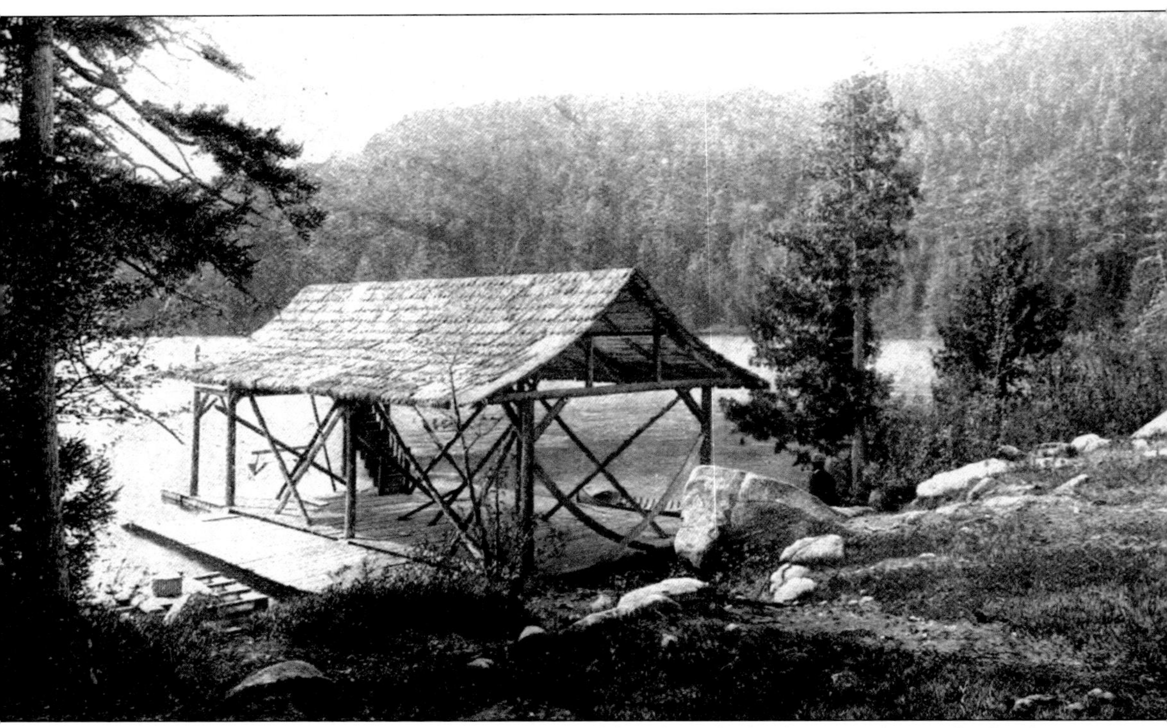

The plethora of boathouses that appear in old Adirondack photographs might lead one to believe that no two boathouses were alike. This rustic boathouse was on Lower Saranac Lake and fits well into the Adirondack environment. The stairway on the front leads to an upper observation deck. Note the Adirondack guide boat moored at the boathouse.

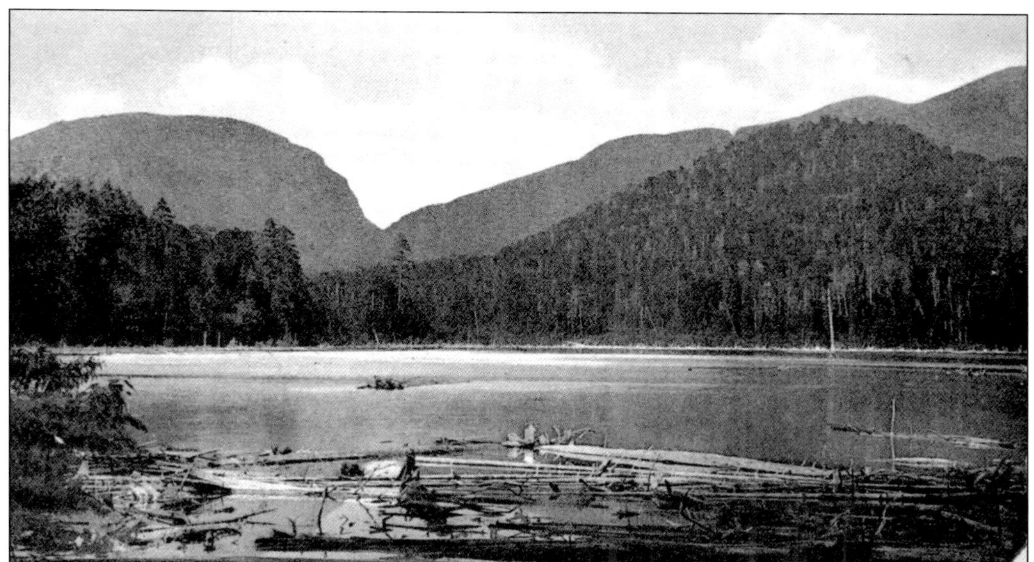

Indian Pass, or the Great Adirondack Pass, was the subject of one of the earliest paintings of the Adirondacks. Charles C. Ingham visited the pass in 1838 and recorded the huge 70-foot-high rocks that had fallen from Wallface Mountain and Mount McIntryre. One rock towers more than 1,000 feet and has attracted other artists, who made the trek through the mountains to paint the pass. The pass, once a Native American trail, was visited by many Adirondack writers, including Alfred B. Street, J.T. Headley, and Nathaniel Sylvester. All who wrote about the pass praised its uniqueness in eloquent prose, such as "sublimely grand beyond description."

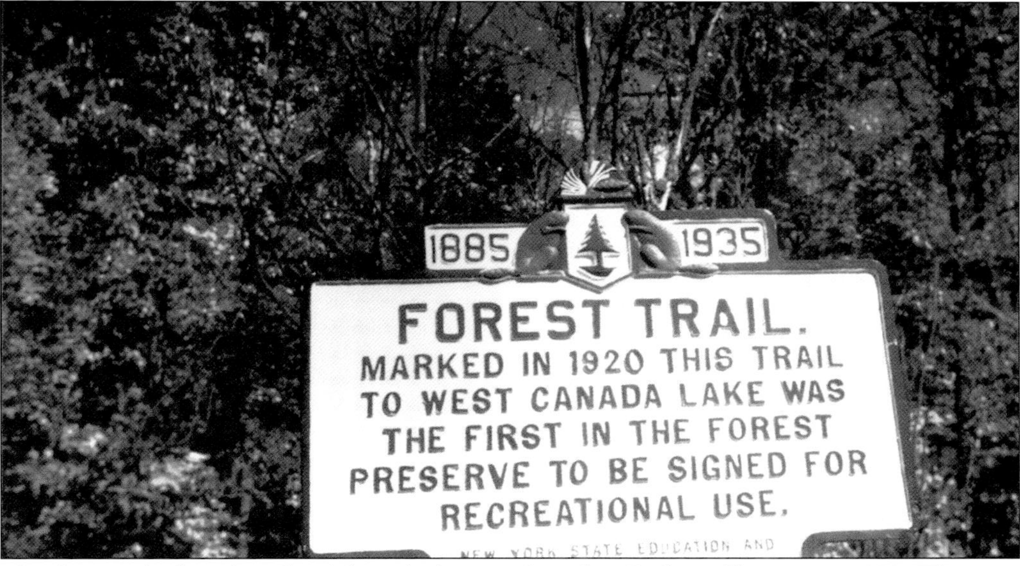

The first marked trail in the Adirondacks was cleared in Perkins Clearing in 1920. The state marker was placed on the site on the 50th Anniversary of the Forest Preserve. Interestingly, one book about state markers notes "there are no state markers in Hamilton County." That author must have missed a good hike into the woods to see the first trail marker. Adirondack trails are marked with small red, blue, or yellow disks fastened to the trees to keep hikers from getting lost in the vast wilderness; it pays to stick to the trails.

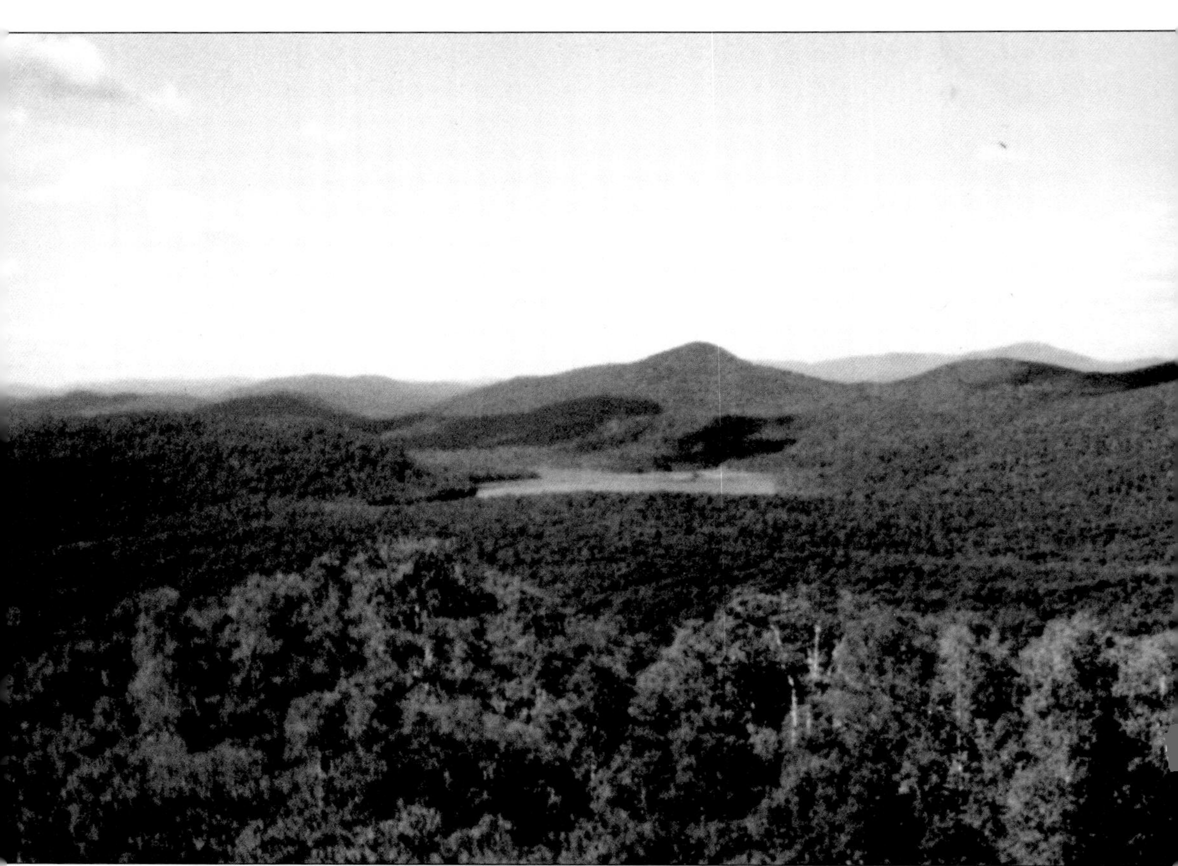

The view from the top of the Adirondacks is like an endless green ocean. Chimney Mountain, near Indian Lake, provides a view of the extensive wilderness of the forested mountains. Little can be seen in this photograph of anything man-made. Almost half of the Adirondack lands are owned by the state of New York and are protected forever from cutting and the building of

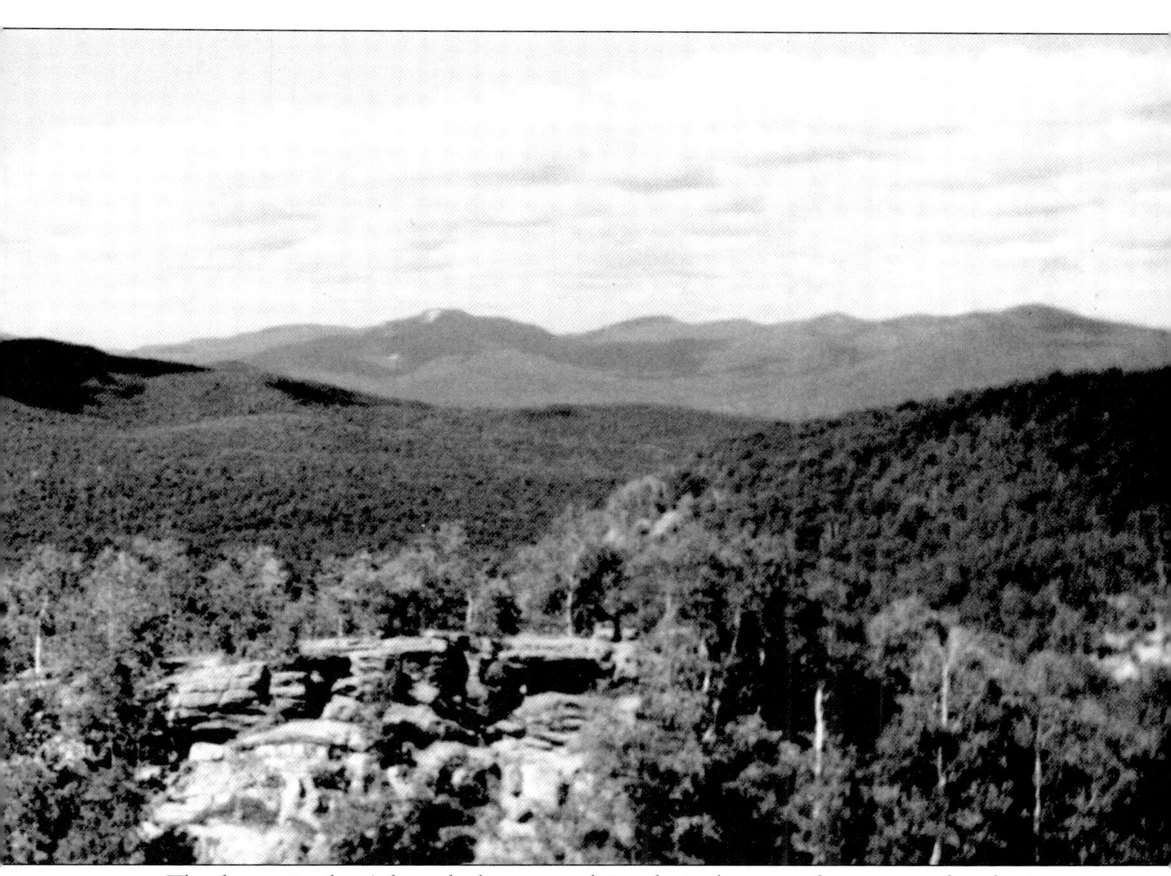

structures. The forests in the Adirondacks are reaching their climax and are covered with giant trees such as maples and white pines. Spruce, firs, beeches, and birches add to the canopy of the Adirondack forest.

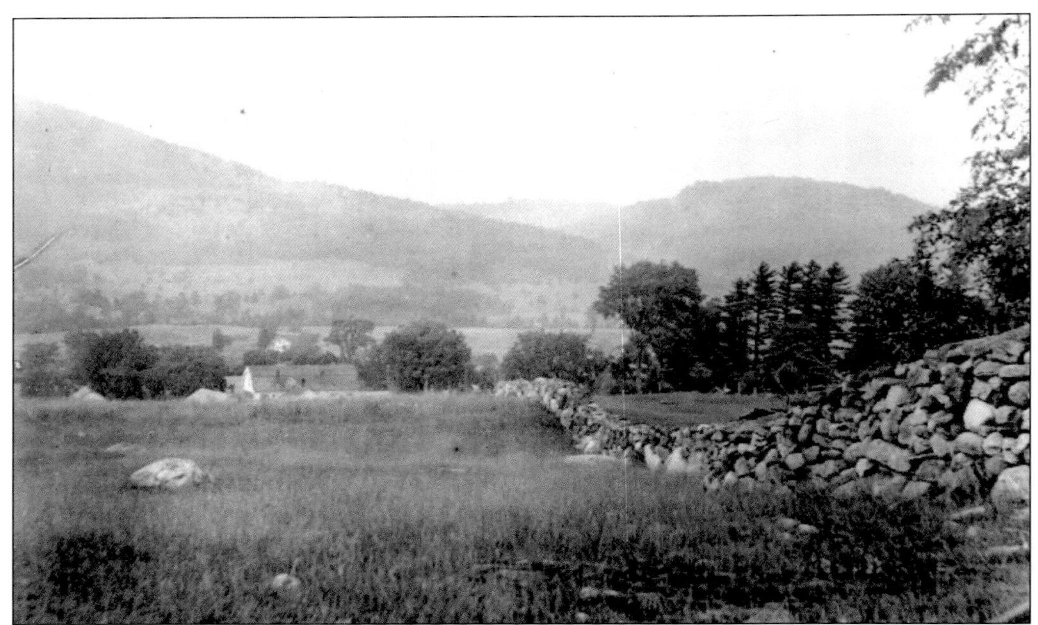

Those who traverse the Adirondack woodlands often find long stone fences ambling throughout the woods. When the early settlers cleared the lands for farming, they built the sturdy fences to confine the animals and to define boundaries. It was a labor intensive job to pick the rocks, carry them to the fence line, lay up two outside rows with a center row, and to build it high enough to keep the animals in. When farming failed, the farmlands were returned to the wilderness and the trees grew up around the old rock fences.

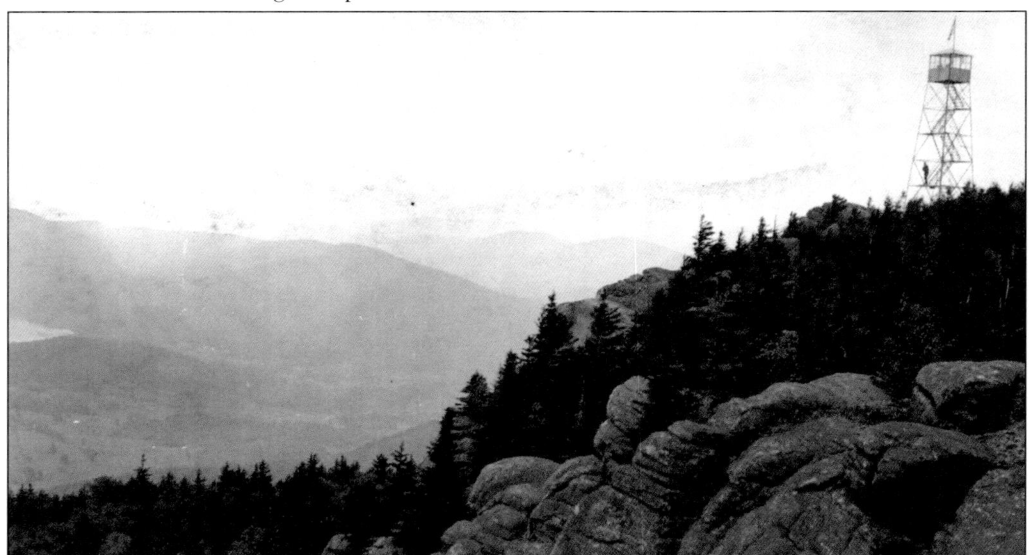

At one time, there were 57 fire towers in the Adirondacks, which were manned by seasonal observers who watched for smoke that indicated a forest fire was starting. Due to the "forever wild" constitutional protection and the surveillance of fires from airplanes, most towers have been removed. "Friends" of the towers have organized to save some of these structures for historical and recreational uses.

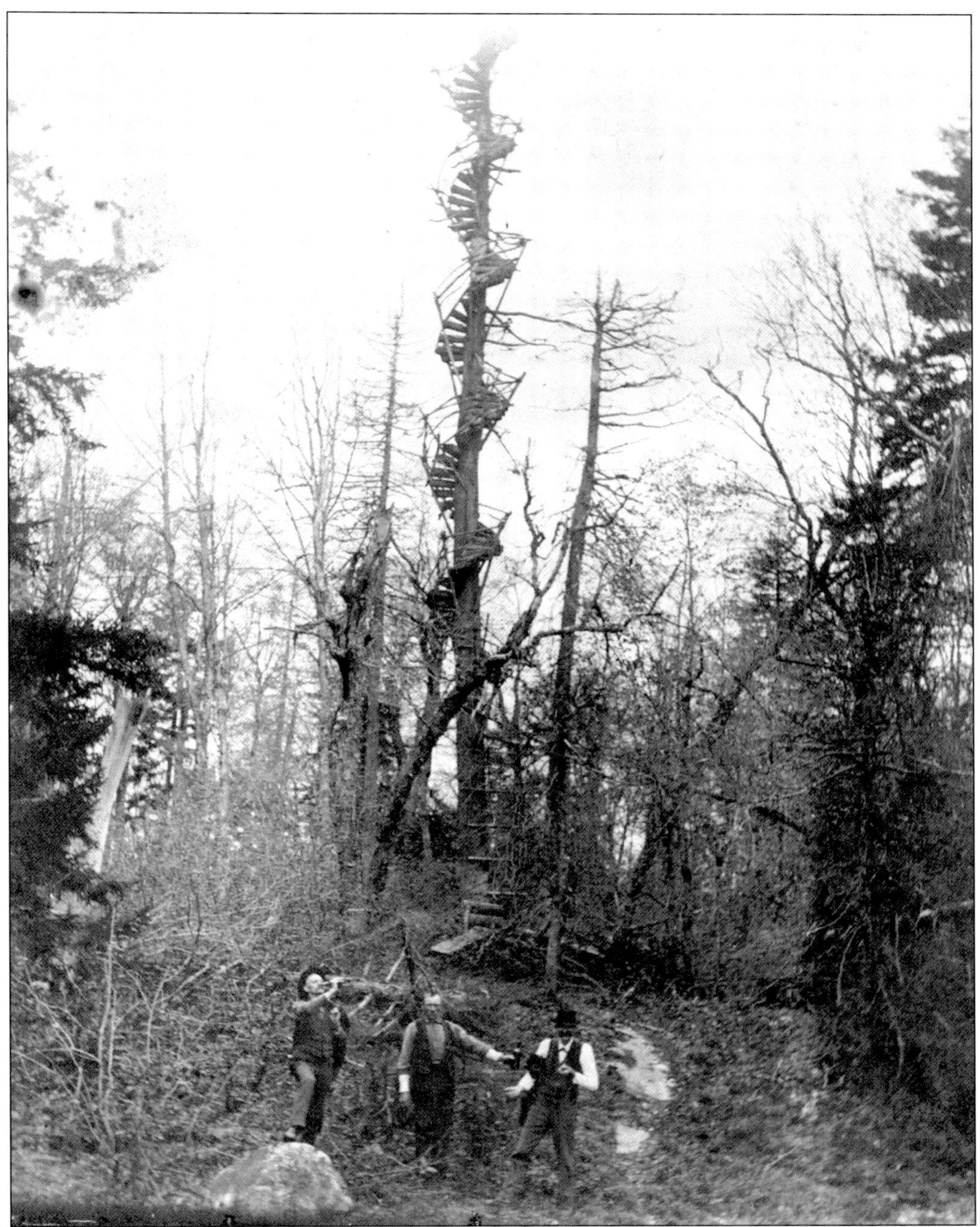

Before the days of the steel fire towers, trees, outcroppings of rock, and wooden platforms served the observers who watched for smoke in the dry woodlands of the Adirondacks. The spiral staircase built around this tree was reportedly once on the top of Tomany Mountain in Arietta. Today, the steel fire tower that was placed on the mountain and the ranger's cabin have been removed, and the trail up Tomany has been abandoned.

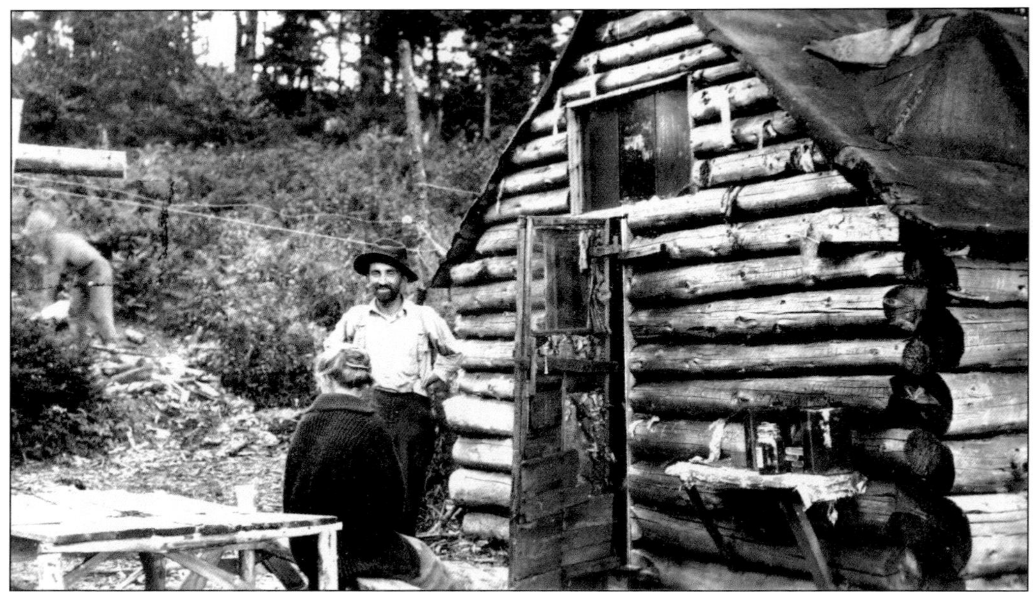

Each of the fire towers on the Adirondack mountaintops had a cabin for the ranger's use. It was a lonely job, and the observers put in long hours during the fire season. They faced hunger, lack of water, wild animals, lightning storms, and the danger of having a serious accident while alone on duty. This 1919 photograph of a ranger's camp was taken on the top of Snowy Mountain, the highest peak in the southern Adirondacks, near Indian Lake.

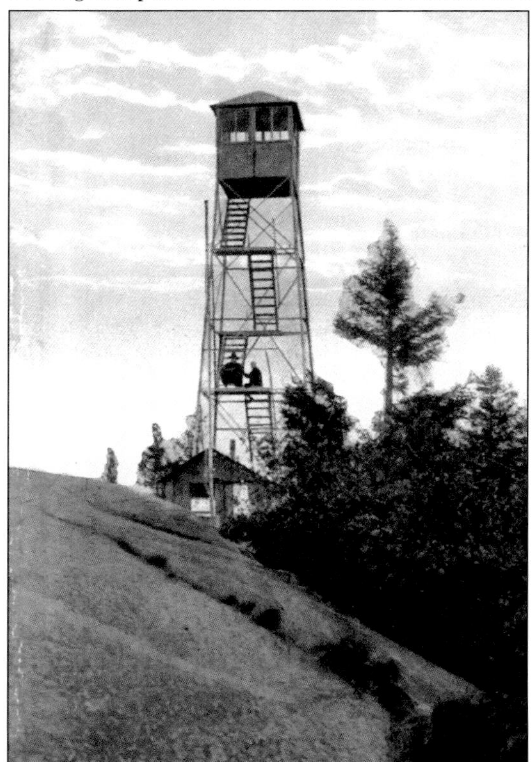

This view of the fire warden's tower on Bald Mountain near Fourth Lake shows the steel tower with its stairways and the observer's cabin nearby. Once found on more than 50 Adirondack peaks, fire towers dwindled to 29 by the early 1990s, and one-by-one they are being dismantled. A fire tower steering committee has been organized to research educational possibilities for the towers that are scheduled to be preserved.

The caption on the photograph of the wooden tower on top of Blue Mountain, "a signal tower," may be in error. The photograph appears to be of one of the early wooden fire observation towers. The steel tower on Blue Mountain, today, is one of the preserved towers and is open for hikers. The two-mile climb leads to the 3,759-foot summit, which provides a great view of the High Peaks.

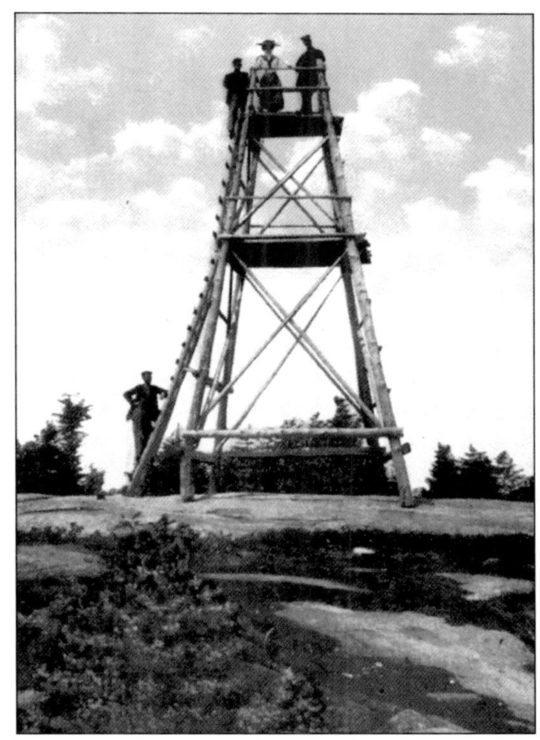

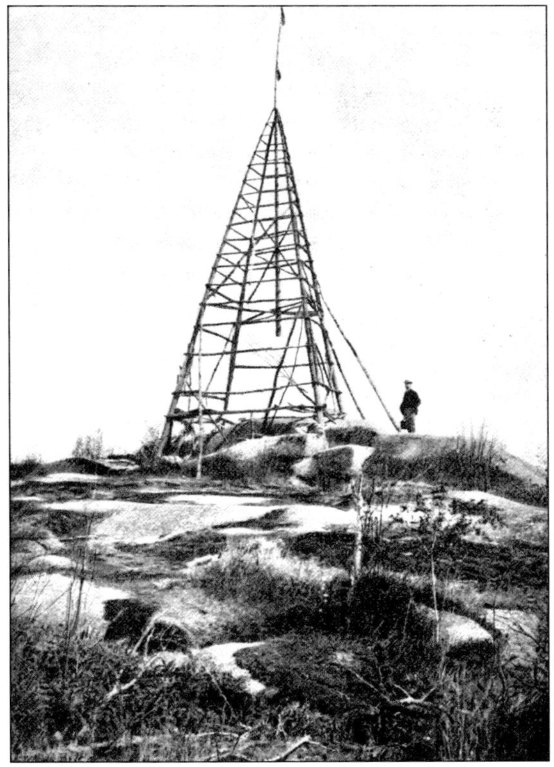

The signal tower on Cobble Mountain, shown in this 1906 view, was placed in use by Verplanck Colvin when he was surveying the Adirondacks. The triangulation method he was using required sightings from mountain to mountain. Note the pointed top instead of the observer's platform found on the fire towers.

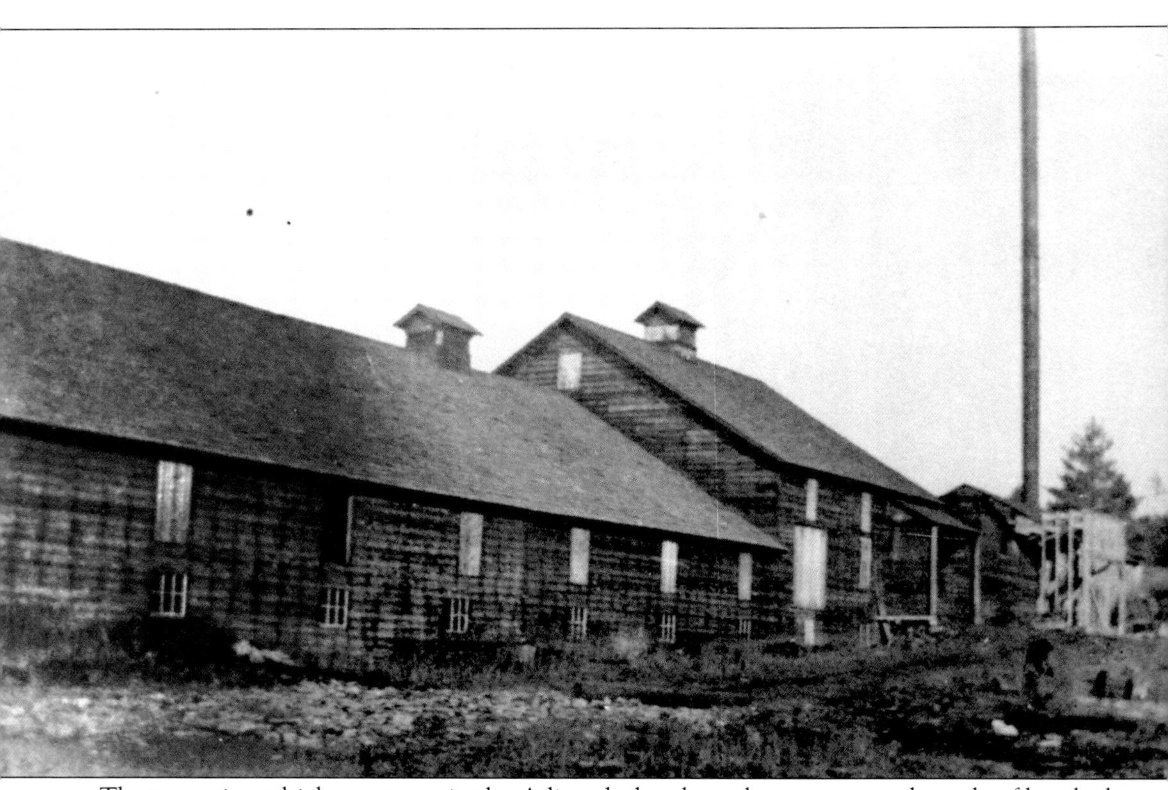

The tanneries, which sprang up in the Adirondacks where there was a good supply of hemlock trees, caused an influx of people who established communities. The bark of the hemlock trees supplied the tannic acid needed in the process of making leather. Two bark tanneries were reportedly in operation in Hope Falls by 1850. Smith and Company had opened a tannery as early as 1845. Some of the Adirondack hamlets that depended on the tanneries could not survive after the hemlock ran out and the tanneries closed. By 1900, the tanneries had left the Adirondacks.

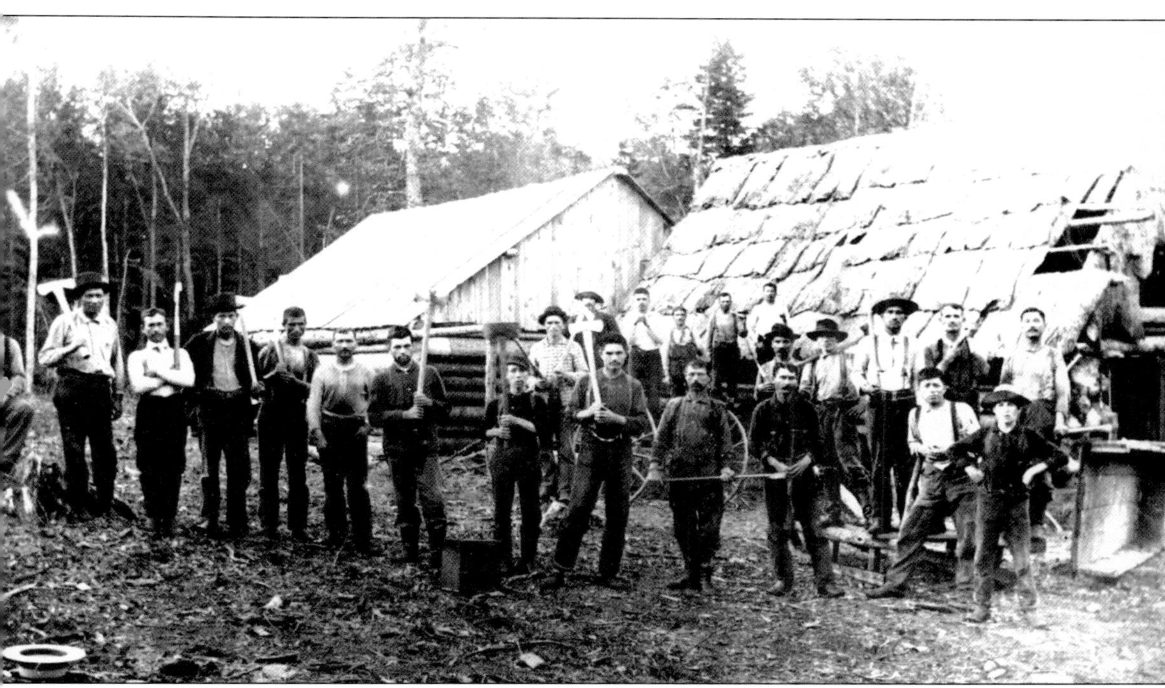

When the Adirondack settlers were not guiding the outsiders in the Adirondack wilds, they were working in the woods. The jobs connected to the logging industry were labor intensive, and it took many hands to tap the resources of the forest. One premier job in the woods was that of the "spudder." The spudder was the one who removed the bark in sheets from the hemlock trees to make tannic acid necessary to tan hides. It was a skilled job and paid the highest wages. The third man from the left is a spudder and is holding a spud, the tool used to remove bark. These axe men and spudders are ready to search out the best hemlock trees and remove the bark in large sheets.

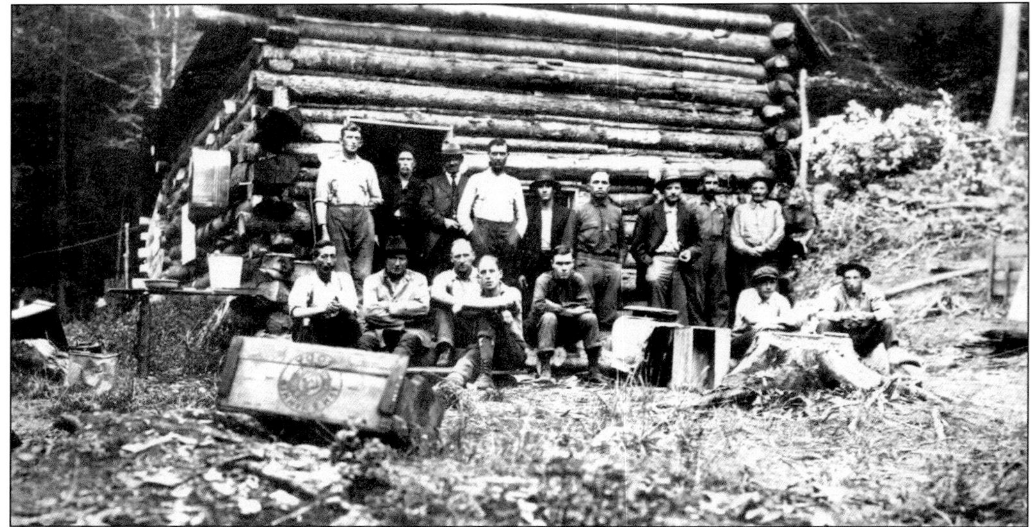

At the height of logging in the Adirondacks in the 1800s, logging camps sprang up throughout the mountains. One old-timer said they took the sawmills to the logs, while today they take the logs to the sawmills. The forested Adirondacks got off to an early start in the lumber industry, with mills as early as the 1700s in Warren, Essex, Herkimer, and Fulton counties. Hundreds were employed in the lumber camps to get the logs out of the woods. The job required workers to select the cuttings, lumberjacks to chop and saw down the trees, and teams of horses to move the logs, as well as road workers, river drivers, and camp cooks. When women were allowed in the camps to cook, a dipper of hot water was always kept ready to keep "snoopers" out of the kitchen; they did not allow the lumberjacks in where the women worked.

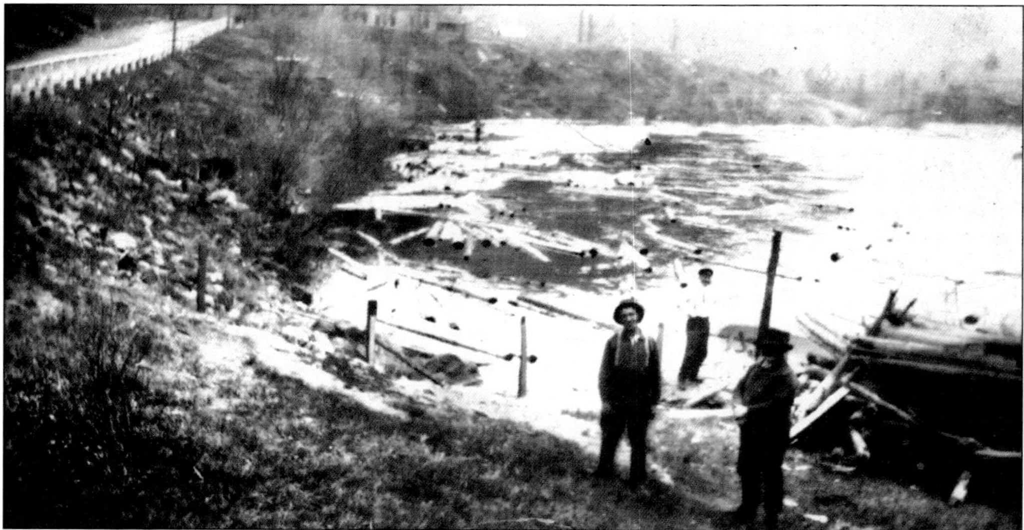

The log drives on the Sacandaga River were big operations and required extensive planning to hire the loggers, river drivers, teamsters, and road builders. They had to be housed and fed along the drive. The rivers of the Adirondacks had been declared "public highways" in the middle of the 1800s to open them up for moving the logs to market. In an 1892 drive on the Sacandaga, 24 men were paid $2 per day to move the logs. In a 1902 drive, 30 men took six days to move the logs through the town of Hope.

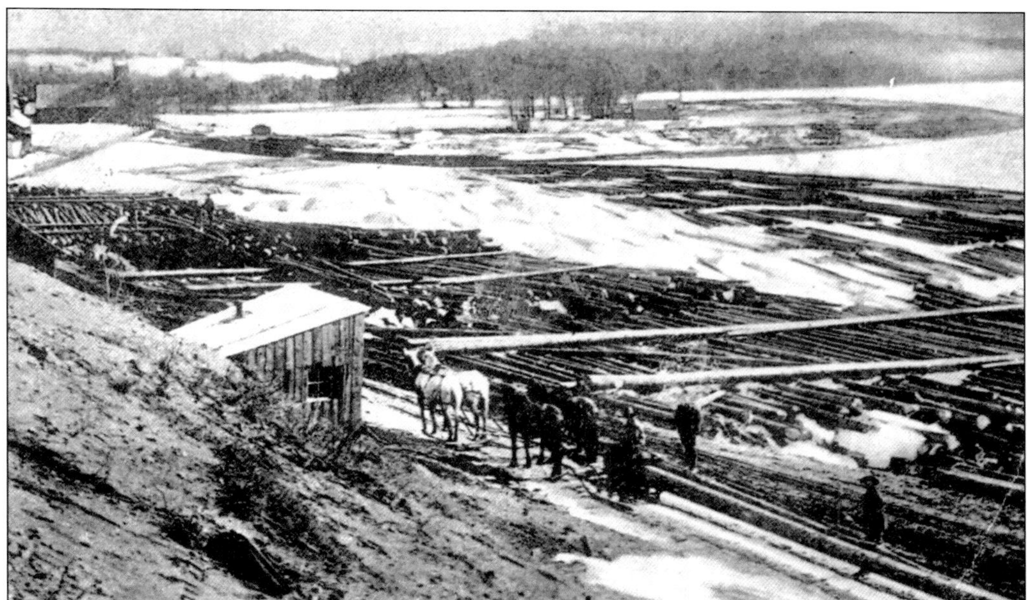

The 1908 "logjam" in this photograph may simply be a log yard where logs are held for the sawmill or for a later log drive down the river. Most logjams are characterized by the logs sticking up high in the air, all in disarray. In some cases, logs were held from one year to another before reaching the downstream sawmill. Local teams of horses were hired to move these logs to the riverbanks.

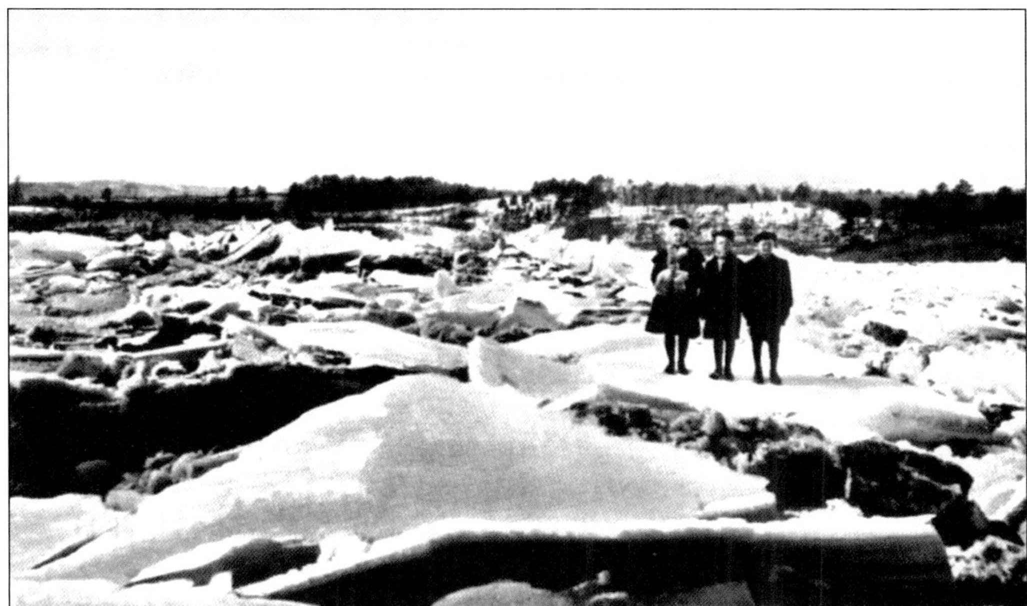

Ice jams were sometimes a bigger problem than the logjams. They were caused when the Adirondack rivers froze to some depth and began to break up due to warming weather or fast currents caused by rains. Huge chunks of ice floated down the rivers until they were stalled by an obstacle, such as a bridge, island, or protruding riverbank. When the water rose, the chunks sometimes moved several feet onto land, often causing severe damage.

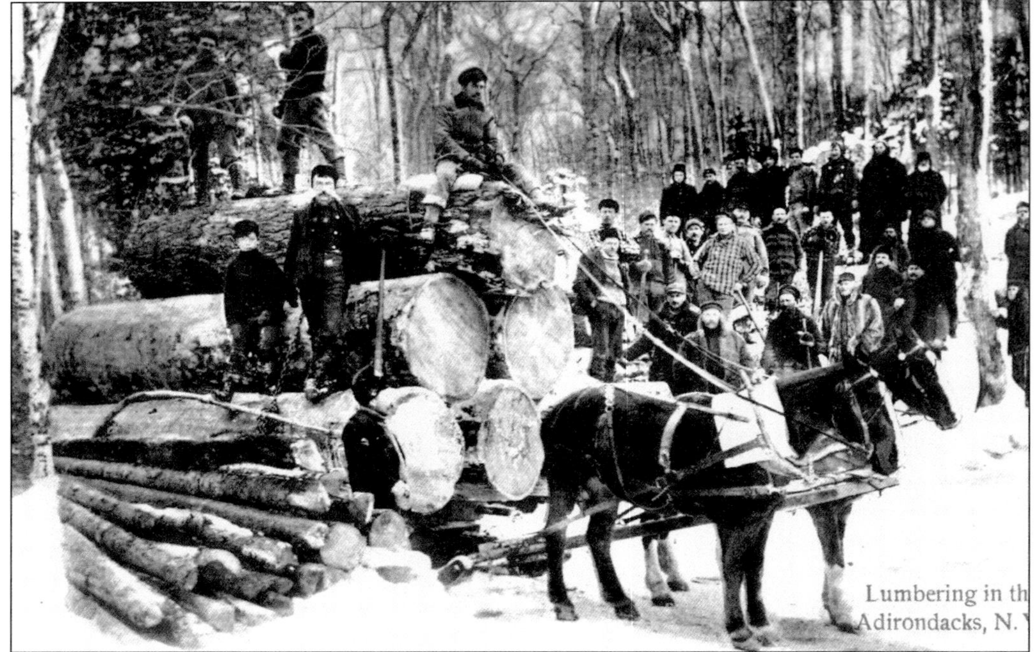

Hundreds found employment in the Adirondack woods during the days of the great log drives. Virgin trees of the forest were cut by crosscut saws or axes and pulled out of the woods by teams of horses or oxen. Life in the lumber camps meant long hours of work and days away from family. It was a happy day when the winter cutting ended, the spring drive was over, and the loggers could take their pay and head to town.

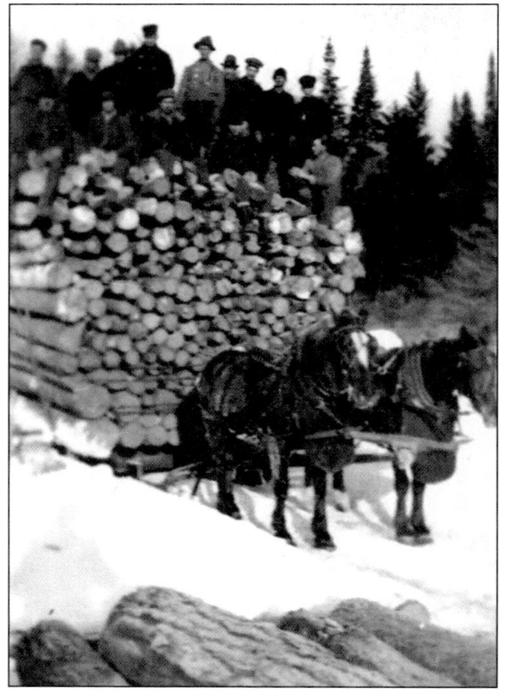

Record loads of logs were taken from the Adirondack hillsides during the height of the logging days. In 1914, one load reportedly had 157 logs, pulled five miles by two horses. The logs were taken to the banks of the Adirondack rivers to be pushed into the rushing springtime waters for transportation to the lumbermills in places like Glens Falls or Northville. They were branded with the owner's mark by use of a branding hammer so that they could be identified at the mill.

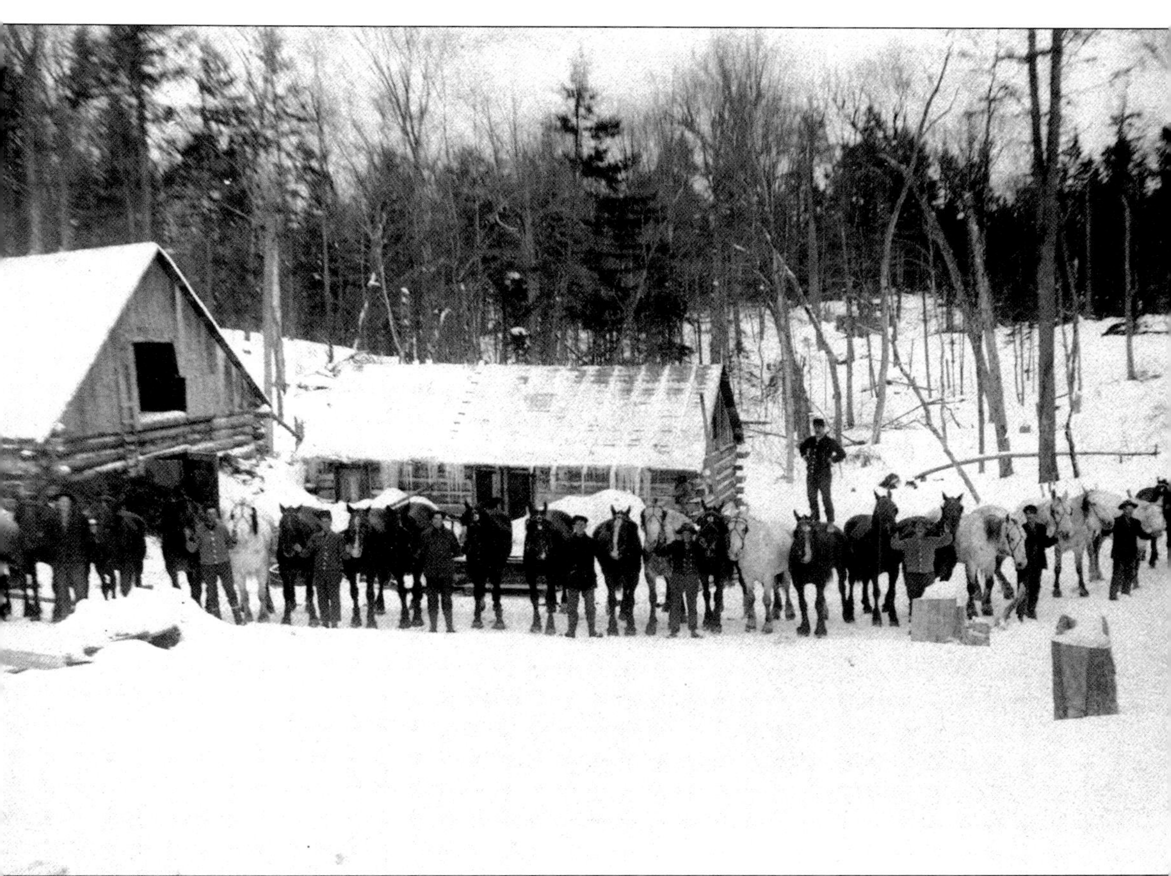

Local teams of horses were hired by the logging company in Long Lake West to haul the logs to the riverbanks. It took all the teams they could find to get the logs out of the winter woods before the spring thaw. Long Lake West lost much of its forestlands in the big Adirondack forest fire of 1908, which burned more than 368,000 acres. The little hamlet was completely destroyed by the fire, which was started by sparks from the New York Central Railroad locomotive.

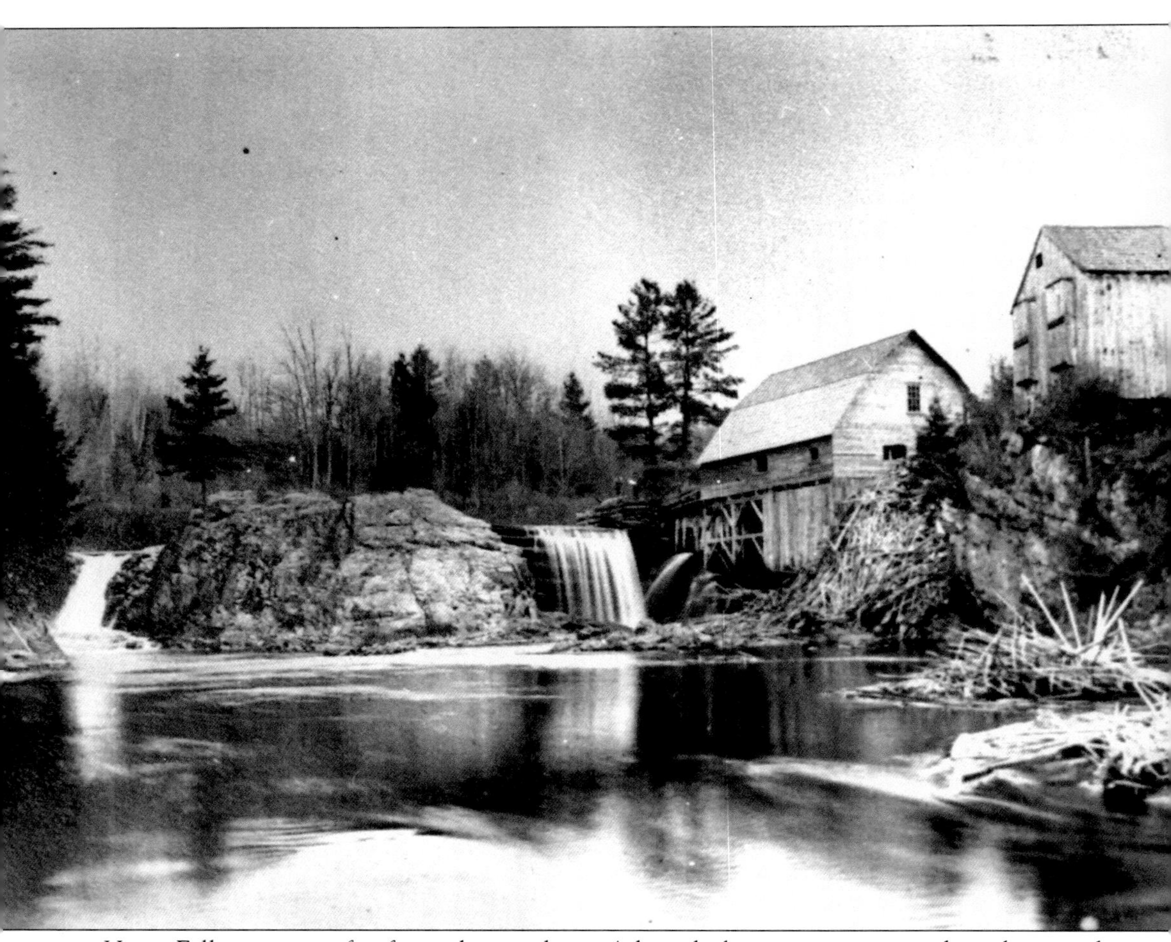

Hope Falls, not too far from the southern Adirondack gateway, attracted settlers at the beginning of the 19th century. It was the center of logging in the region and soon had seven sawmills in operation to handle the growing demand for lumber from the Adirondack forests. Water power was readily available in Adirondack country, making it possible for the early industries to thrive.

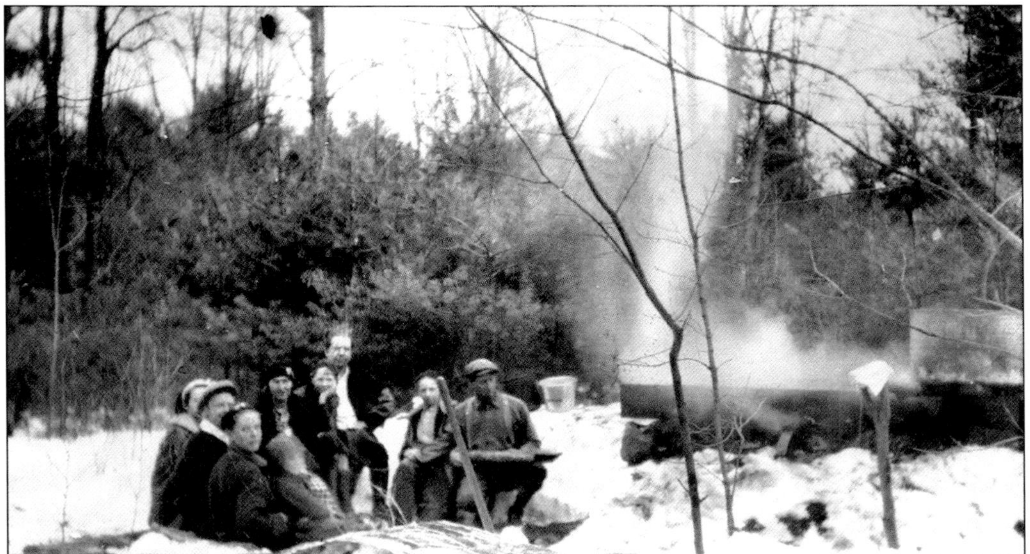

Boiling the maple sap from the maple trees was a family affair in the Adirondacks. The giant maple trees in the sugarbush were tapped with sumac spiles, and 30 gallons of sap was extracted, one drop at a time, for each gallon of syrup. Open-air sap houses, with their big kettles and pans, were often used for the endless boiling, which removed the water from the sap. Family members and friends gathered during the spring season to help gather the sap, cut the wood, and enjoy "jackwax," concentrated syrup poured on snow and eaten like taffy.

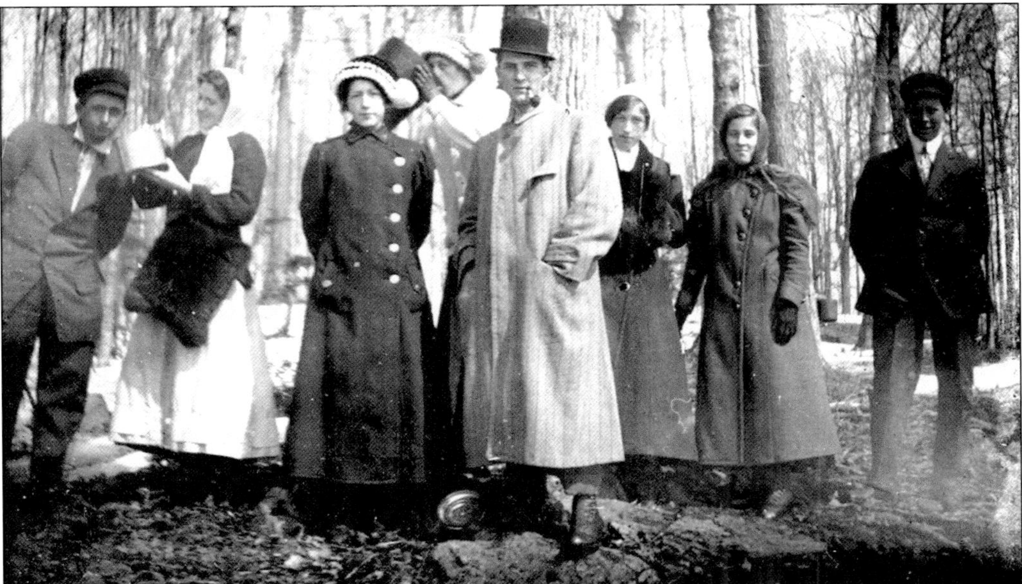

Taking an outing to an Adirondack sugarbush was a favorite activity in the springtime. When the sap from the giant maple trees was being boiled into syrup in the sap house, visitors could enjoy some jackwax twisted around a maple stick. It appears from the dress that this may be a Sunday afternoon outing to the sugarbush. Note the bucket on the tree in the background and the man drinking sap from a bucket, as well as the young woman offering her friend a drink of the raw sap.

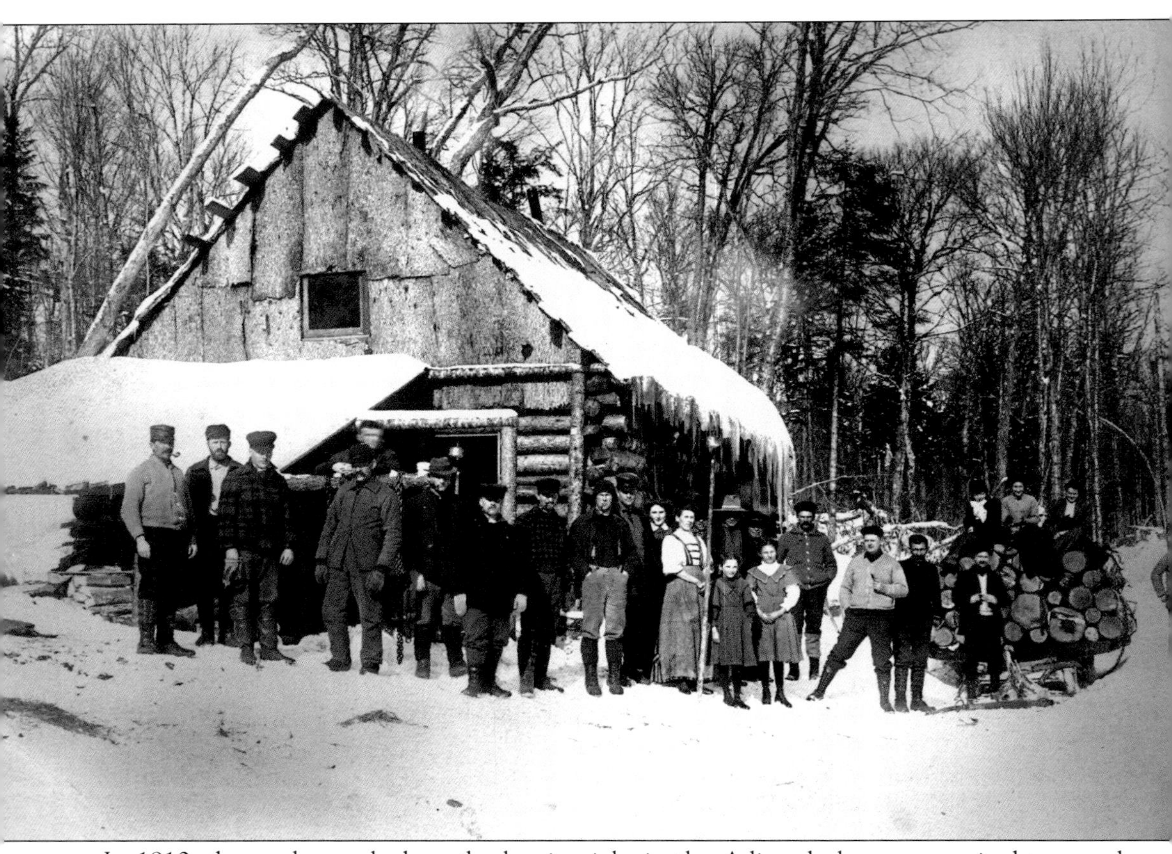

In 1910, those who worked on the logging jobs in the Adirondacks were required to spend several months in the woods. Some female members of the family would work in the camps as cooks, getting up at dawn to feed the hungry lumberjacks before they headed out for the day. Mealtime was for eating: the food had to be ready, and the men were not allowed to talk while eating. Pack lunches often had to be made and taken out on the job so time was not wasted returning to the logging camp to eat. They worked from dawn to dusk, and one owner was said to have turned the time back so far on his clock to get his men up earlier that he had gone back to the previous day.

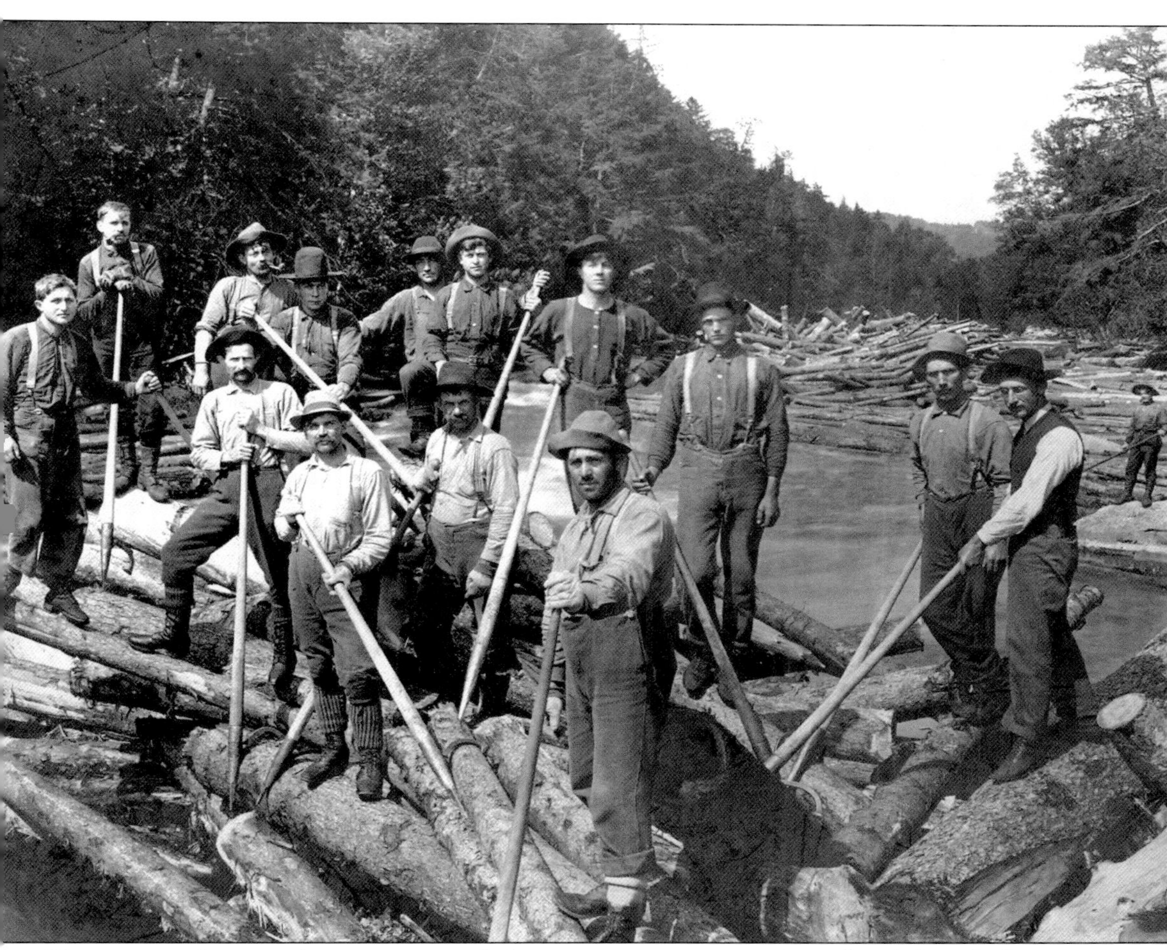

Transporting logs in the waterways of the mountains originated in the Adirondacks on the Schroon River, which led to the Hudson River to reach the mills at Glens Falls. The Adirondack waterways were soon opened for transporting logs, and this cheaper way of transporting logs was instituted. The river drivers were the brave men who walked the logs to break up the jams, to push logs back into the water, and to keep them moving. Lives were lost when a jam unexpectedly broke and the drivers lost their footing. Much like the cattle in the old West, the logs had to be branded with a special branding hammer of the owner's identifying mark. Also like the old West, rustling took place and brand marks were sawed off and replaced with other brands to steal the logs on the way to market. One enterprising rustler was said to have used the sawed-off parts of the log to burn in his steam engine that ran his mill. One river driver, upon reaching the mill, jumped up and down on a log shouting, "This year I ran the whole drive without getting wet!" whereupon one of the other drivers reached over with his peavy, the tool they use to roll the logs, and pushed the bragger into the water.

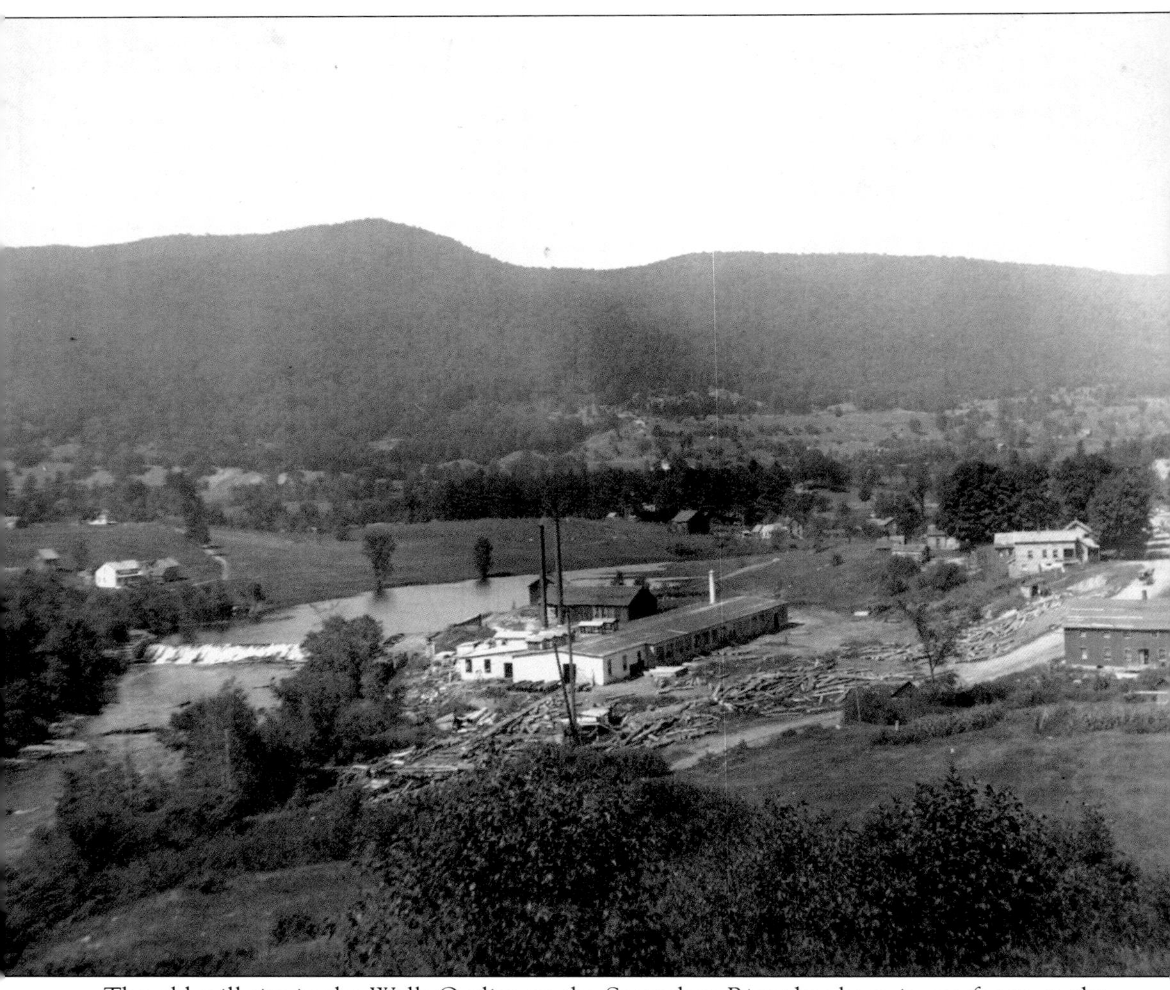

The old mill site in the Wells Outlier on the Sacandaga River has been in use for more than 200 years. Verplanck Colvin, the state surveyor, noted the mill on his 1898 map of the area. Back in 1871, an old clipping tells of the death of Elias Straus, a clothing peddler, who was swept over the dam at the site when it was a tannery. The mill has served many purposes over the years.

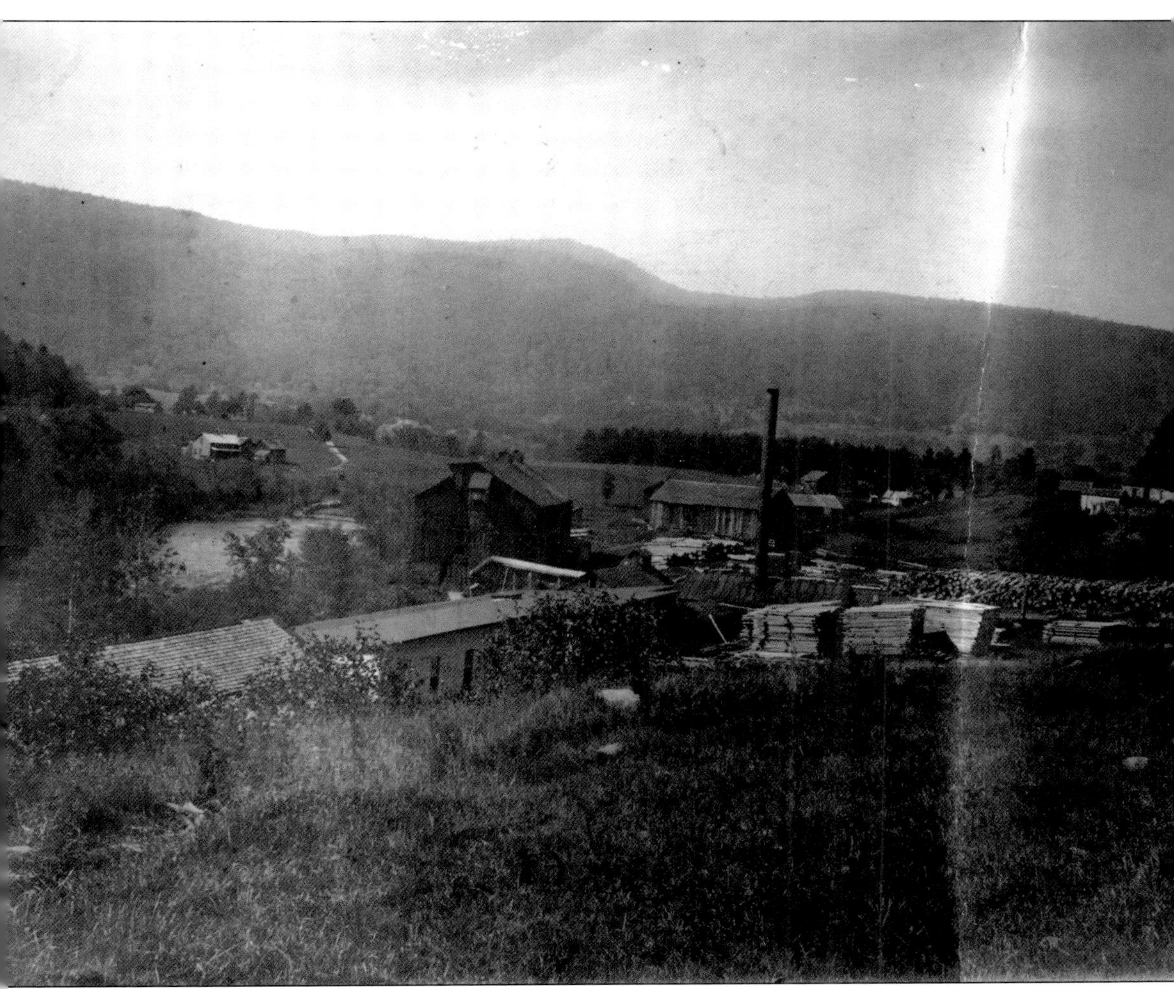

The old sawmill in Wells was built by Nicholas Bratt in the beginning of the 1800s. By 1830, a gristmill was added to the site and 10 years later the mill was also making pottery. When it burned down in 1866, a tannery took its place. In 1904, the tannery became a veneering mill. Other wood products were added in 1915. Two years later the mill burned.

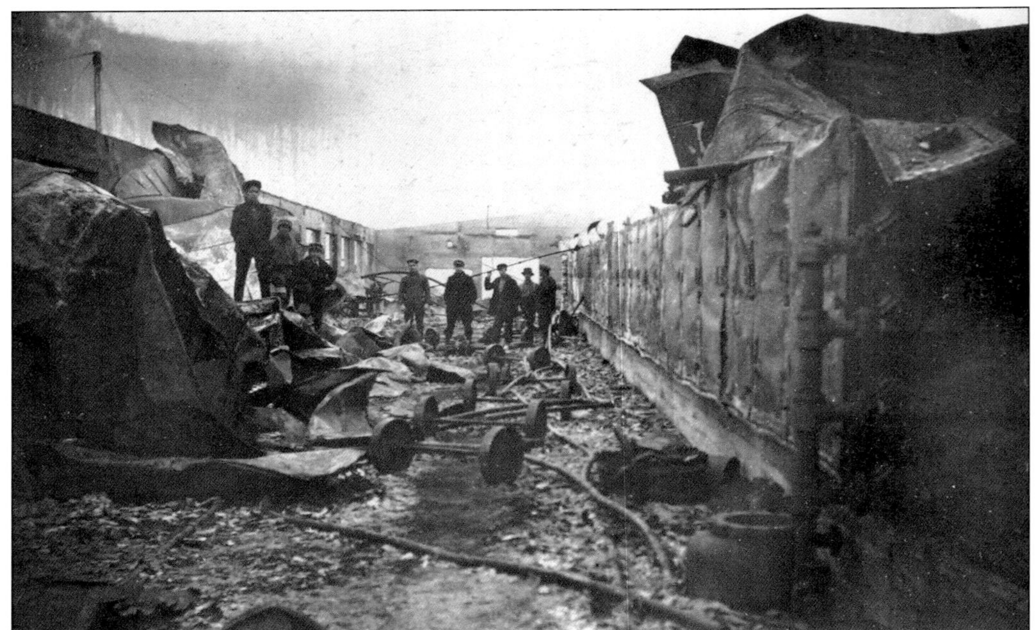

Fire was the greatest enemy of the original industries and the old hotels in the Adirondacks. Many buildings have been lost over the years. A fire in 1917 ended the production of veneer and other wood products at the old Wells mill site. Carl L. Fry and Charles B. Hanley purchased the site and opened the Adirondack Lumber Company, which remained in operation for the next 59 years. Souvenir matchbox holders given out by the company advertise "Rough and finished lumber, Roofing, Cement, Etc."

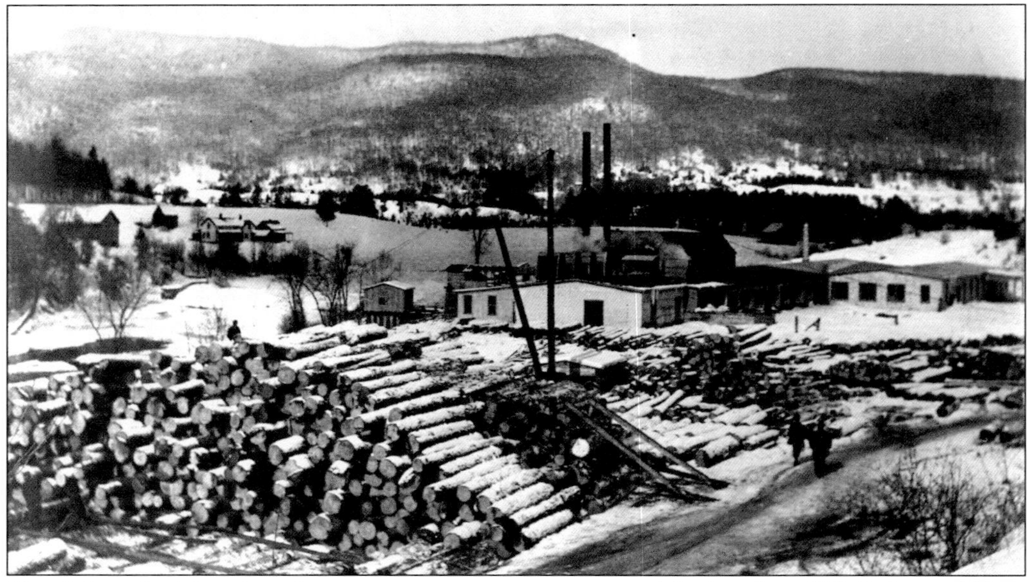

The Adirondack Lumber Company was an important part of the hamlet of Wells from 1917 to 1976. The site had been used since the early 1800s for a sawmill, a gristmill, a pottery, a tannery, a veneer mill, wood products, and a bobbin factory. Today, it has a new life as the studio and gallery of sculptor John Van Alstine and his wife, artist Holly Hallman.

Two

Camps and Cabins and Clubs

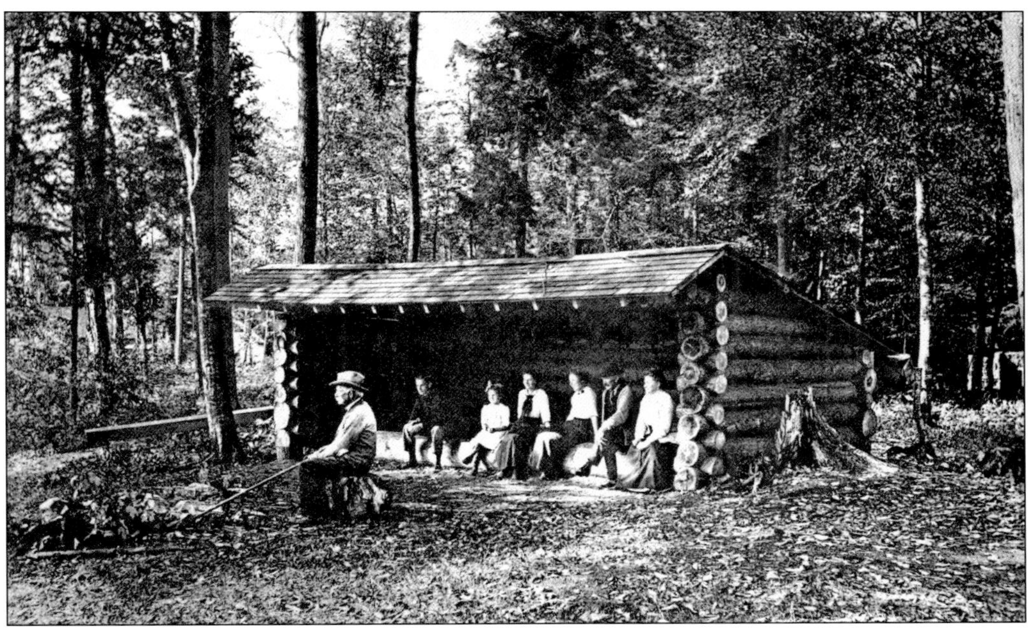

The lean-to is the shelter of choice in the Adirondacks. The first state lean-to, or open camp, was built in 1919. Some called these early shelters "three-sided shanties." New York State constructed lean-tos along the Adirondack trails and on the peaks to provide shelter for campers and hikers. Guides and hunters had been using these log shelters since the early 1800s. They also made simple three-sided shelters covered with evergreen branches for temporary use. Beds were made of balsam twigs placed vertically in the floor of the shelter. Today, many private camps have their own lean-tos.

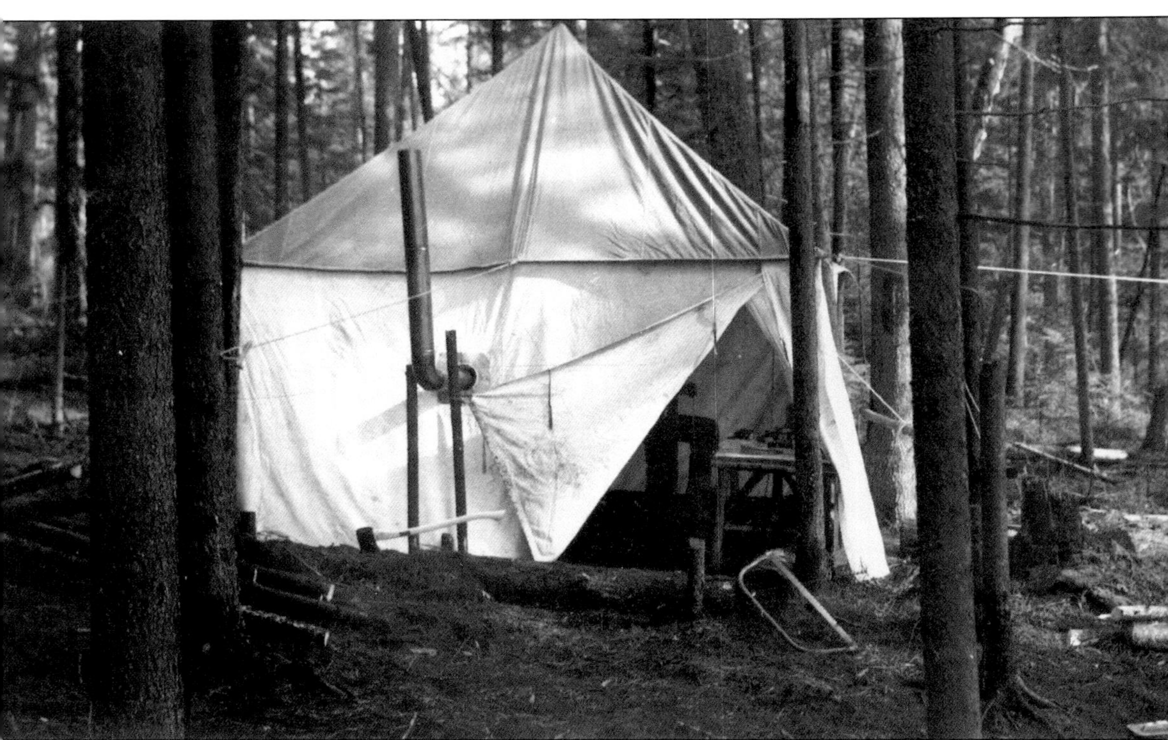

Canvas tents played an important role in the early Adirondack days and made Adirondack habitation possible. Tents were used for family vacations, for those who came for the tuberculosis cure, in children's camps, and by the sportsmen. Often they were placed on wooden platforms with carpets spread on the floor. Furniture and flowers were added to make them more homelike. At one time, the platforms were erected on state land and used year after year. Hunters added a wood stove with a protruding stovepipe to keep warm during the hunting season.

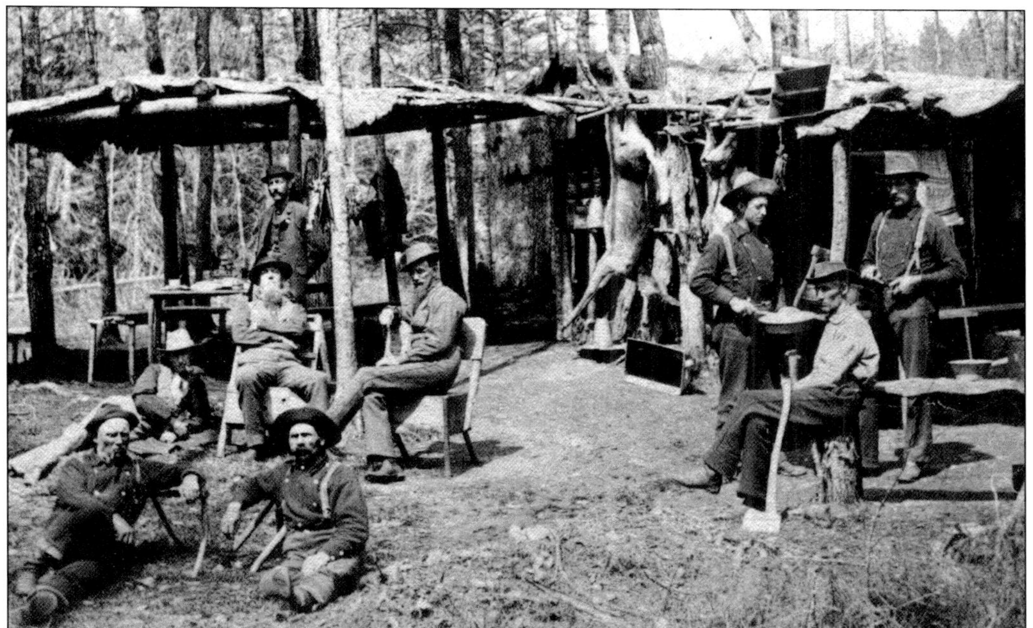

"A Home in the Woods—Adirondacks" was the title of many late-19th and early-20th-century photographs. The "home" could mean anything from an evergreen branch lean-to to a palatial great camp. Hunters used native tree branches, bark, scrap lumber, and tarpaper to build temporary hunting camps. Many returned to the same deer-hunting territories year after year. The ideal home in the woods was the 20- by 20-foot log cabin.

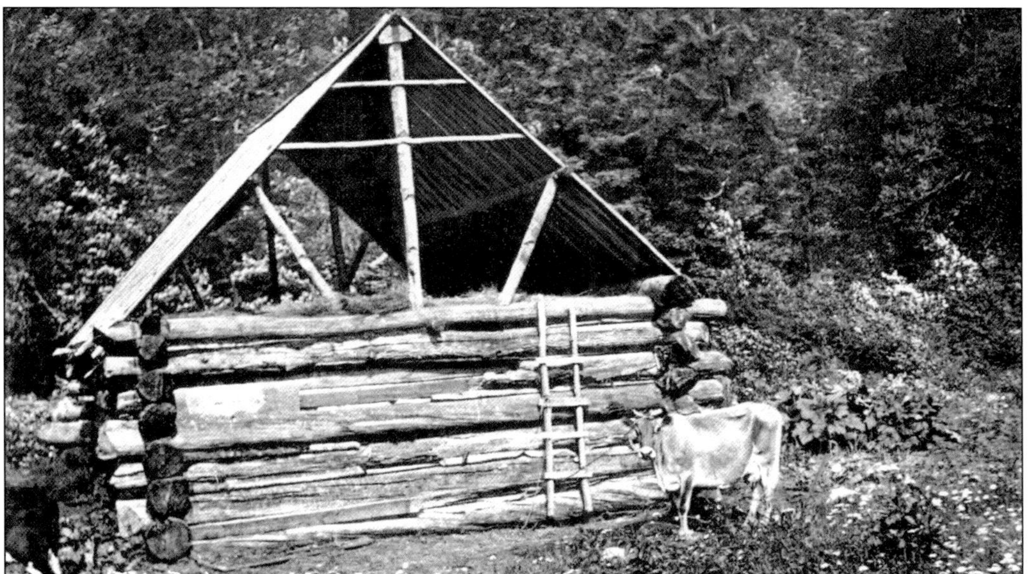

The dairy at Mud Creek Camp is shown in this early-1900s photograph. Cows were valuable in the Adirondack camps for a supply of fresh milk, cream, and butter. Local farmers, who kept cows to supply their family's needs, often operated a "rent-a-cow" business. Renting a cow to the hunting or lumber camps for the season provided good income to the farmer when money was scarce.

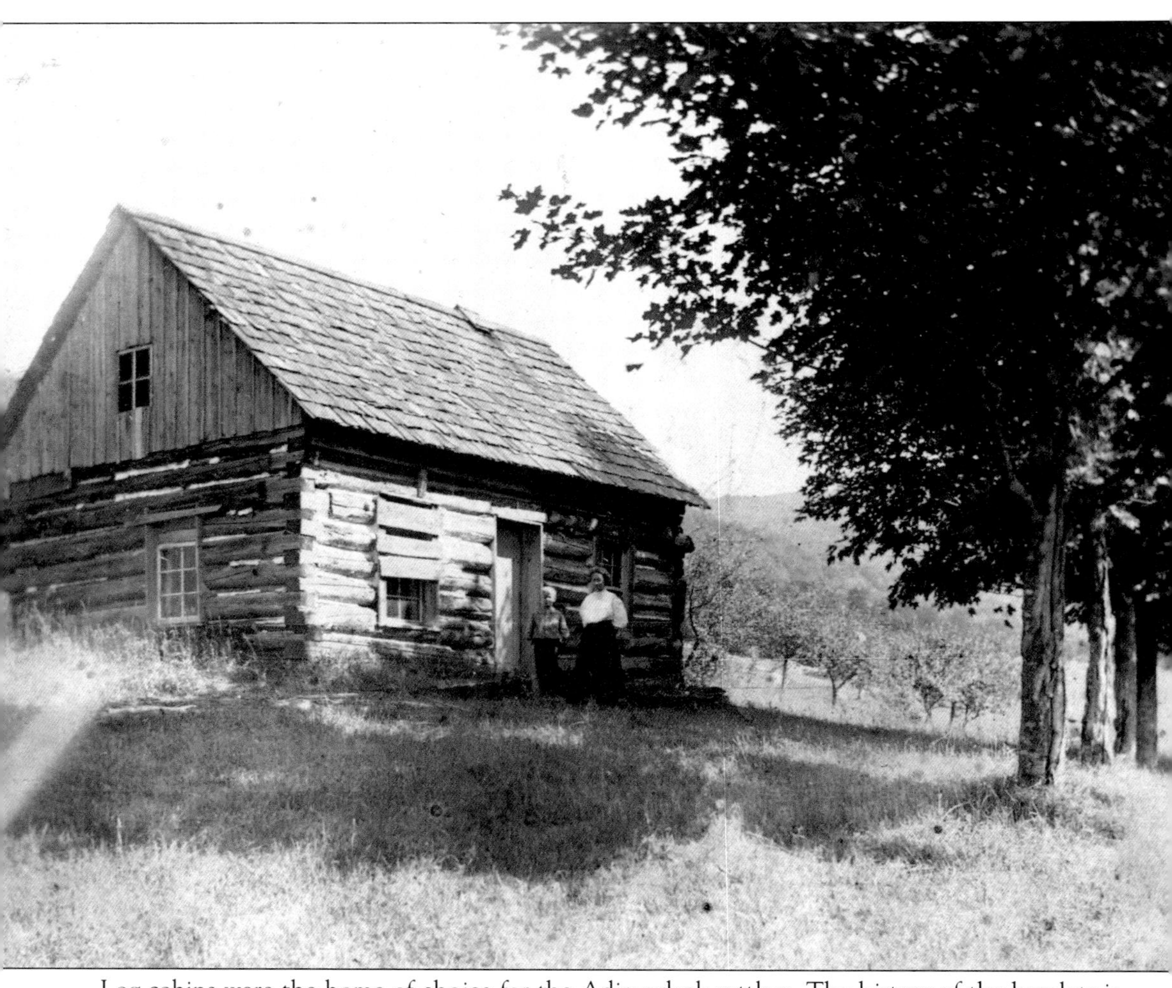

Log cabins were the home of choice for the Adirondack settlers. The history of the hamlets is a history of log cabins being the first buildings in the settlements. In 1835, Griffin consisted of four log houses. When the Reverend John Todd visited Long Lake in 1841 he reported eight families living in little log cabins. The cabins, made of native logs and stone, often had a dirt floor and a sleeping loft. The quickest and easiest corners were made by cutting out a square chunk about halfway up the log and fitting the next log on top of it. The cracks between the logs were caulked with local clay or sphagnum moss. Note the apple orchard behind the cabin. Many families had apple orchards, as they relied on nature for much of their food.

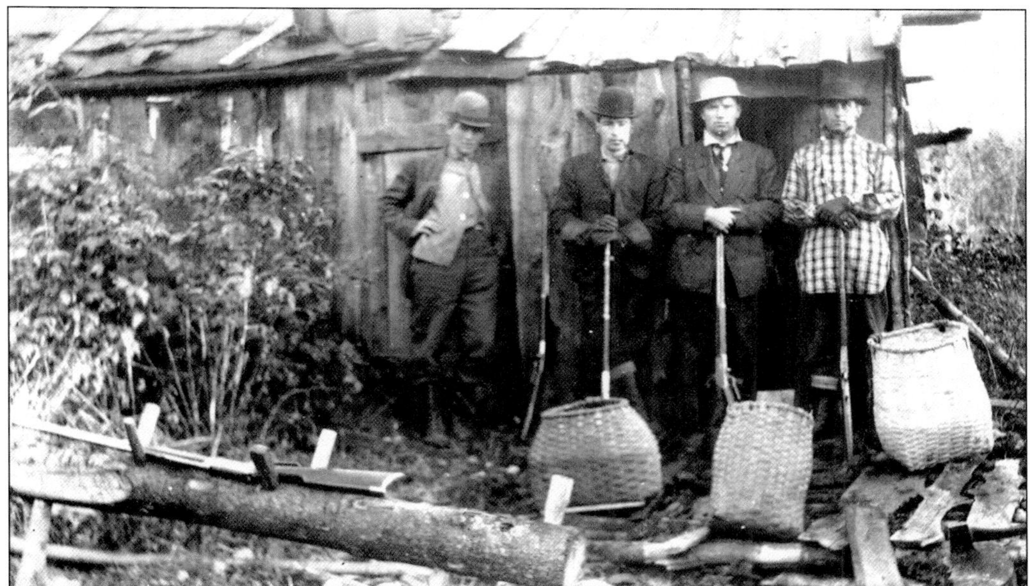

Hunting camps were often made from scrap wood left by the early lumber camps. Bark and boards were layered on the roof to keep out the rain and a stovepipe, stuck through the roof, was used to remove smoke from the wood stove. The well-dressed hunters each had their own hunting rifles. Adirondack pack baskets were used to carry in the supplies and food. Members of this early-1900s hunting party, from left to right, are George Besaw, Fred Bennett, Henry Besaw, and Henry Van Avery.

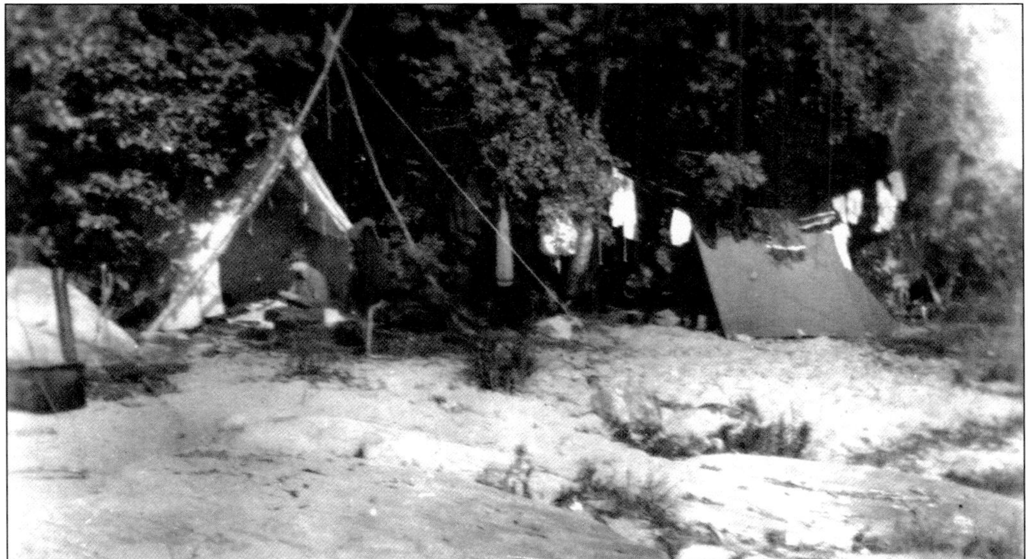

Lewey Lake has a long history of attracting sojourners to the Adirondacks. French Louie and Sam Seymour moved to its shores in the 1870s. A *Journal of a Hunting Excursion to Louis Lake* was written in 1851 and published by the Adirondack Museum in 1961. Camping at Lewey Lake began with roadside tents and was well-established before the development of today's New York State campsite in the 1920s. A cabin colony and hotel has been operated on Lewey Lake by the Galusha family off and on from 1913 to the present.

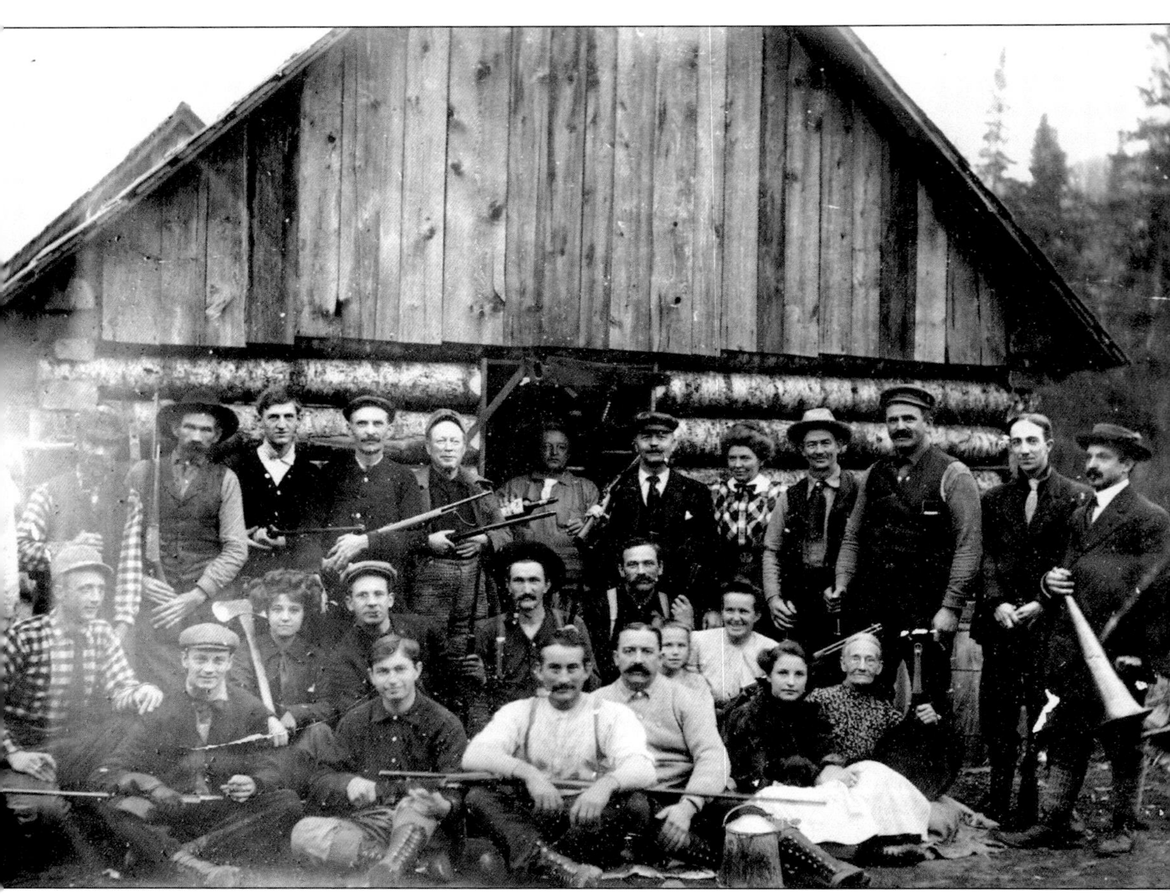

Most who pushed the voting lever "yes" in 1979 to consolidate the New York State holdings in the Perkins Clearing area had little knowledge of the popular Perkins Camp that gave it its name. Isaiah Perkins ran a hunting and fishing camp in this west Canada area for many years. Hundreds found the camp over the years to be typical of the Adirondack hunting enterprises found throughout the mountains. Good accommodations, good food, good guides, and congenial hosts brought people back year after year. In this photograph, taken at the Perkins Camp on Jessups River, the guides, sports, and cooks pose together. It appears that one young woman is holding an ax; she is probably responsible for keeping the wood box filled with wood for the cookstove.

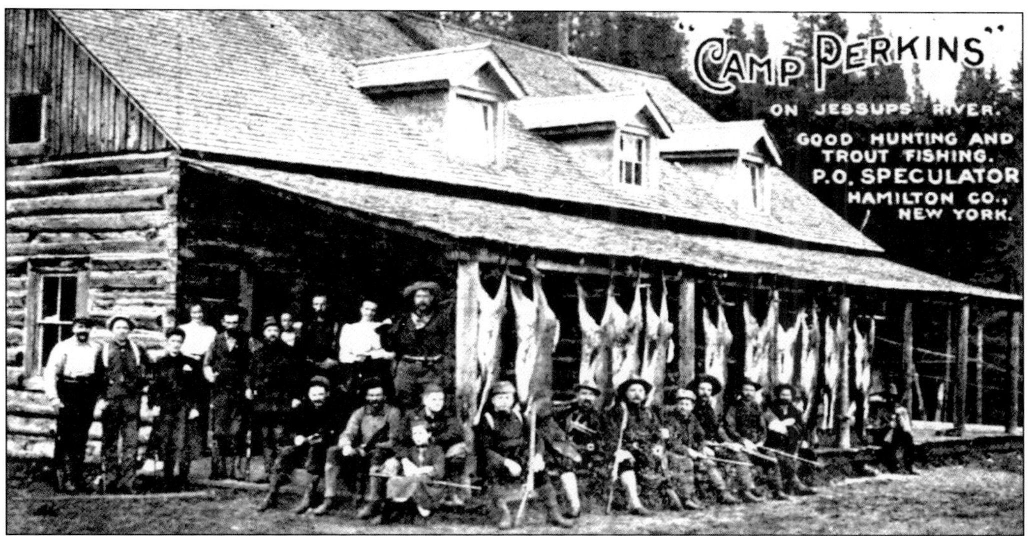

Camp Perkins was on an old road that led to Indian Lake from Lake Pleasant or over to Old Forge country. The camp was an imposing log building that provided a woodland home for those who came to hunt and fish in the Adirondacks. The photograph illustrates another Adirondack practice, that of forming hunting or fishing clubs. It shows the annual hunt of the Jessups River Gun Club.

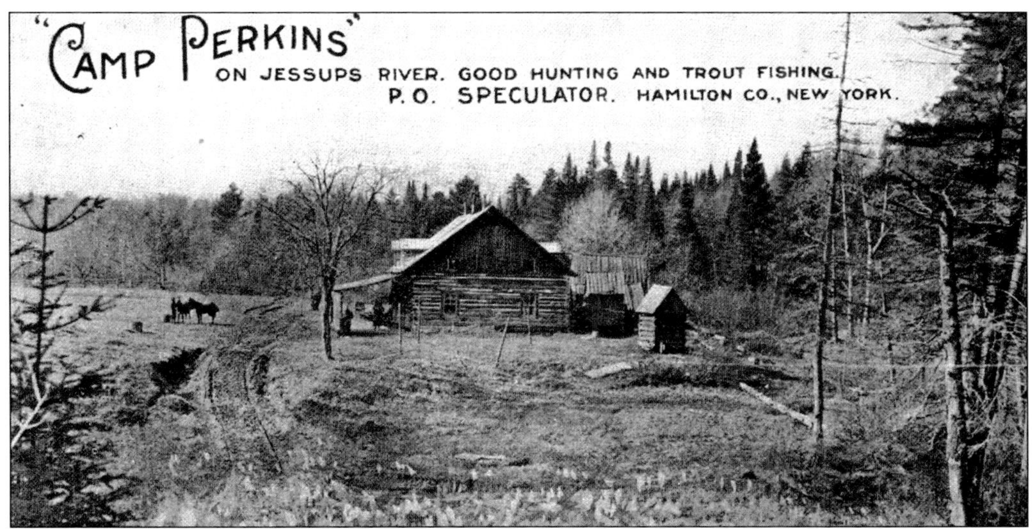

Postcards were a good way of advertising Adirondack destinations in the early 20th century. This 1909 postcard promotes good hunting and trout fishing at Camp Perkins on Jessups River. Indoor plumbing was unknown in the early Adirondack camps and hotels. Note the privy, or outhouse, standing behind the camp. Three stovepipes protruding from the top of the roof indicate the use of wood stoves to heat portions of the building.

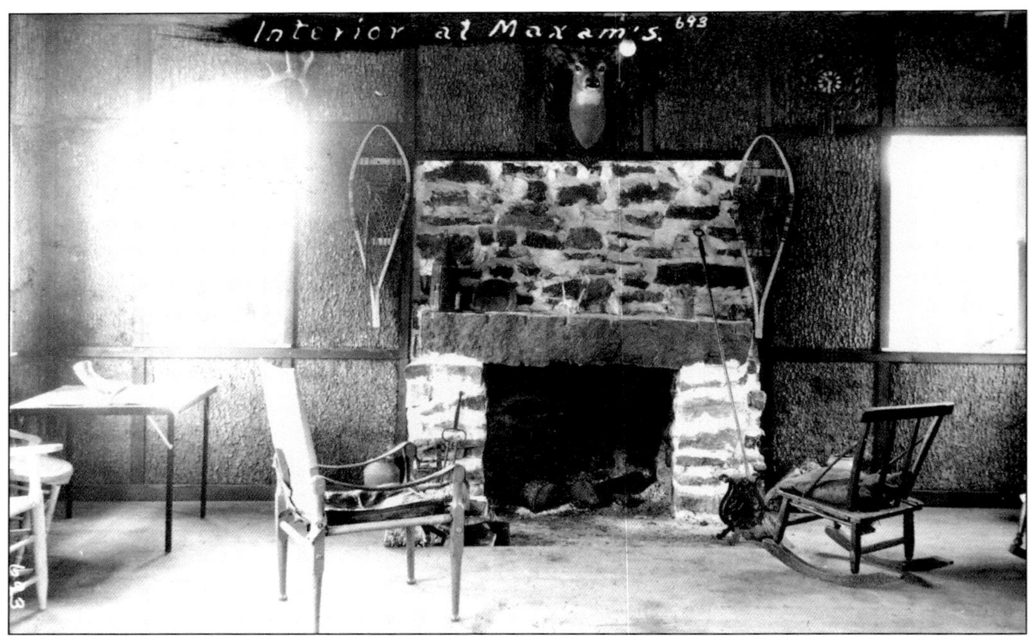

Maxam's Camp at Garnet Lake had several bungalows on the shores of the lake. The interiors consisted of several attributes common to many Adirondack camps. Note the large stone fireplace, the bark-covered walls, the mounted deer head above, a hanging pair of snowshoes, a card table with reading material or jigsaw puzzle, and assorted furniture.

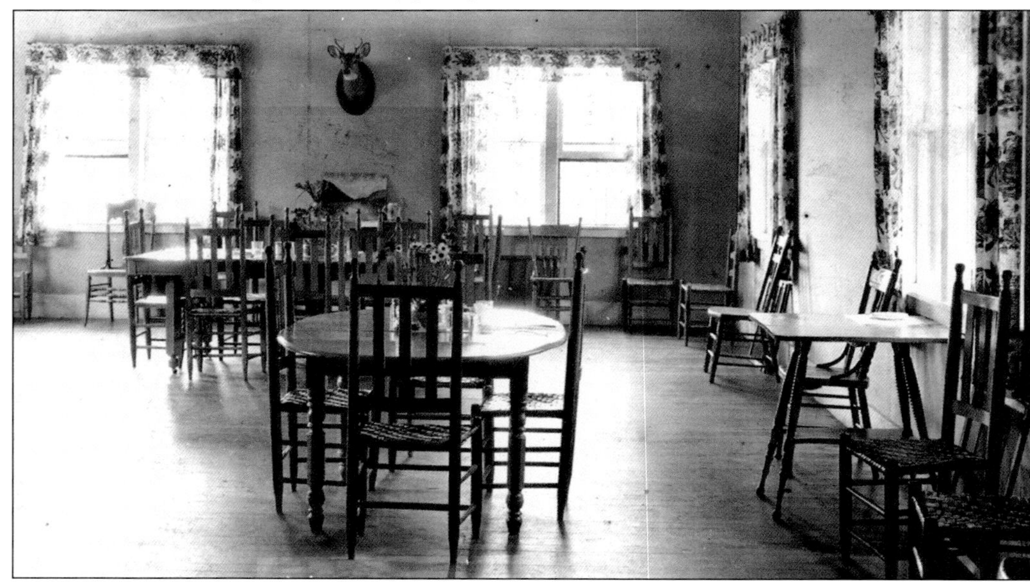

One of the drawing cards of the Adirondack resort destinations was to stay where there was a common dining area. Campers could eat the meals provided by the hosts and avoid the daily task of preparing food. This spacious dining room at Maxam's Camp at Garnet Lake is well furnished with tables and chairs, and has wildflowers on the tables. The dining room would not be complete without the traditional mounted deer head on the wall. Open windows with light, airy curtains allowed the sunlight and fresh air to come in.

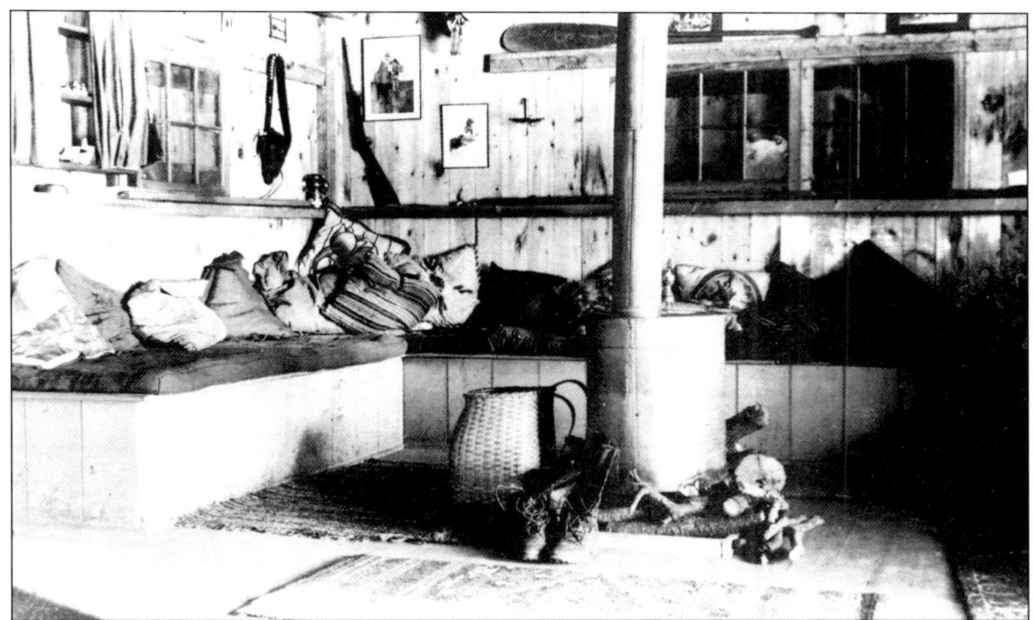

Typically, the Adirondack camps shared the same interiors. The message on this postcard is "Just to show you what a real good interior is!" Built-in couches with cushions provided adequate seating room and sometimes sleeping bunks. Boat paddles and guns often hung on the walls, and an Adirondack pack basket would be close by. The wood stove heated the camp and dried the L.L. Bean hunting shoes. Indian rugs were scattered on the wooden floors.

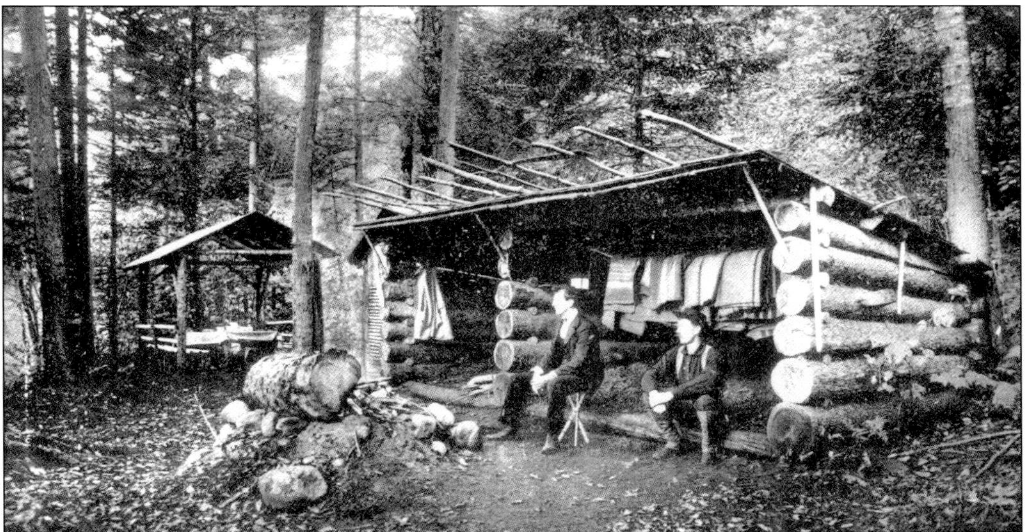

The interior of the open camps were somewhat different than the permanent buildings. This 1907 scene provides a picture of a rather elaborate lean-to, which appears to have two rooms with a log wall in between. The balsam mattress can be seen on the floor. To make the mattress soft, the ends of the twigs were placed in the ground, allowing the branches to stick up for a cushion. The hanging blankets and carpets could be spread over the evergreens for a clean, soft, sweet-smelling bed. The other building was the summer kitchen and dining hall. Cooking was done on the big stone fireplace that also heated the lean-to.

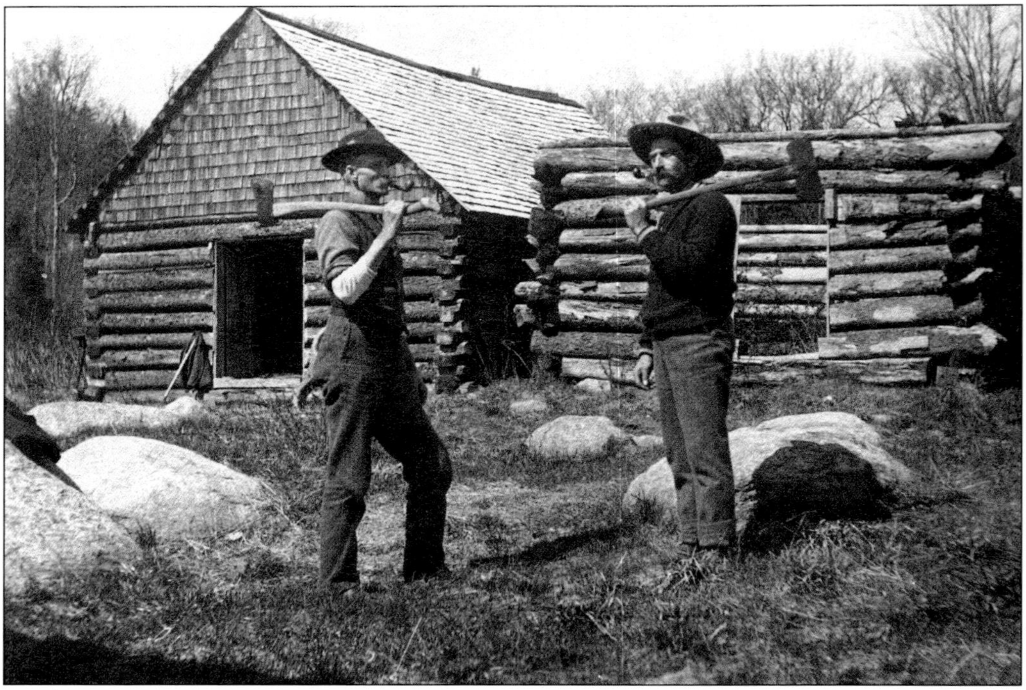

Workers with axes were needed to construct Adirondack log homes and outbuildings. It appears these axe men are replacing a crumbling building (right) with a new log building. They are using a smoking pipe as part of their work. While they are chopping a log, the smoke keeps the mosquitoes away. They cannot chop wood and swat flies at the same time.

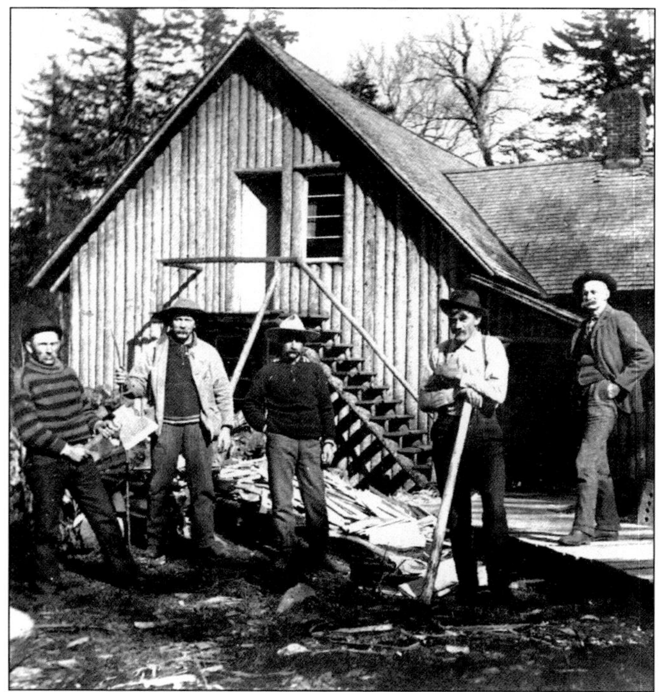

A building the size of this one requires a team of builders. Some of the great camp log building crews consisted of 200 workers. This crew has constructed a unique log building with vertical logs. The worker on the left shows off his broad axe, a tool used to hew the logs. Handles for the broad axes were customized for their users. The long-handled tool held by one of the other workers may be a peavy used to move the logs.

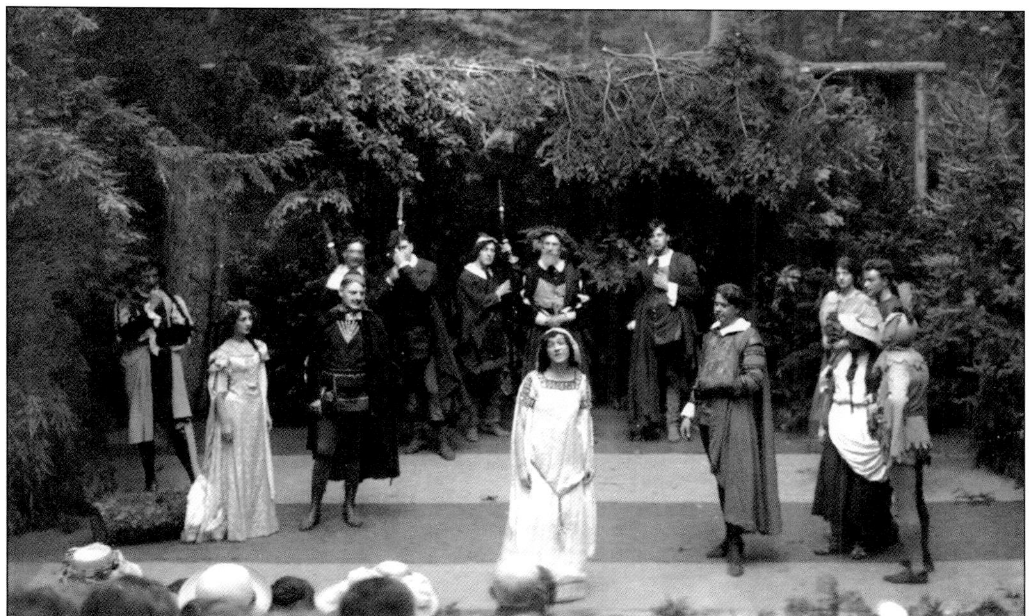

Melvil Dewey's Lake Placid Club had its own theater with a pipe organ and presented the popular shows of the day. This production features the Coburn Players in *As You Like It* at the club's 1,200-seat Forest Theater. The club also had four outdoor theaters.

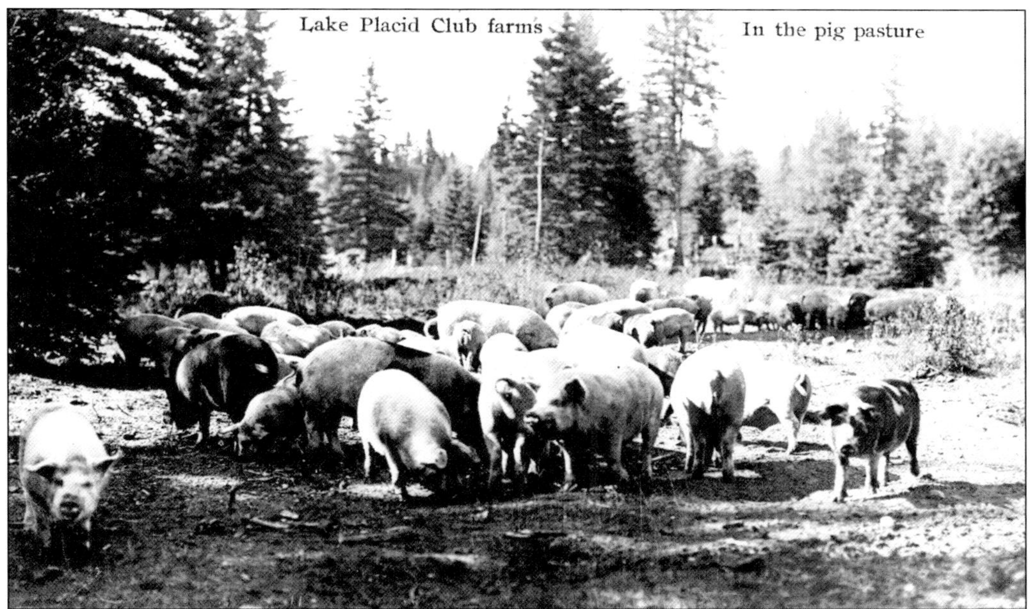

Many of the early Adirondack hotels and resort facilities had their own farm for fresh produce, eggs, dairy products, and meat. Melvil Dewey's Lake Placid Club maintained its own pig farm for supplying pork to its members. Dewey purchased 42 farms and consolidated them into 8 farm centers to supply food for the club.

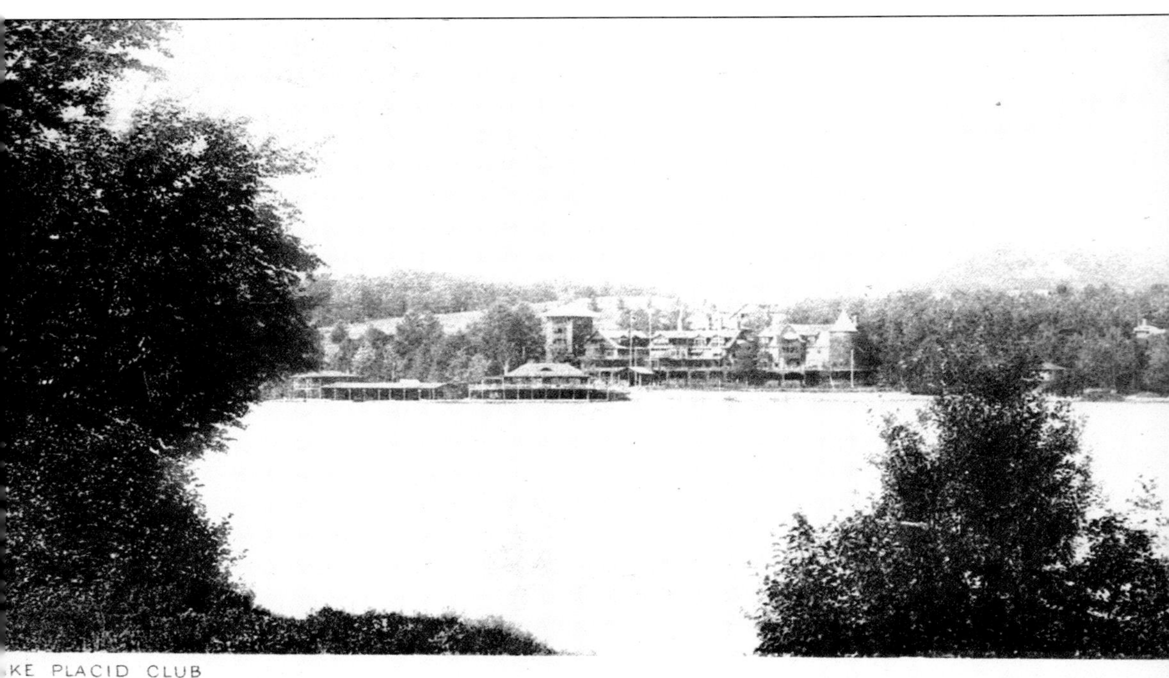

One of the Adirondacks most successful enterprises began with a sneeze. Seeking relief from hay fever and rose cold, Melvil Dewey and his wife founded the Lake Placid Club in the Adirondacks. In 1890, acting on a recommendation from hotelkeeper Paul Smith, the Deweys selected a site on a little hill by Mirror Lake. In order to reach the site, they hired a guide and guide boats, went through seven carries, and rode the buckboard 20-odd miles through the woods. The club grew into a resort with 400 buildings and 2,000 members. The Deweys built a second club in Florida for those interested in escaping the Adirondack winters. The

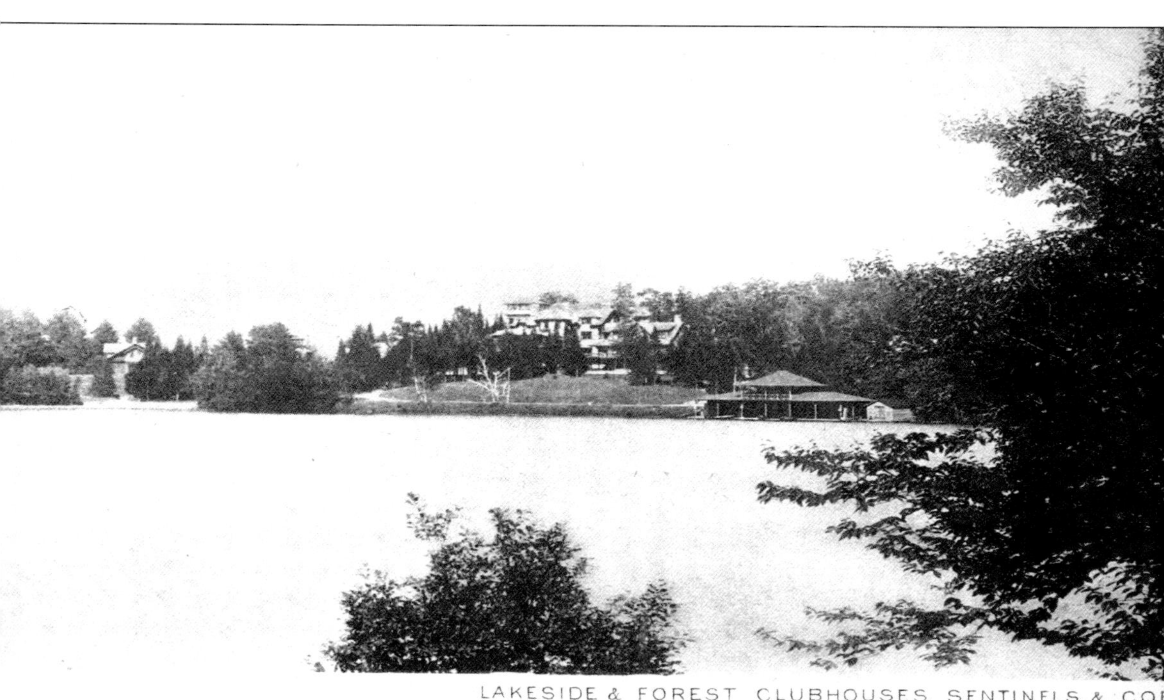

club was opened at Lake Sterns in 1927, and the name was changed to Lake Placid. The Adirondack branch of the Lake Placid Club became well-known for its winter sports program and promotion, started in 1905, which led to bringing the winter Olympics to Lake Placid. Melvil Dewey gained fame with the development of the Dewey decimal system of cataloging for libraries. His club had a 15,000-volume library. Also on the club site were five golf courses, forty tennis courts, a winter sports area, shooting and fishing facilities, riding trails, restaurants, and a water sports complex.

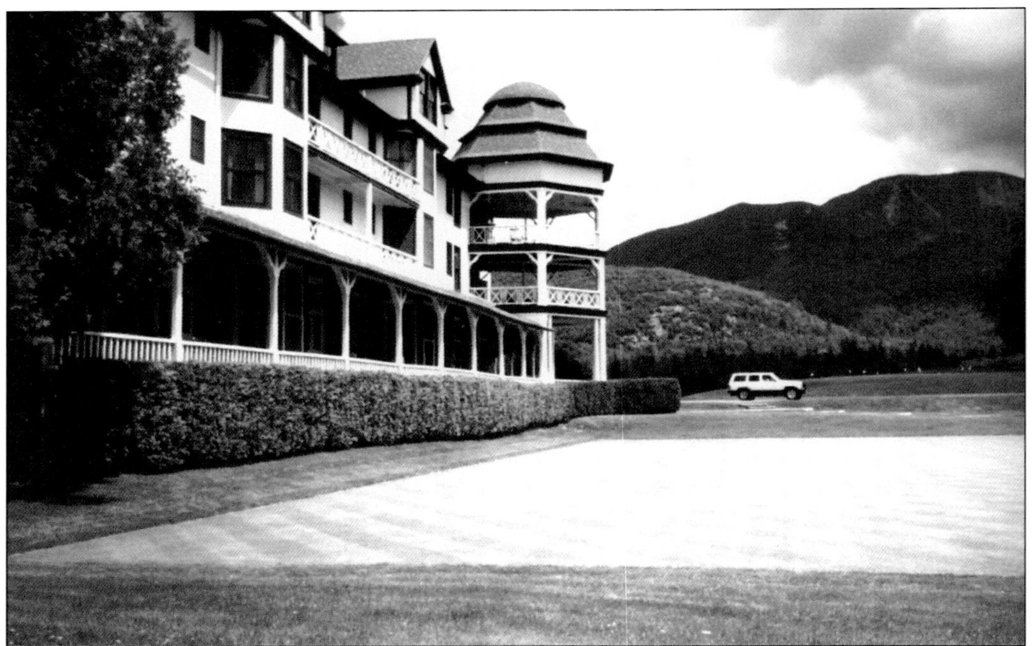

The St. Huberts Inn was purchased by the Adirondack Mountain Reserve, a stockholder preserve established in 1887, for the AuSable Club in 1906. Still in its original state, the inn is a rare example of the mountain resort hotels built in the United States in the late 19th century. Once a tract of 40,000 acres, the Adirondack Mountain Reserve has sold off all but 7,000 acres, most of it going to New York State. The members of the club have wisely chosen to maintain the old inn.

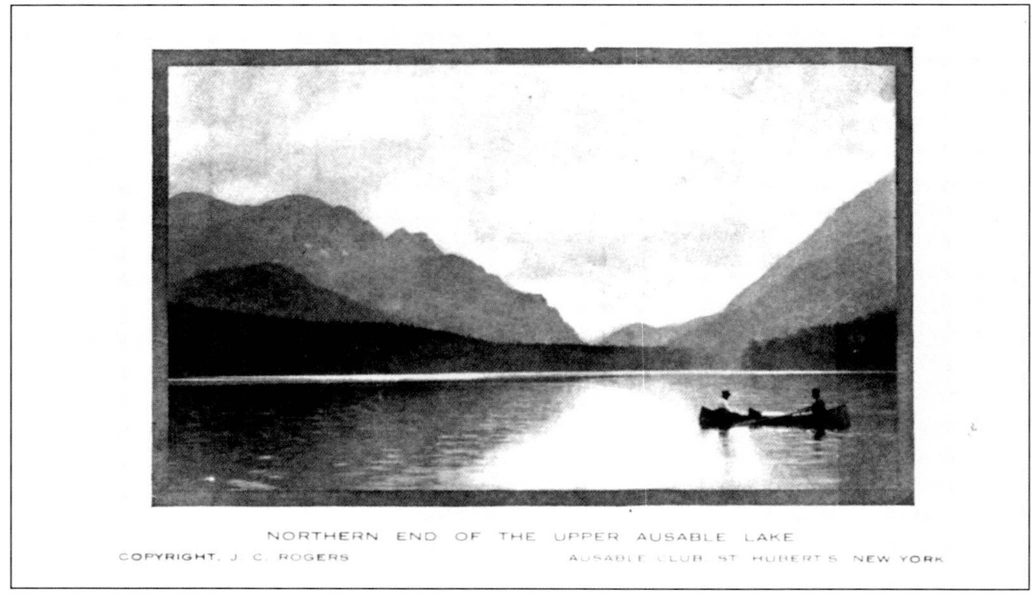

The AuSable Club very kindly sold choice mountaintops and trails to New York State for public use beginning in 1921. Access to the trails has generously been kept open to the public, and the lakes and woodlands have been kept as a retreat for club members.

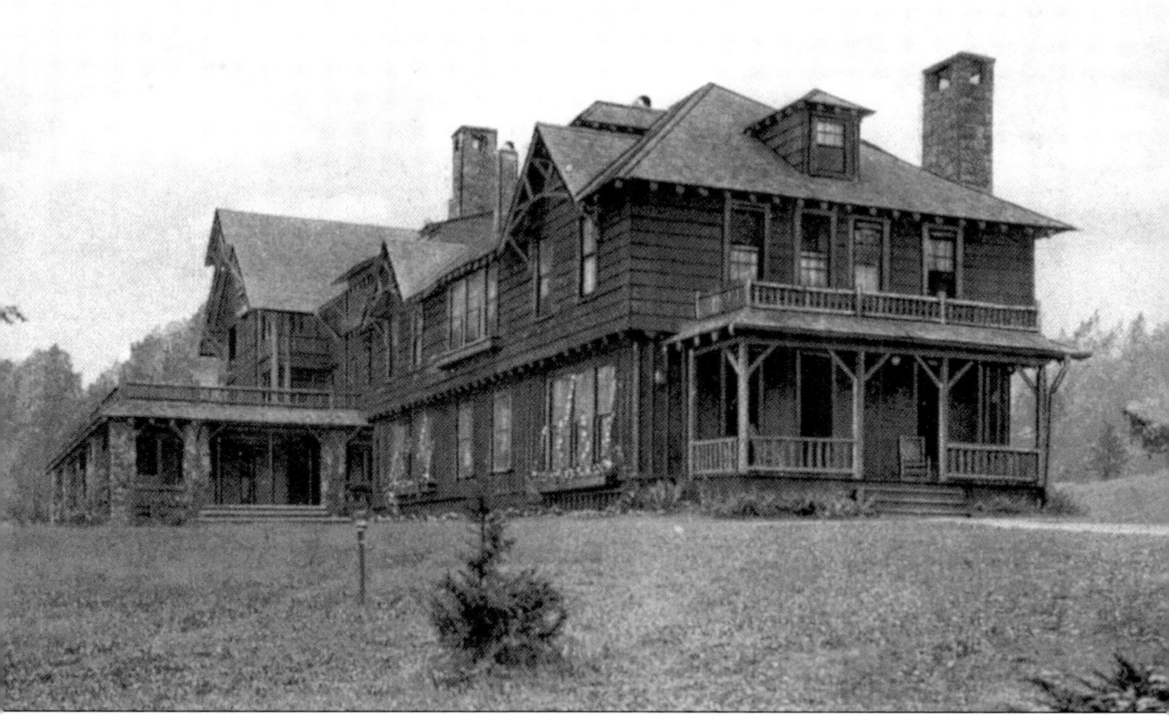

The Adirondack League Club near Old Forge was founded in 1890 and merged with the 1878 Bisby Club in 1892. The club has been considered the largest proprietary sporting club in the Adirondacks and possibly the world. The 300-member club still owns some 50,000 acres of the original 200,000 acres and leases an additional 22,000 acres. The holdings include 56 lakes and ponds. Oral tradition tells of Adirondack guide Nick Stoner naming one of the lakes "Nicks Lake," because he did not like a name change on one of the club's other lakes. The Adirondack League Club, much like other private land clubs, is a good steward of the Adirondacks. It was organized "to preserve and conserve the forest, protect the game and fish, promote scientific forestry, and to maintain the preserve for its members."

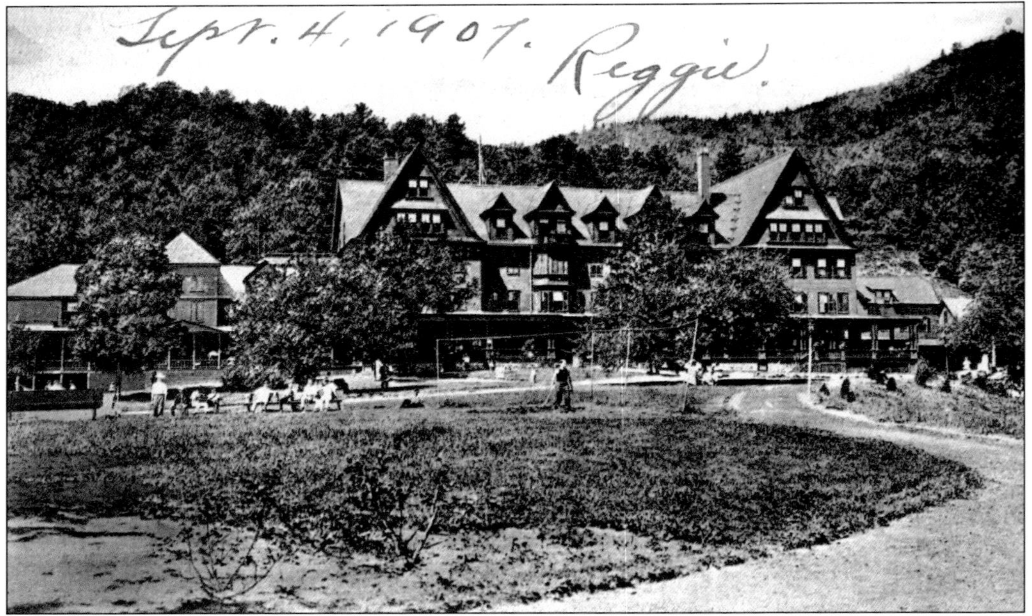

Silas Paine, a vice president of Standard Oil, developed a hotel complex on Lake George at Silver Bay in the late 1890s and created a conference center in 1900. The property had evolved in a typical Adirondack way. Part of an original patent, it was claimed by squatters, became a tourist home, grew into a hotel, and ended up a conference center. It was purchased by the YMCA in 1902 and became the Silver Bay Association Christian Conference Center. The center has attracted thousands for vacations, programs, conferences, and seminars.

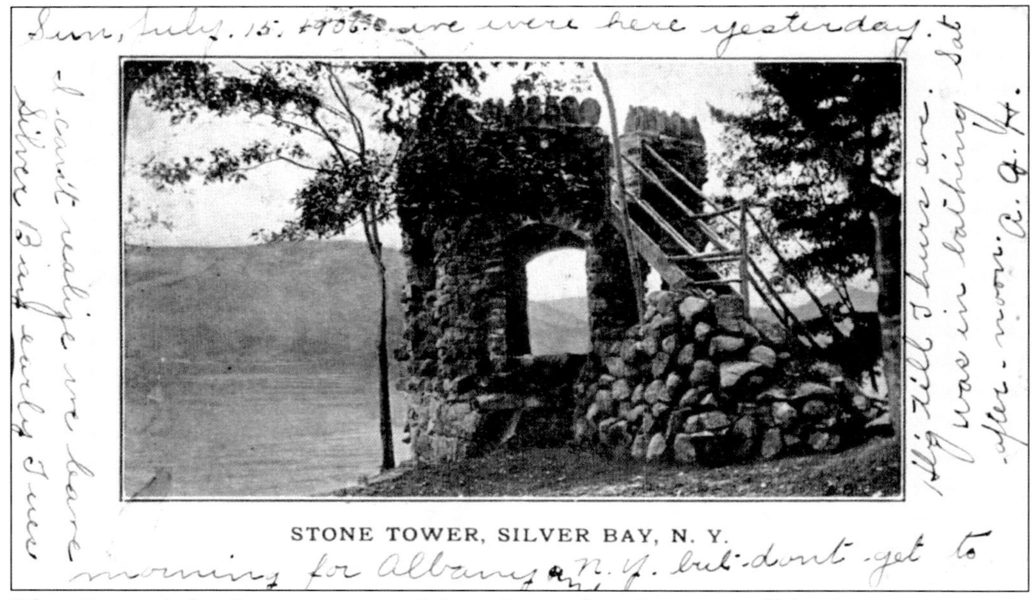

Silver Bay on Lake George was named from the sunshine bouncing off the shimmering waters of "the world's most picturesque lake." Lakeside pavilions, towers, and docks attract those who attend the YMCA Silver Bay Conference Center in the summertime. The peaceful shore is an ideal place for Adirondack solitude and inspiration.

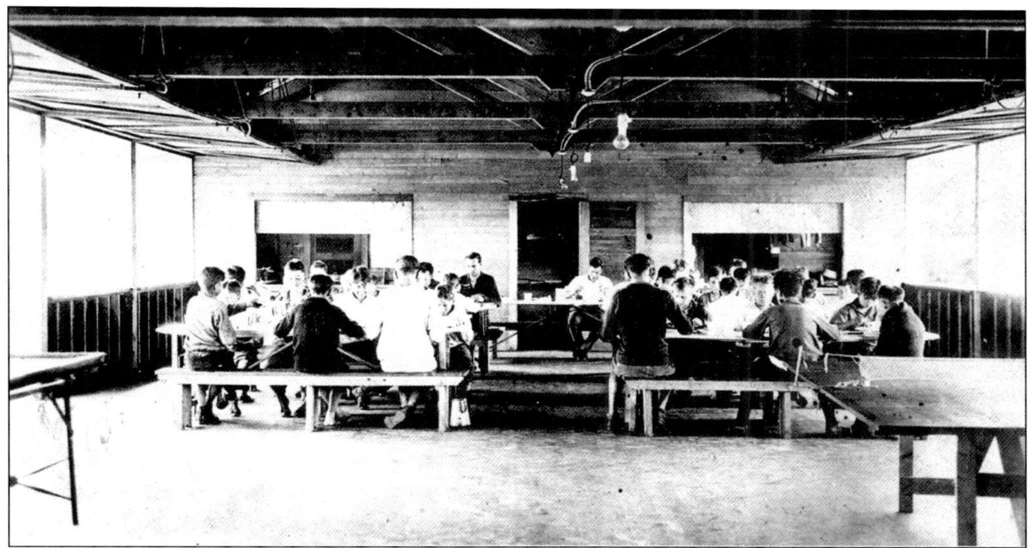

Camp Agaming, a Native American word for "on the shore," was opened on Lake Pleasant in 1923 by the Gloversville YMCA. When it opened, the cabin-type camp was attended by 95 boys, and it eventually grew to house 200 boys each season. The campers enjoyed crafts, swimming, sports, mass games, movie shows, and building friendships. Camp Agaming provided an Adirondack experience for boys from the city for many years but was forced to close when attendance dropped off and expenses went up. This was representative of the fate of many of the original Adirondack children's camps.

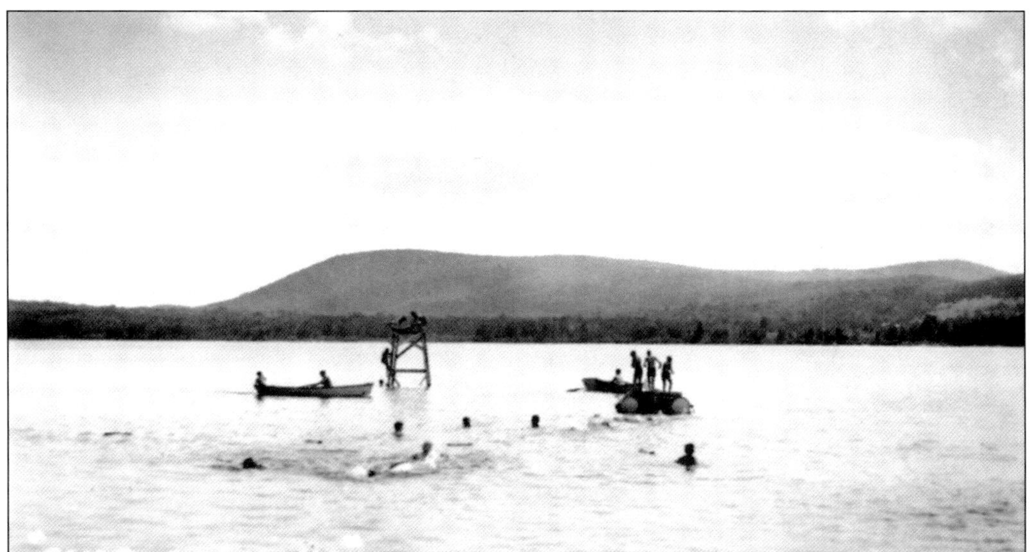

Camp Agaming offered swimming activities in cool and refreshing Lake Pleasant for boys from the city. Many boys developed lifelong friendships at the camp, which was sponsored by the Gloversville YMCA. Many remember swimming out to the raft and enjoying the water away from the city during the hot summer months.

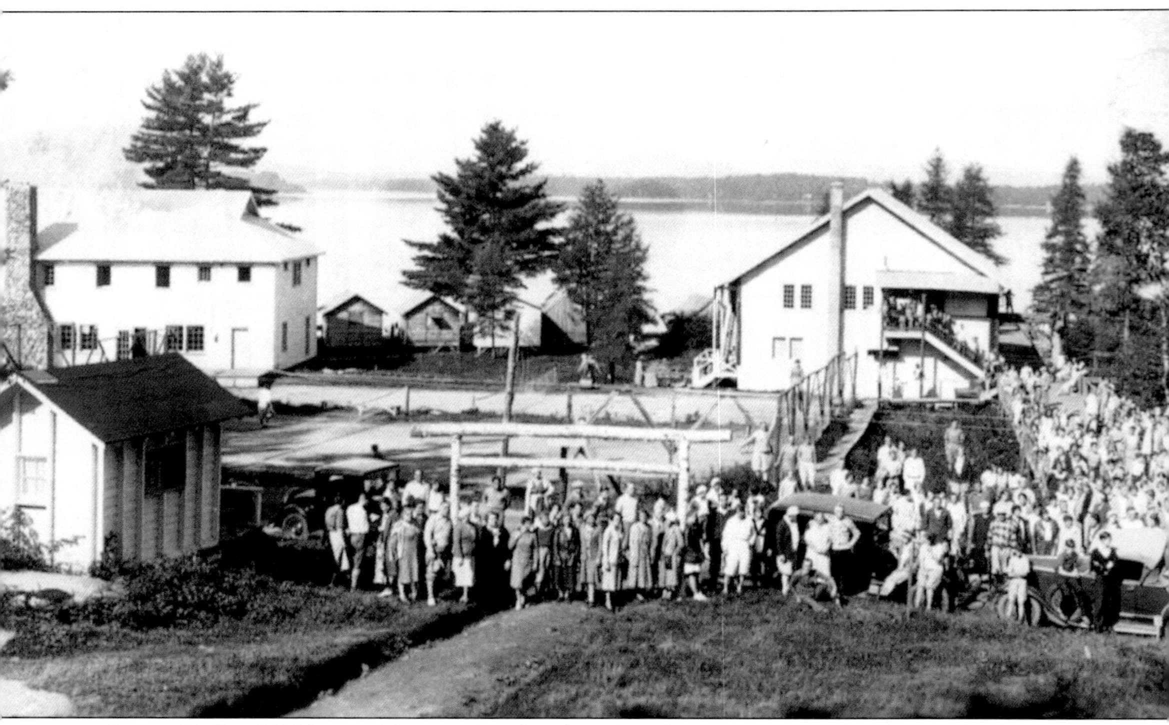

George F. "Pop" Tibbitts of the YMCA developed a religious camp on the shores of Lake Pleasant in 1917. He had already been instrumental in developing YMCA Camp Dudley, the Silver Bay Conference Center, and Camp Glen Eyrie on Lake George. He called his Lake Pleasant camp Camp-of-the-Woods. Shown are some of the camp's cabins and service buildings. Much of the camp consisted of tents on platforms along the beach of Lake Pleasant or on the hillsides. For many years Tibbitts also operated a Florida branch called Park-of-the-Palms. He had made the decision to "build an altar to Jehovah on the shores of Lake Pleasant" while in company with Charles B. Knox of Knox Gelatin fame. When Tibbitts passed away in 1948, his longtime secretary and friend, Gordon Purdy, took over and continued the camp.

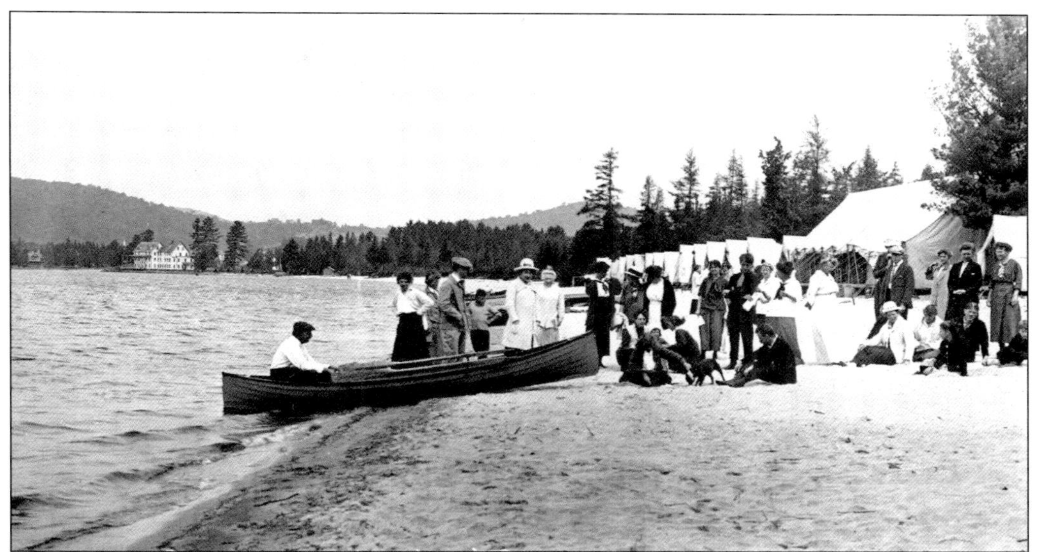

The vision to build a religious camp on the shores of Lake Pleasant would have died if it were not for the determination and ability of Pop Tibbitts. By 1917, Tibbitts had purchased 50 acres for a camp of the woods "where city dwellers could enjoy the beauty and health-giving qualities of the Adirondacks as a living testimony to the glory of the Divine." It was soon to become the well-known outdoor religious center, where words and music in a recreational setting attracts thousands to this day.

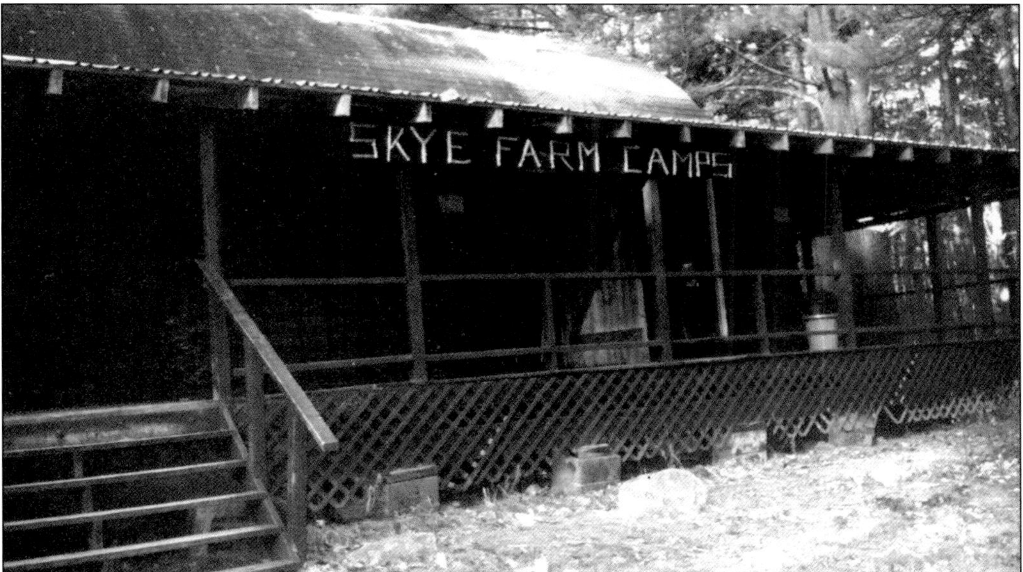

Religious church camps, where hundreds of our nation's youth could spend some time in the Adirondacks each summer, played a major role in the development of the Adirondacks. The camps were sponsored by a variety of denominations and offered programs of crafts, swimming, hiking, and other outdoor activities, along with attention to their spiritual development. The Methodist Skye Farm Camp, shown here, is located on Sherman Lake near Chestertown. The camp was built through the efforts of several ministers on a 148-acre farm. The old stone fences and decaying farm machinery can still be seen in the fast-growing woodlands.

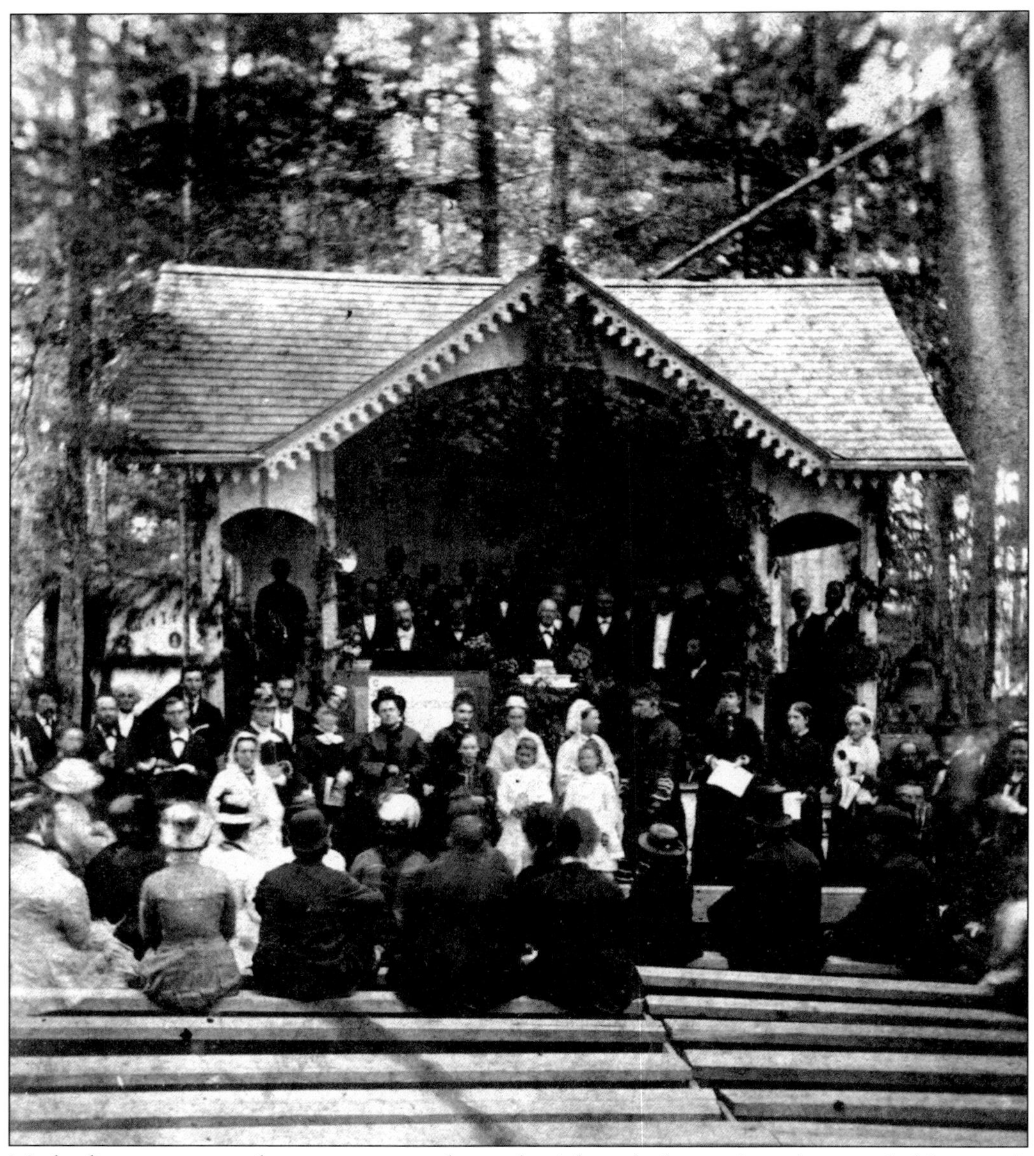

Methodist campgrounds sprang up in the early Adirondacks, with gatherings held in such places as Riverside on the Hudson River at Riparius and Sacandaga Park near Northville on the Sacandaga River. Riverside campground, at Riparius, was founded in 1868, and the tent meetings at Sacandaga began *c.* 1884. Church groups came by foot, wagon, and railroad to gather under the tents or open sky to hear the word of God. A plot was cleared, planks were placed on the stumps for benches, elevated boxes called lumberjacks were scattered around the yards to be filled with cobblestones to hold the fires for lighting the evening services, and a pulpit stage was constructed to elevate the speakers. Tent meetings became so popular that tabernacles were erected and the tent platforms were turned into cottages.

Three

Adirondack Style

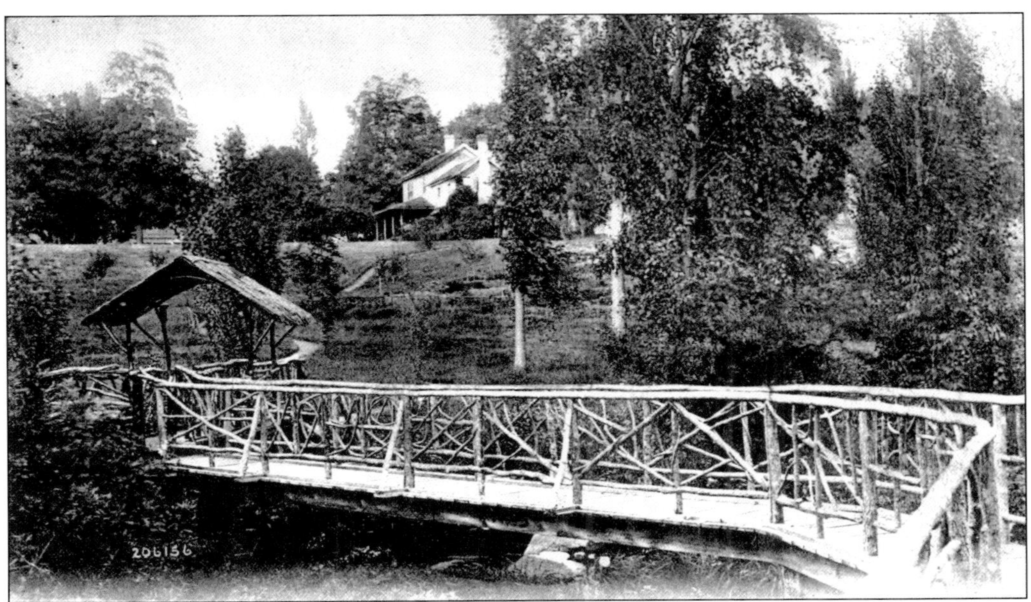

The use of native materials was a natural occurrence in the Adirondacks. Existing materials grown in the forests were inexpensive and available. Rustic twig furniture, logs and rustic trim on houses, rustic gateways, fences, and bridges were commonplace. This rustic bridge in Broadalbin is typical of what could be seen in parks and across bays or streams throughout the Adirondack settlements.

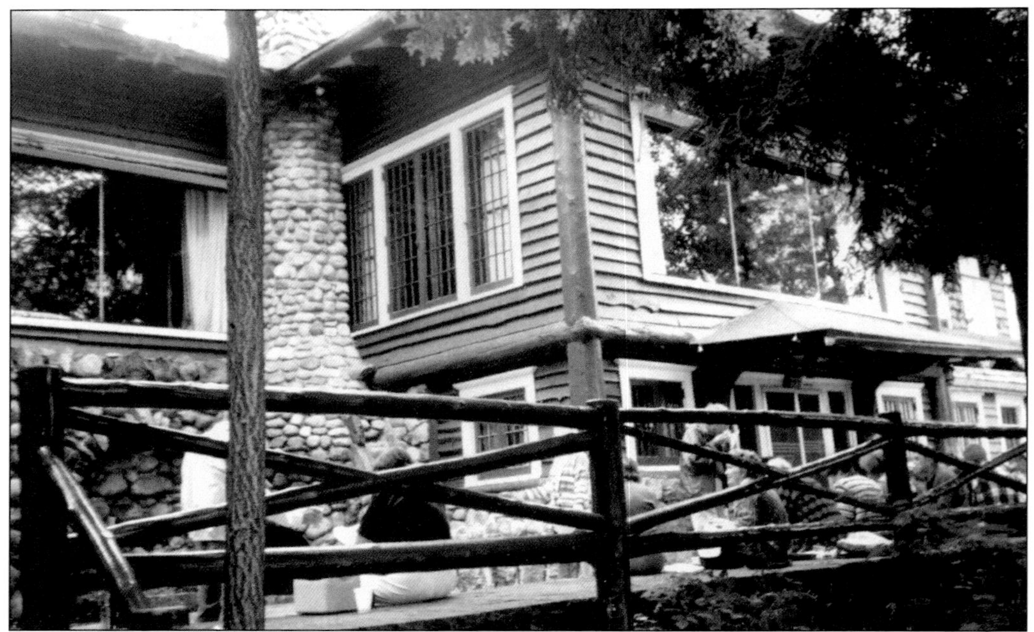

Much has been written about the "great camps" of the Adirondacks. From the mid-1800s to the 1930s, our nation's wealthy came to the Adirondacks to build massive camp complexes, most with a giant main building made of logs and surrounded by 20 to 70 support buildings. Camp Hutridge, commonly known as Camp Topridge, on the St. Regis Lake, gained fame as the home of Post Cereal fortune heiress Marjorie Merriweather Post, whose extensive collection of Native American artifacts in her 80- by 100- foot living room is now in the Smithsonian. Camp Topridge was once willed to the state of New York but is now in private ownership.

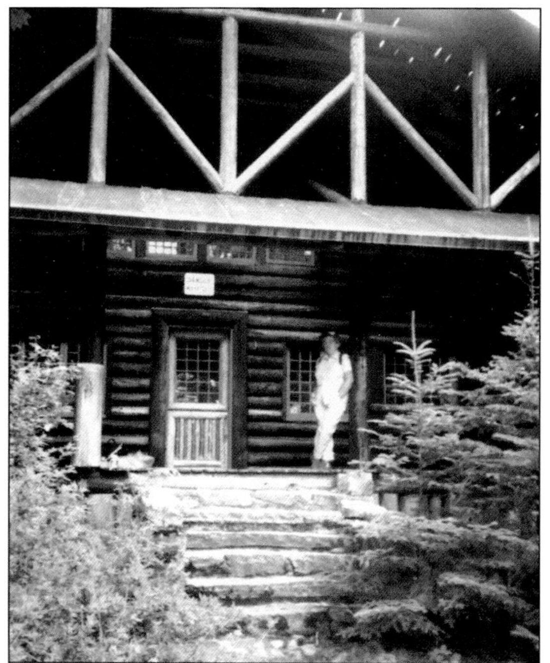

The people of New York State own a great camp. It is Camp Santanoni, near Newcomb, once the summer home of the Robert Pruyn family. A fine example of rustic Adirondack architecture, it is made of native logs and includes a series of buildings connected by a common veranda, or porch. A farm complex was also constructed on the estate. Today, the entire great camp estate serves as an interpretive site on the heydays of the wealthy in the Adirondacks. It is open with guides during the summer season for those who want to make the four-mile hike, horseback ride, or bicycle trip in to the camp.

Fox Lair, on Route 8 between Wells and Weavertown, has become overgrown and a part of the surrounding wilderness. It was once the site of the wealthy estate of the Hudnut cosmetic clan. Richard Hudnut, who developed a famous perfume, bought 1,200 acres on the East Branch of the Sacandaga River in 1900 and built his baronial mansion. It had a 50- by 50-foot living room filled with French furniture. The photograph shows some of the exquisite stonework and the balcony of Lady Hudnut's room.

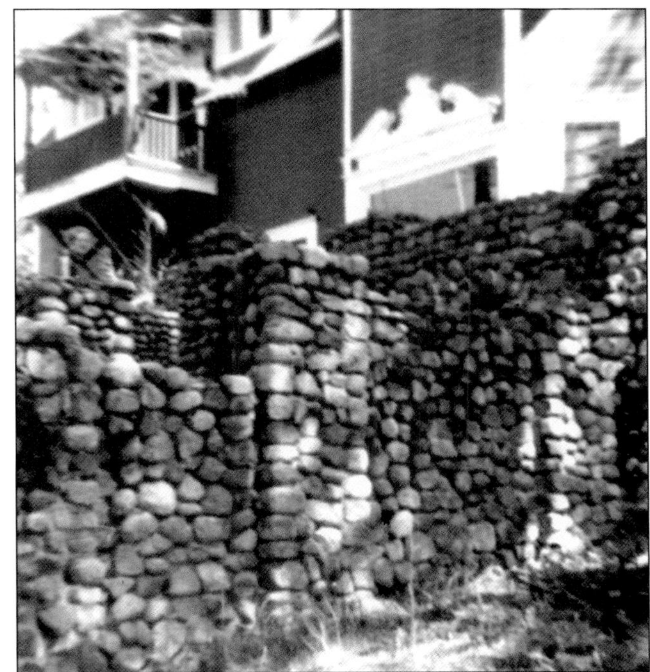

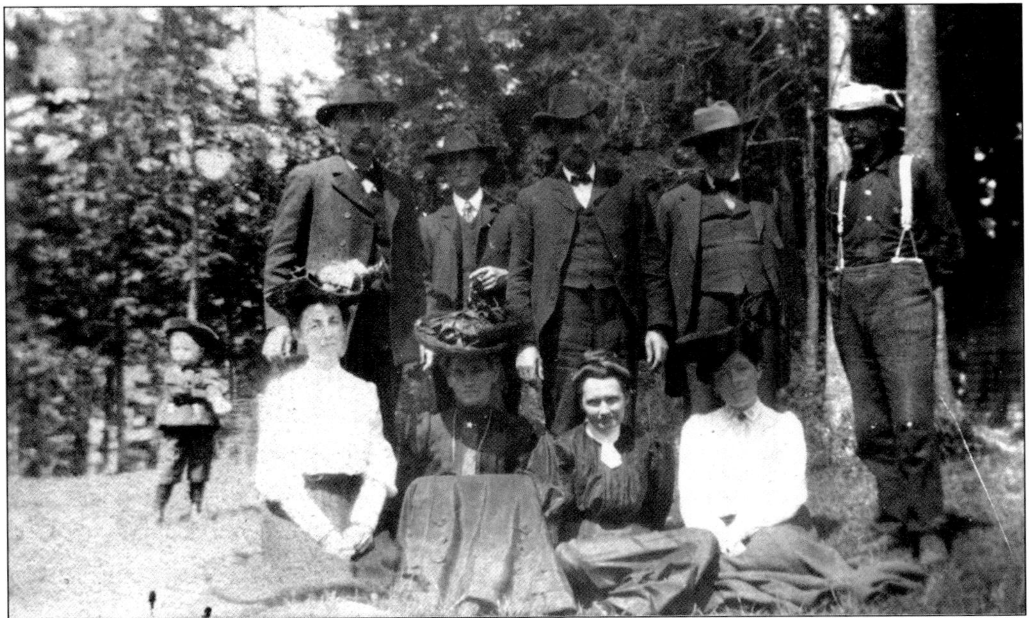

Great camp owners and their friends enjoyed their rustic retreats in the Adirondacks. Edward H. Litchfield, a Brooklyn lawyer who found the Adirondacks to his liking in 1866, built a massive chateau near Tupper Lake in 1905. The man wearing the suspenders might be the caretaker-guide, an important position in the year-round care of the 8,600-acre estate. Oral tradition tells of Litchfield surrounding his Adirondack property with an eight-foot-high chain-link fence to hold his wild game farm. In later years, the fence company wanted to photograph the fence still in use but unsuccessfully searched for it near Litchfield, Connecticut.

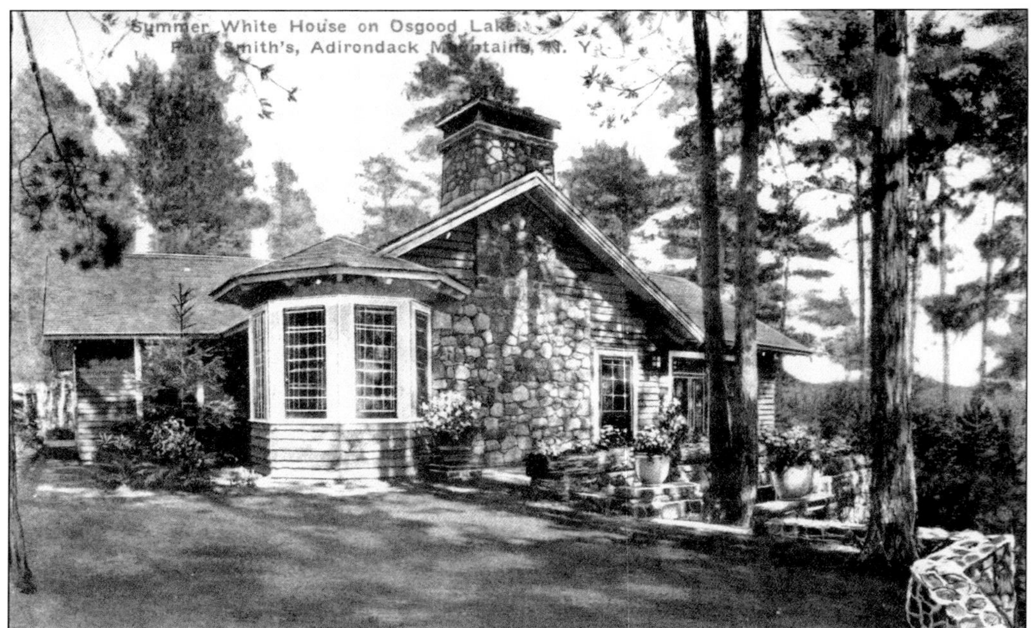

In 1926, Calvin Coolidge took up fishing and accepted the loan of White Pine Camp, on Osgood Pond near Paul Smiths, for use as a summer White House. The president's wife, Grace, son John, and the family's two white collies, Rob Roy and Prudence Prim, accompanied him. His visit was a big event in its day for the remote Adirondacks and was covered by the major newspapers. The camp is opened for tours or lodging today.

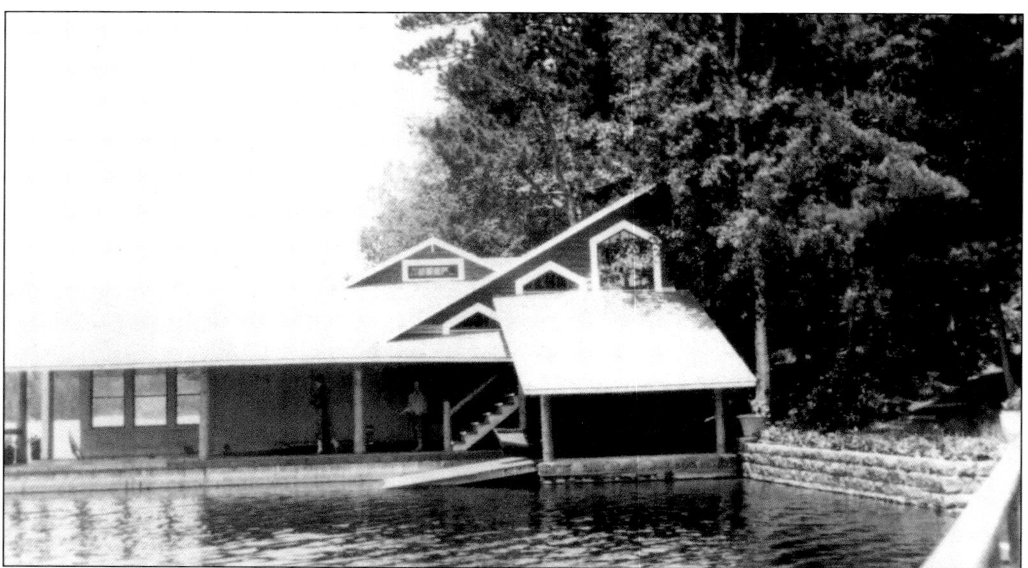

White Pine Camp has 3,400 feet of shoreline on secluded Osgood Pond. The boathouse, much like the early Adirondack boathouses, sits in the water, allowing the boats to be driven under cover. Many of the boathouses also included a stairway to an observation deck, where guests could get a good view of the lake and boats.

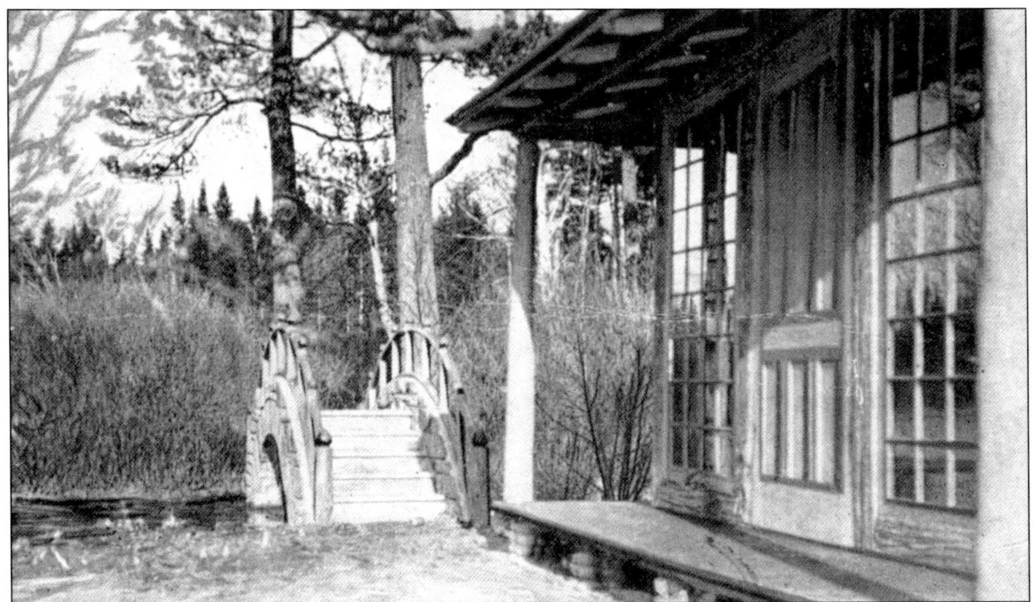

This postcard of the tea garden at President Coolidge's summer White House was mailed in 1926 while the first family was in residence. The message on the back reads, "Do you drink tea? This is where the President takes his tea."

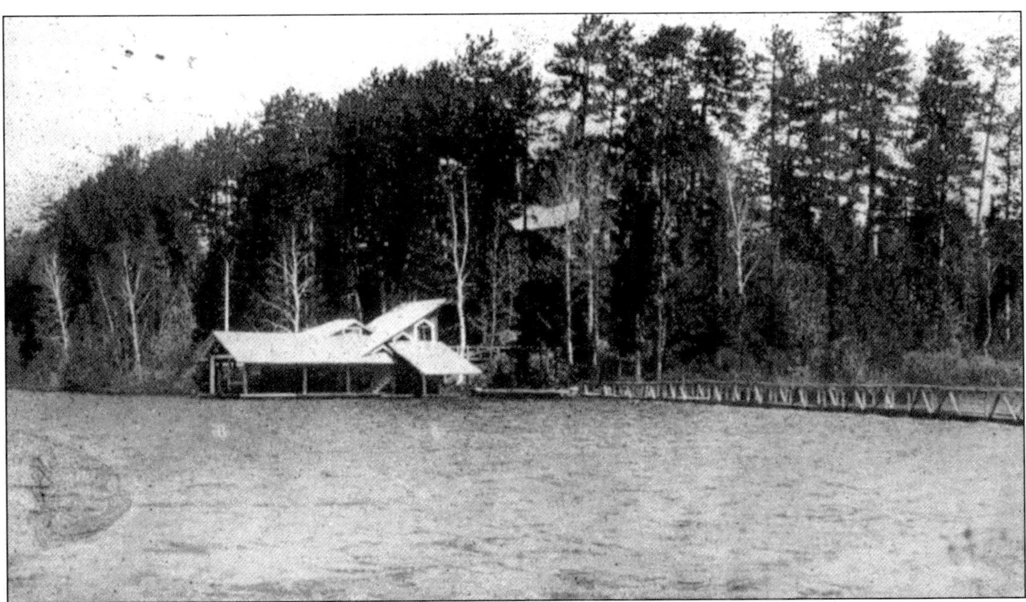

This footbridge, 300 feet long, stretches across the lagoon at White Pine Camp. The bridge, along with some 20 other buildings, has been restored. The camp, built in 1907, featured brainstorm wood siding, lumber cut with one edge left in its rough natural state. The development of the siding, which spread to other Adirondack camps, was the brainstorm of builder Ben Muncil, who refused to use white clapboard siding on an Adirondack camp.

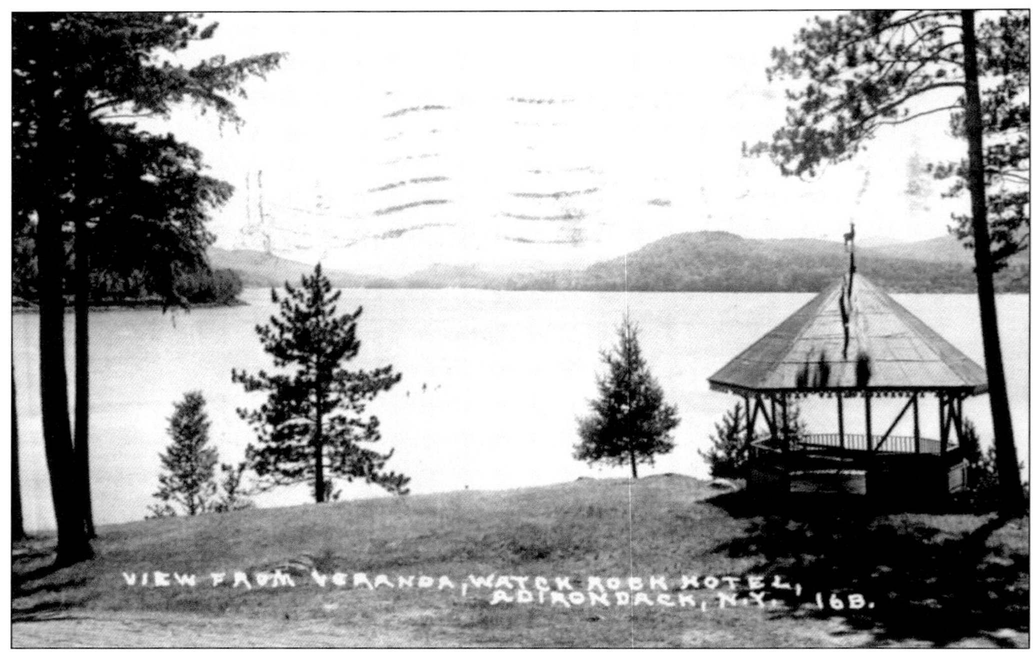

In their heyday, gazebos flourished throughout the Adirondacks. Most camps had a gazebo in the woods, on the lakeshore, or attached to the main building by a covered walkway. Some called them summer sitting rooms or summerhouses; the larger ones were called pavilions. Gazebos were perfect places for slowing down, savoring the view, enjoying a little company, or reading a book.

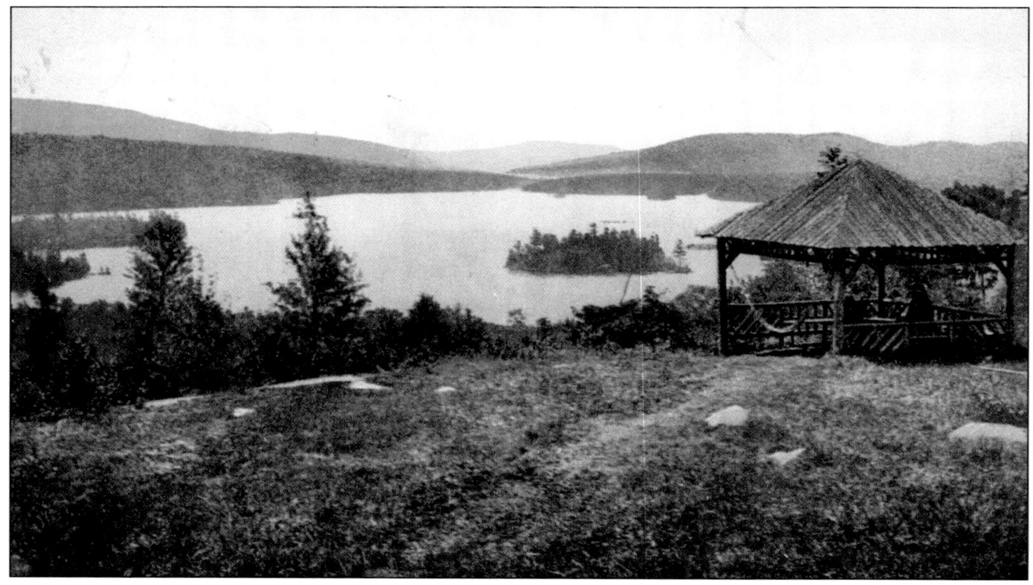

The original gazebo at the Adirondack Museum in Blue Mountain Lake has been restored. It commands a wonderful view of Blue Mountain Lake and the surrounding forested hillsides. It appears in the earliest pictures of what became the museum grounds with the one here from 1905.

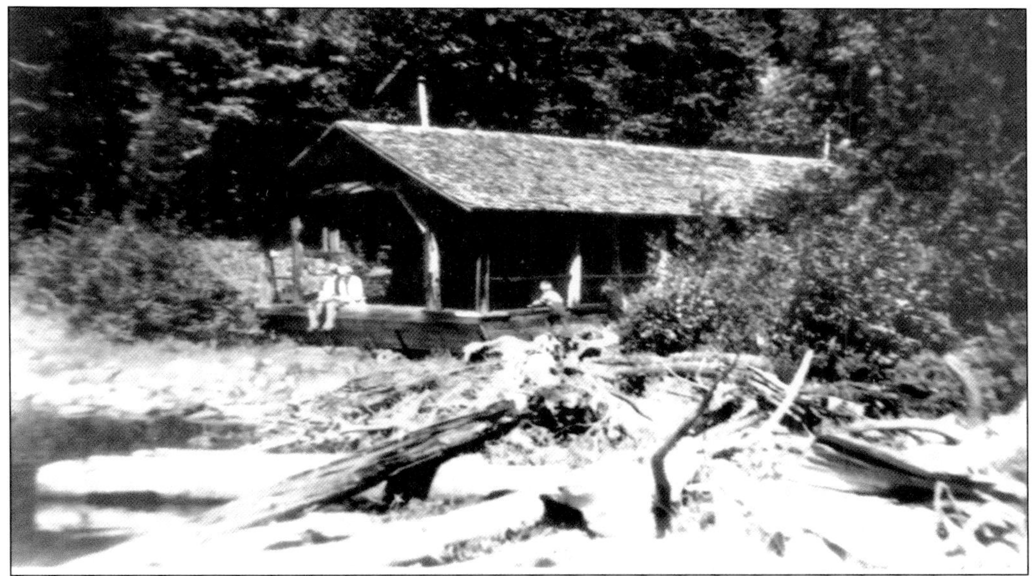

A strange-looking craft was found in the woods at Cortland College's Camp Pine Knot on Raquette Lake. It was the Barque of Pine Knot, a houseboat built in the 1870s by William West Durant, an Adirondack great camp builder. The houseboat was used during the black fly season to escape the flies. It seems that the flies do not like to travel to the center of the lake, so the boat was parked out in the lake for the family's use. It was complete with three rooms, a kitchen, and a bath with running water.

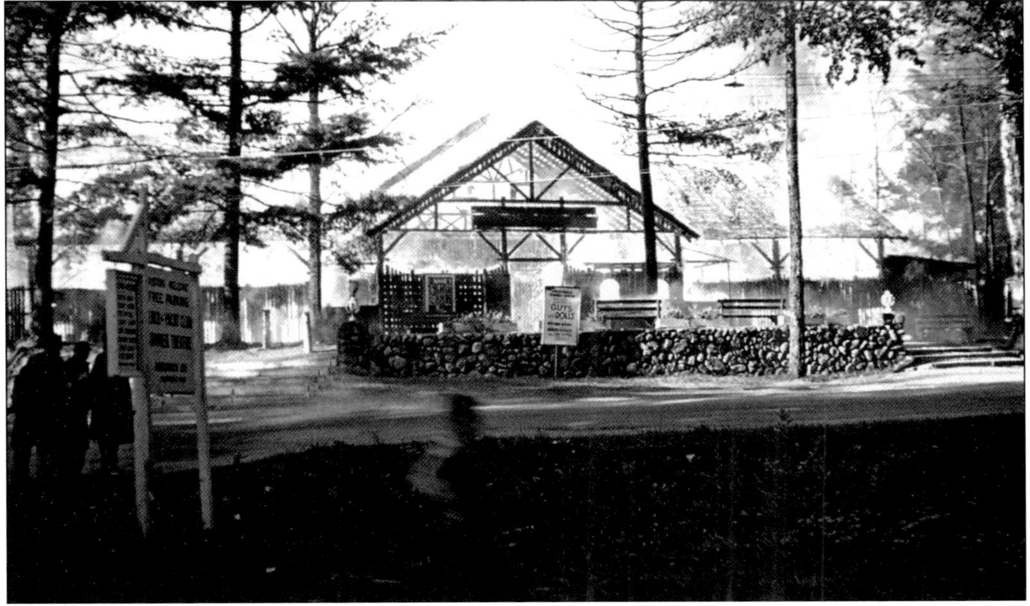

Another unique Adirondack rustic structure was the Rustic Theater at Sacandaga Park. It was built of giant Adirondack logs with an open space halfway up the wall to the roofline. The theater offered concerts and vaudeville twice a day beginning in the early 1900s. Silent moving pictures were shown during the evening. Live theater followed, with stars like Marlene Dietrich. The theater burned in 1955, after a performance of *Guys and Dolls*.

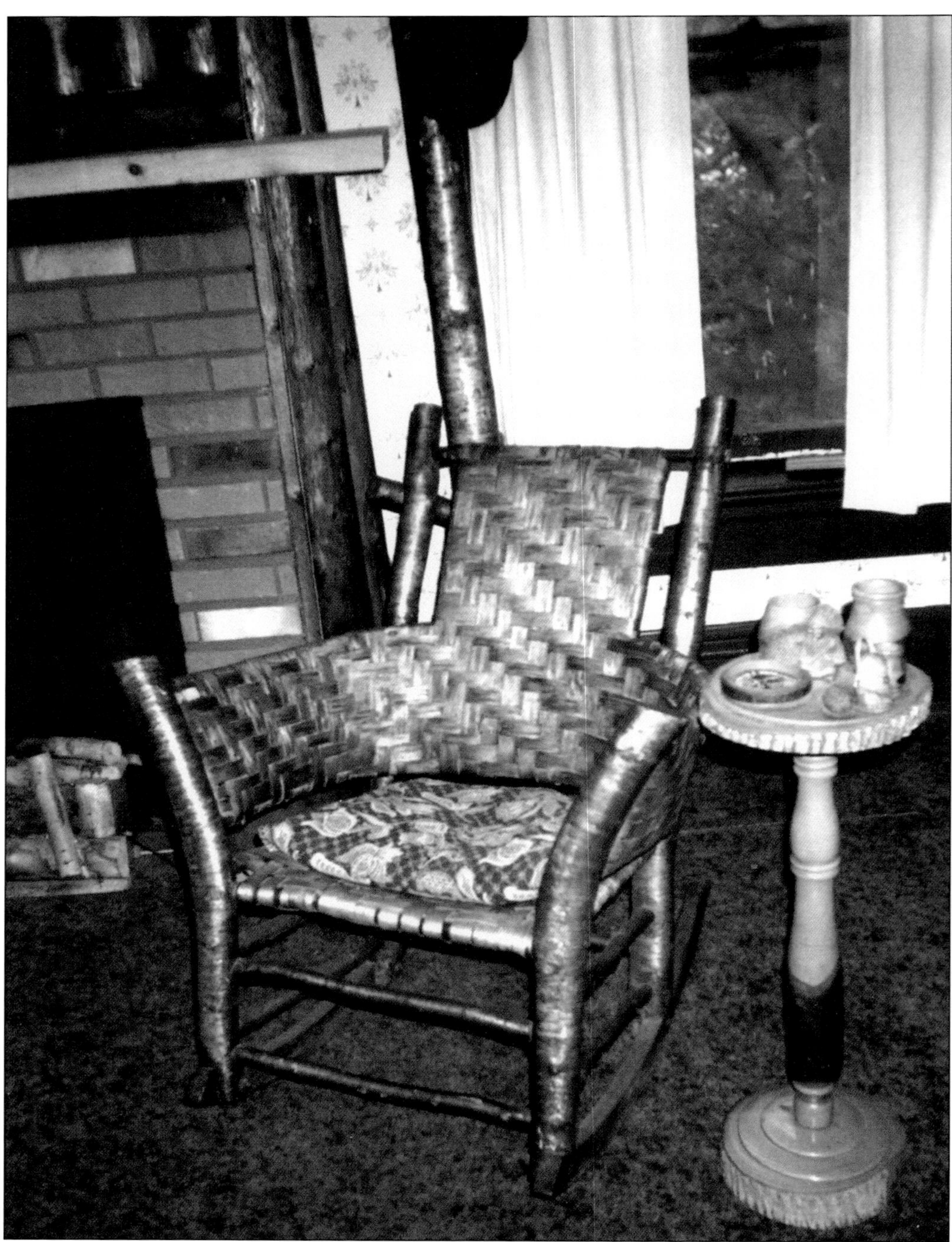

Makers of rustic furniture started up in all parts of the Adirondacks. Although they had no contact with one another, much of their furniture was similar. Native materials appear to dictate somewhat the finished product. Using the available native trees, the furniture makers created useful furniture for their homes and for the camp owners. One such maker, Lee Fountain of Wells, became best known for his yellow birch rocking chairs, which, at one time, graced many Adirondack porches and living rooms.

Four

HAMLETS, VILLAGES, AND SETTLEMENTS

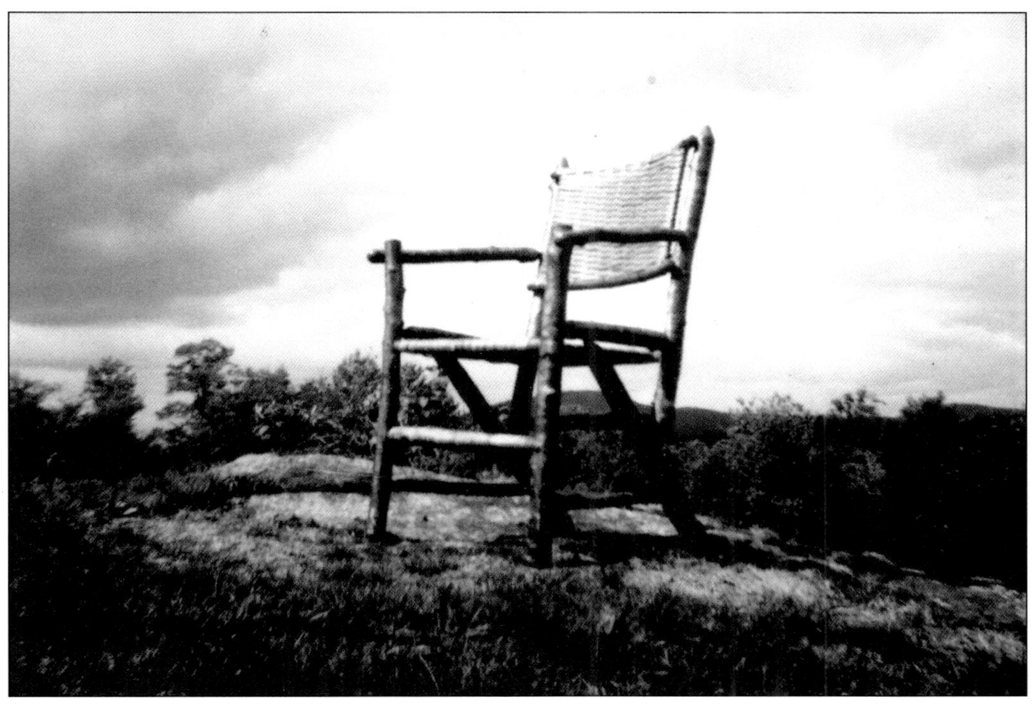

The clever Adirondack craftsmen who made furniture from native materials knew when to cut the wood to keep the bark forever tight. Lee Fountain fashioned the legs of this chair with diagonal back legs to keep it tight through use and to stop it from tipping back. The seat and back splints were stripped from long-lasting ash logs.

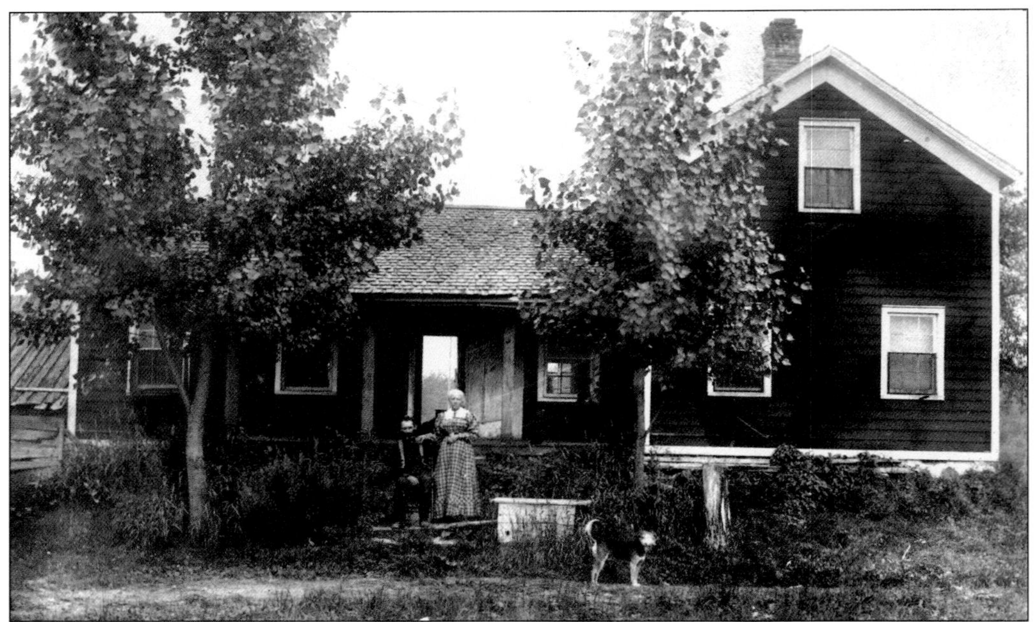

When William and Laura Whitman had their picture taken in front of their Osborn Bridge home in 1910, little did they know that by 1930 the property would be under water. When the Sacandaga Reservoir (Great Sacandaga Lake) was created, the entire village of Osborn Bridge had to be moved or destroyed. The site of the village can be visited in the fall of the year when the Sacandaga waters are at their lowest.

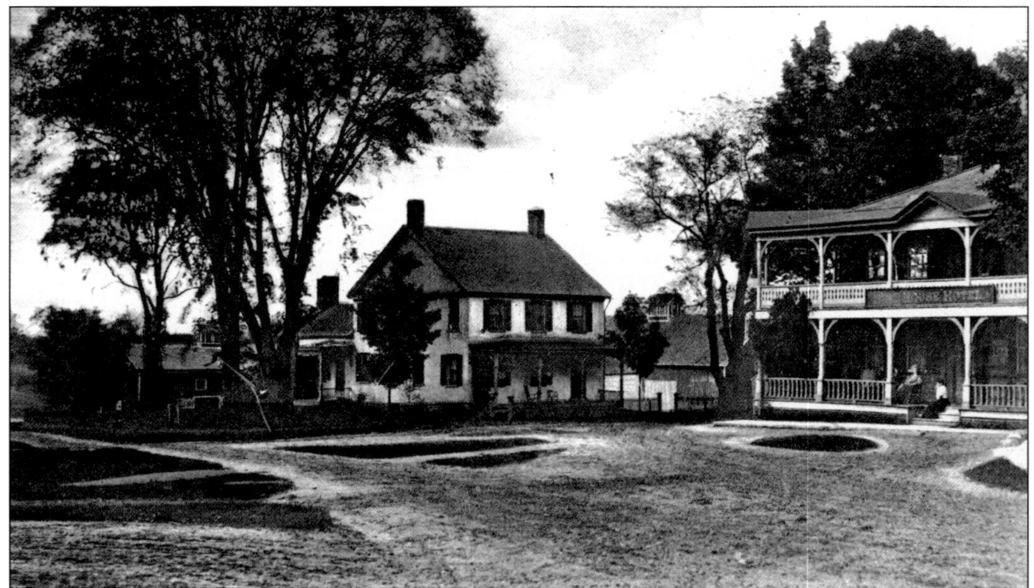

Sir William Johnson, who settled in Johnstown in 1763, had his fish house in the town of Northampton. The village, first settled in the 1770s, became known as Fish House while the post office was called Northampton, from the original patent. In 1961, the village was officially declared Fish House. When the Great Sacandaga Lake was constructed in 1930, three quarters of the village was covered by water, including the village square.

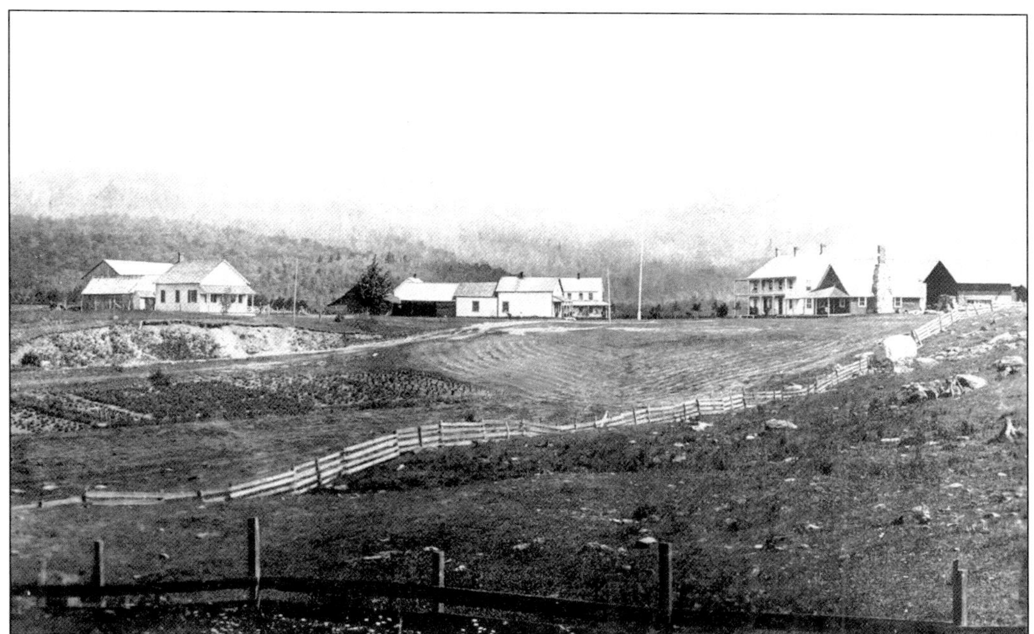

Stony Creek was a sparsely populated town with scattered buildings when it became incorporated. The early wood-centered industries eventually gave way to a tourist economy as the forests were used up and the tanning industry changed. Over half of the town today belongs to the state of New York.

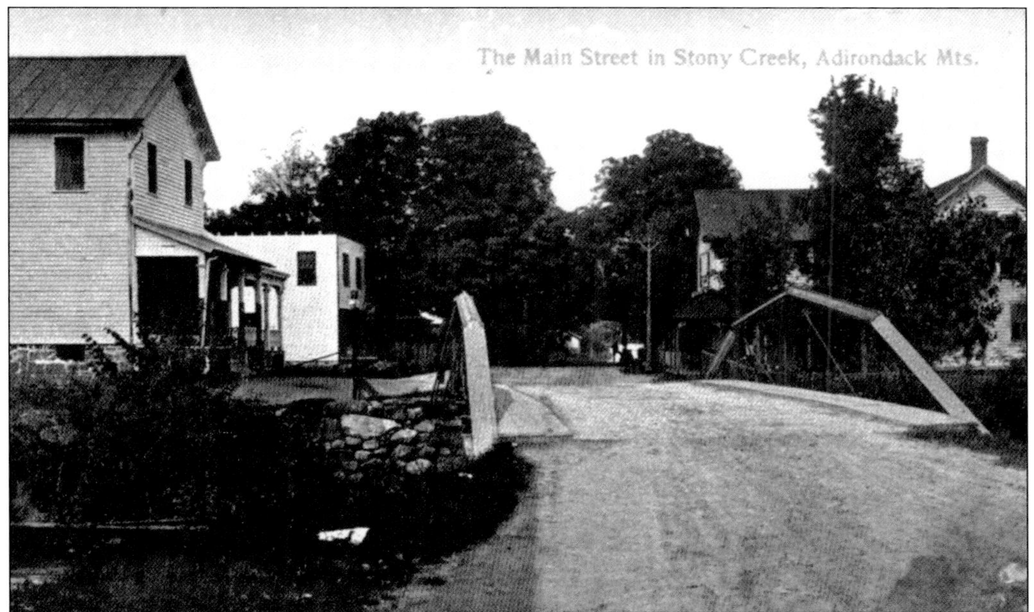

The town of Stony Creek became official in 1853. The industries in the town, related to the forest, included several sawmills, potash production, a broom factory, and the biggest industry, a tannery, which depended on the hemlock bark. When the industries closed down, the 20th century brought the summer tourists, the principal livelihood in Stony Creek today.

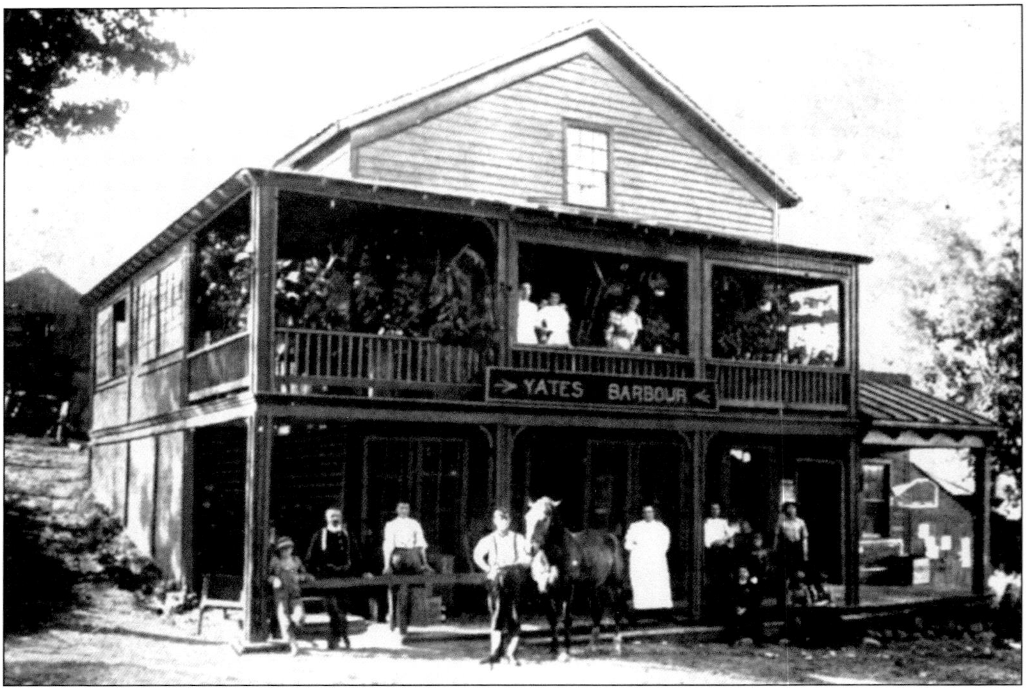

Corinth is one of the southeastern gateways to the Adirondacks. It got its beginning with the early Adirondack logging operations in the 1770s. Permanent settlers arrived in Corinth c. 1775, during the American Revolution. In 1818, Corinth became an official town in the Adirondack wilderness. At its second town meeting, a bounty of $10 was placed on wolves. Corinth became the "snowshoe capital of America" in the 1970s.

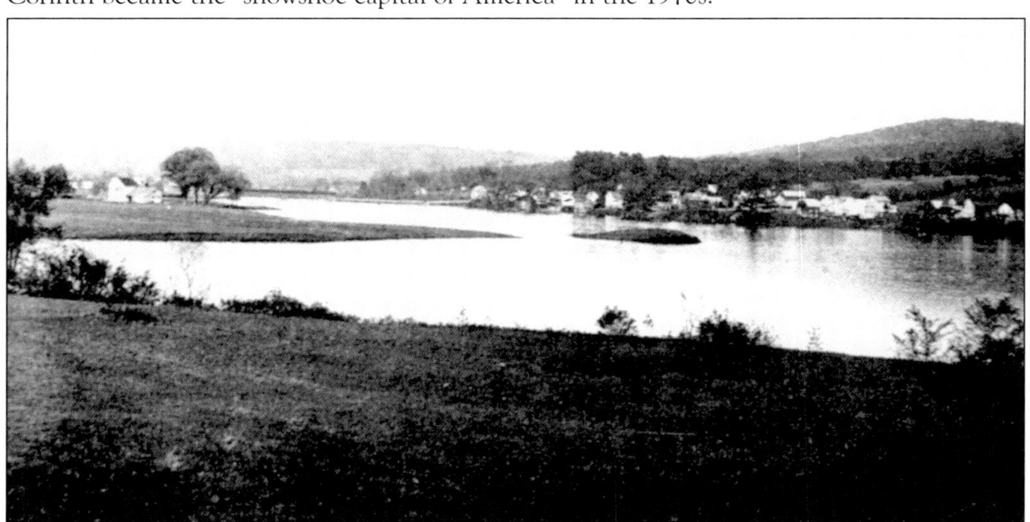

In this early-1920s photograph, the hamlet of Wells can be seen on the banks of the Sacandaga River. Brush and trees were being removed from the river flats to get ready for the construction of the proposed dam and lake. The long covered bridge across the river can be seen in the distance. At one time, the farmers grew so many cucumbers along the riverbanks that part of the settlement was called "Pickleville."

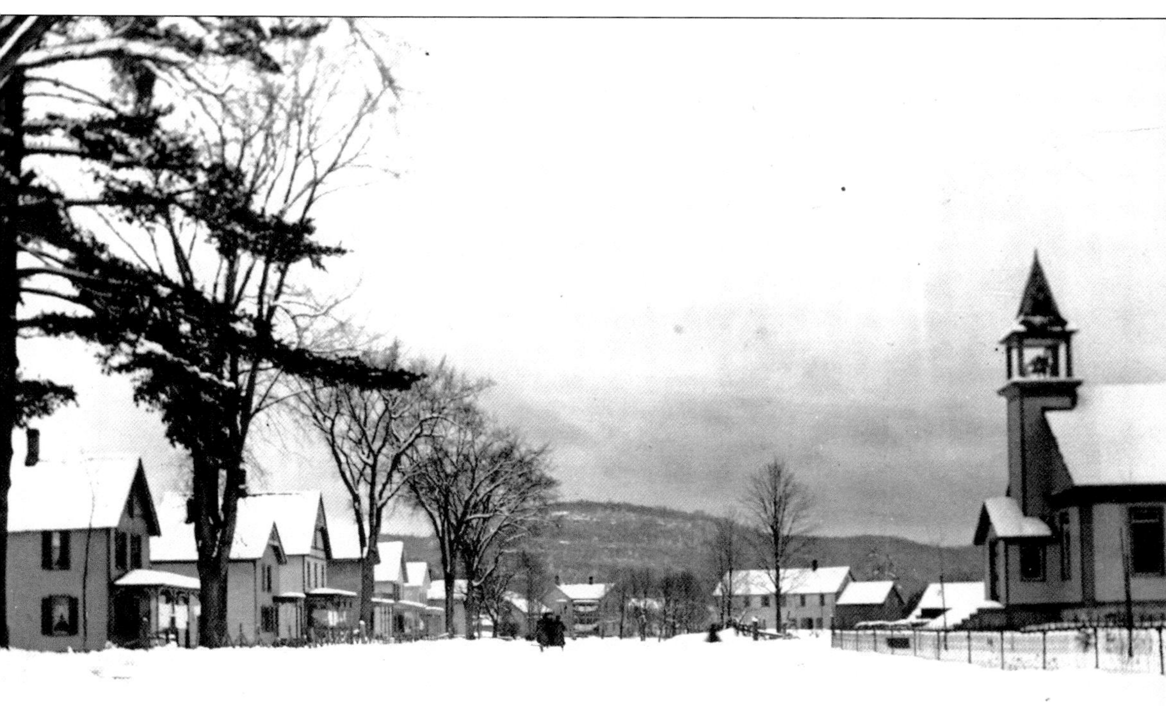

The hamlet of Wells in Hamilton County is situated at the bottom of an ancient sea. The unique geology of this sedimentary "island" in the midst of the metamorphosed Adirondacks has been examined since the 1842 study of Prof. Ebenezer Emmons. Settlement began just before the start of the 19th century when Isaiah and Hannah Whitman came from Long Island to build the first tannery. William Wells built a grist- and sawmill, and the town became organized in 1805, the first town in Hamilton County.

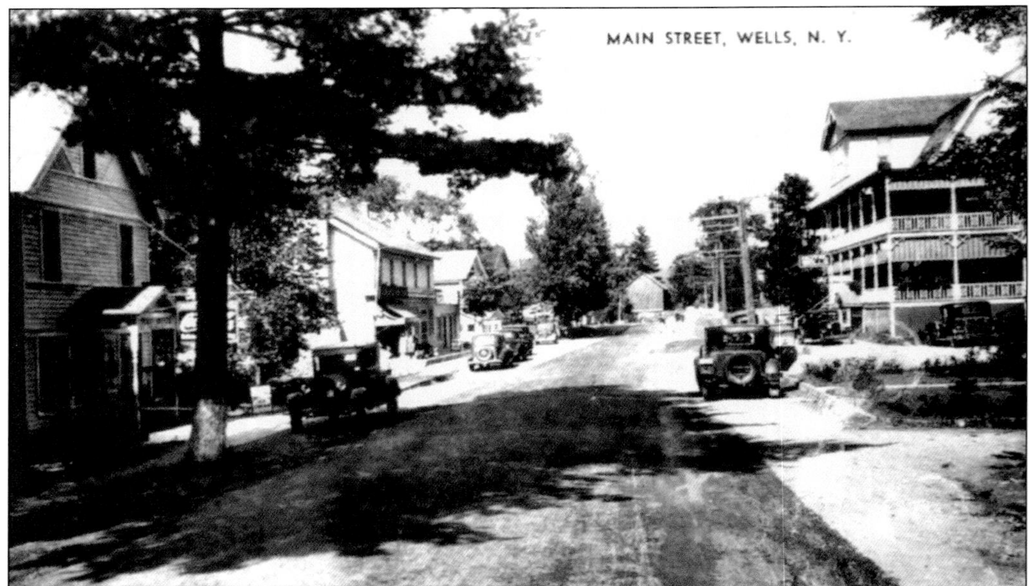

Main streets in the Adirondack hamlets were the commercial centers of their day. A hotel, general store, drugstore with an ice-cream parlor, and the post office could be found on Main Street. The barn at the end of the street was part of a nearby farm, which provided a place to change horses for the stage that passed through with passengers and mail for the Adirondack settlements.

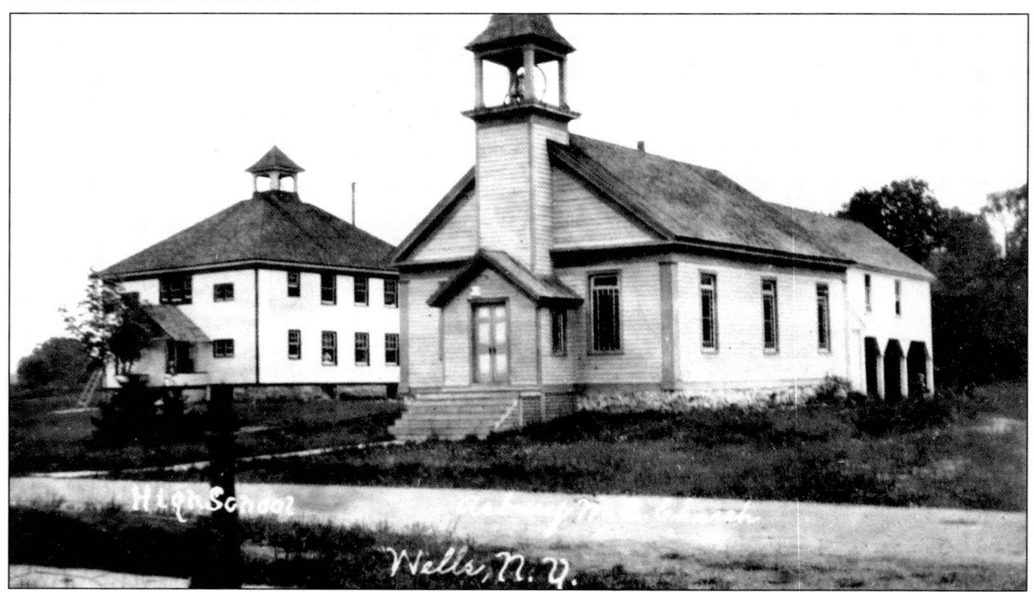

Wherever the Adirondack settlers chose to live, churches and schools soon followed. The Wells Union Free School was constructed in 1907 and enlarged for the high school in 1926. The Wells Methodists held services in their homes before 1840 and built their church in 1852. The old Wells High School building was added to over the years and, in 1964, was replaced by a completely new building. The shelter behind the church provided a place for horses; today, it has been replaced by a dining hall and Sunday school rooms.

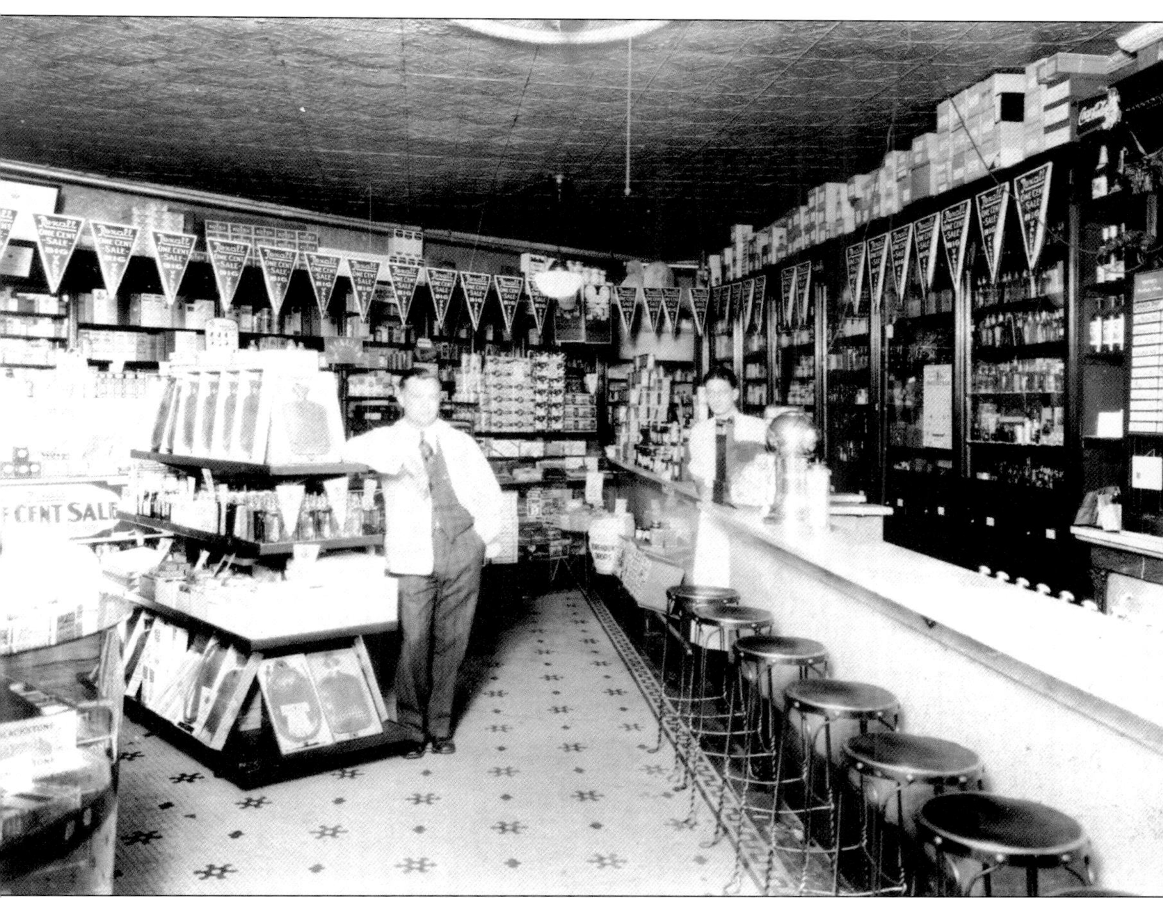

Drugstores were a welcomed addition to the Adirondack hamlets, where access to medical help and medicines often meant a trip to a distant community. The drugstore carried a wide range of products and often had a soda fountain. Fred Sawers is the druggist in the photograph. Note that the Rexall "one cent sale" is on. Other brands of note include Blackstone cigars, Coca-cola, Canada Dry, and the popular Horehound drops.

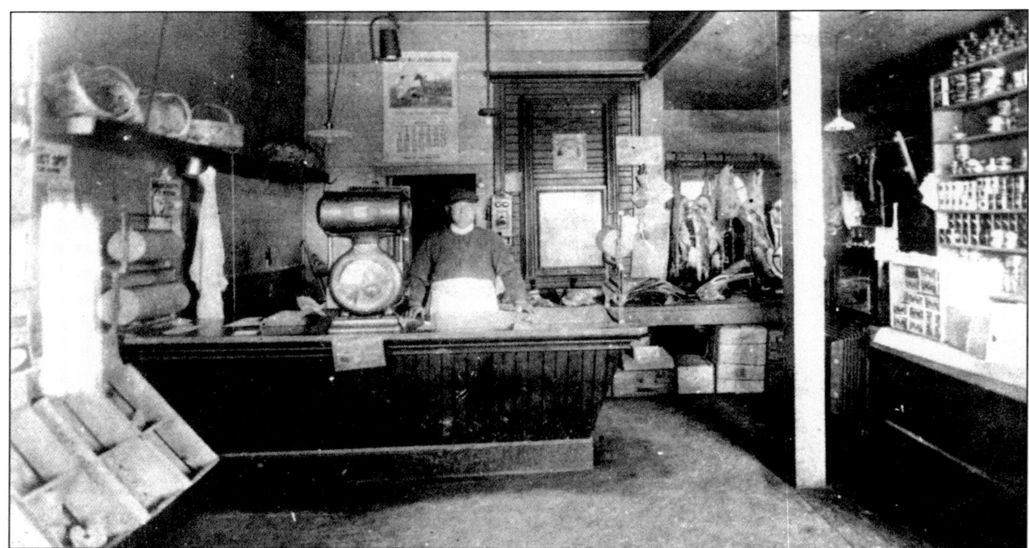

The old general store was common to the Adirondack hamlets and met the needs of the surrounding rural area. The store supplied food and clothing, tools and garden supplies, hardware and sewing needs, along with feed for animals. The general store became the gathering place for news and fellowship, and often had a checker board, an old potbelly stove, and a nearby spittoon for tobacco chewers. Note the old wooden telephone on the wall over the left shoulder of owner L.L. Buyce.

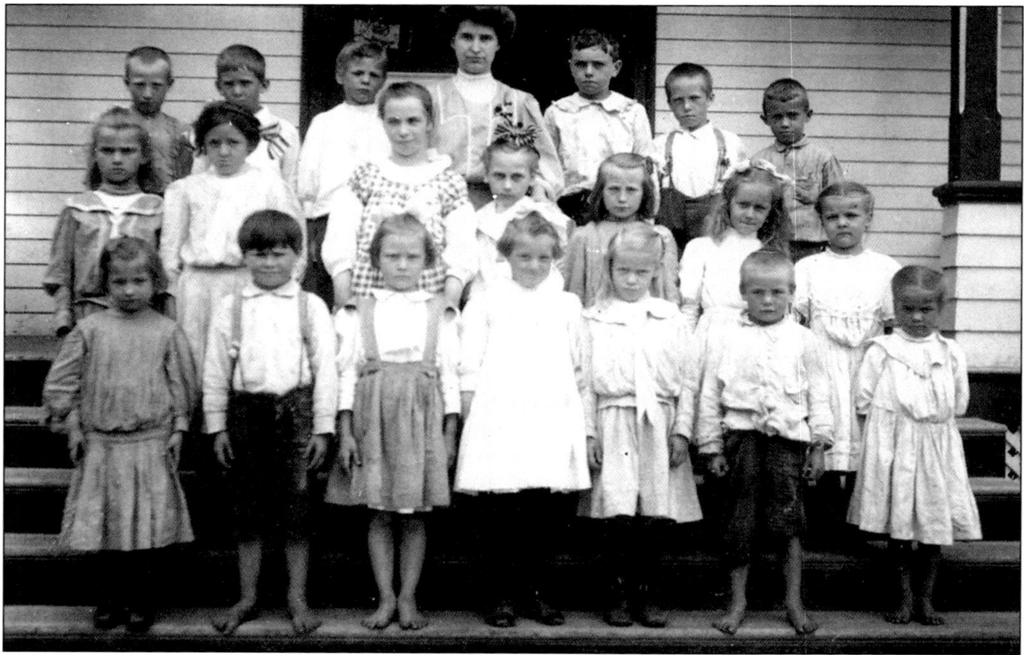

Children dressed up to go to school and, with the closing of the one-room schools, they attended central schools in the Adirondack settlements where classes were much larger. Teachers were young and often boarded with someone in town. These children attended a school in Wells. Note the bare feet on some of those in the front row.

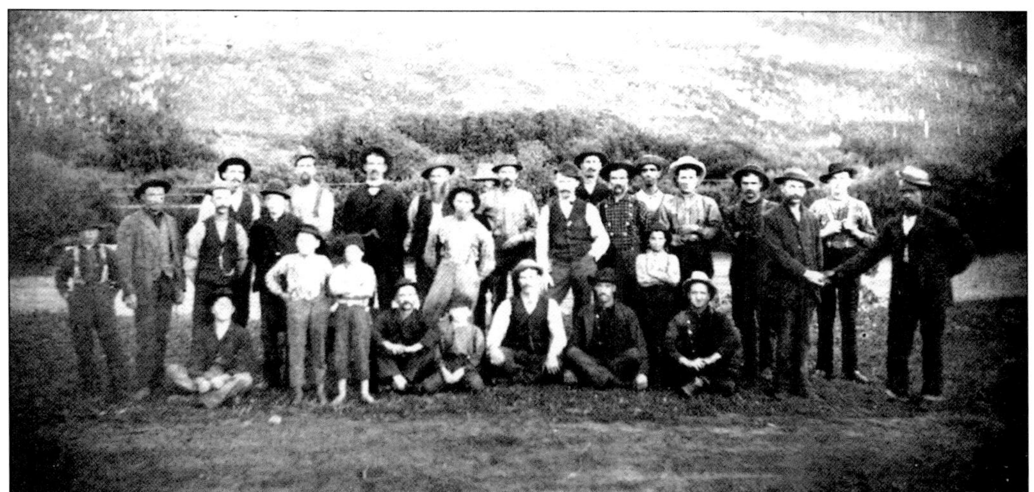

Frank Girard (second from right, holding onto his suspenders) once ran a hunting and fishing camp in the former Morgan Lumber Company boardinghouse. The two well-dressed men flanking Girard apparently have made a deal and are sealing it with a handshake, often better than a contract in those days. Like Girard, the others in this early photograph may have been residents of Griffin—before it became a ghost town—who worked in the tannery or lumber camps of the two men shaking hands.

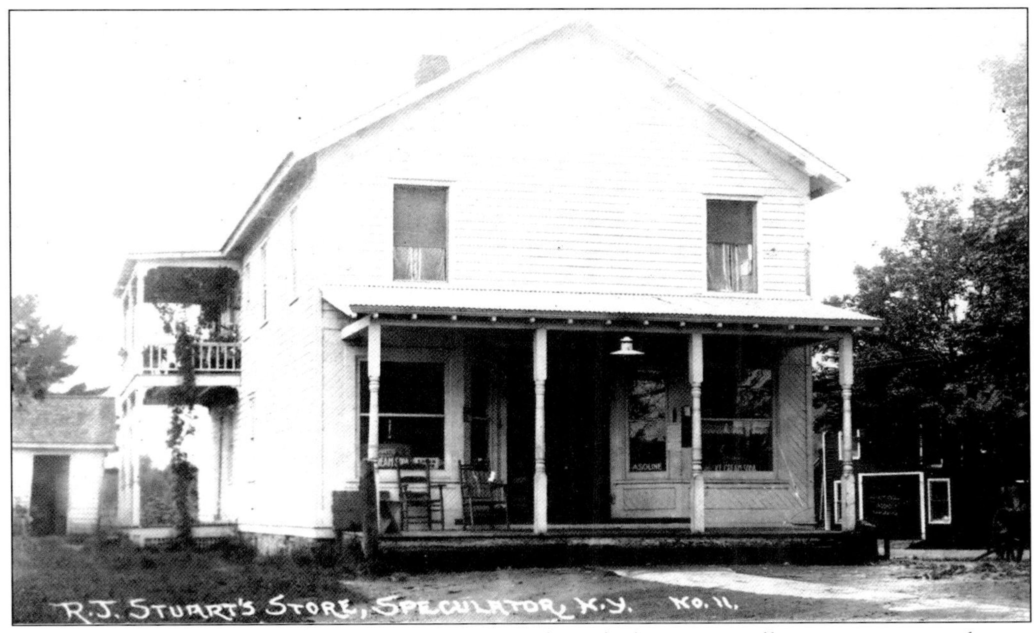

Robert J. Stuart left his position of running the Adirondack Inn in Wells to open a general store in Speculator c. 1913. Some years later there were three additional general stores in town. One old-time general store owner was heard to say, "when one general store opens in the Adirondacks and they begin to make money, three others open up and they all starve together!"

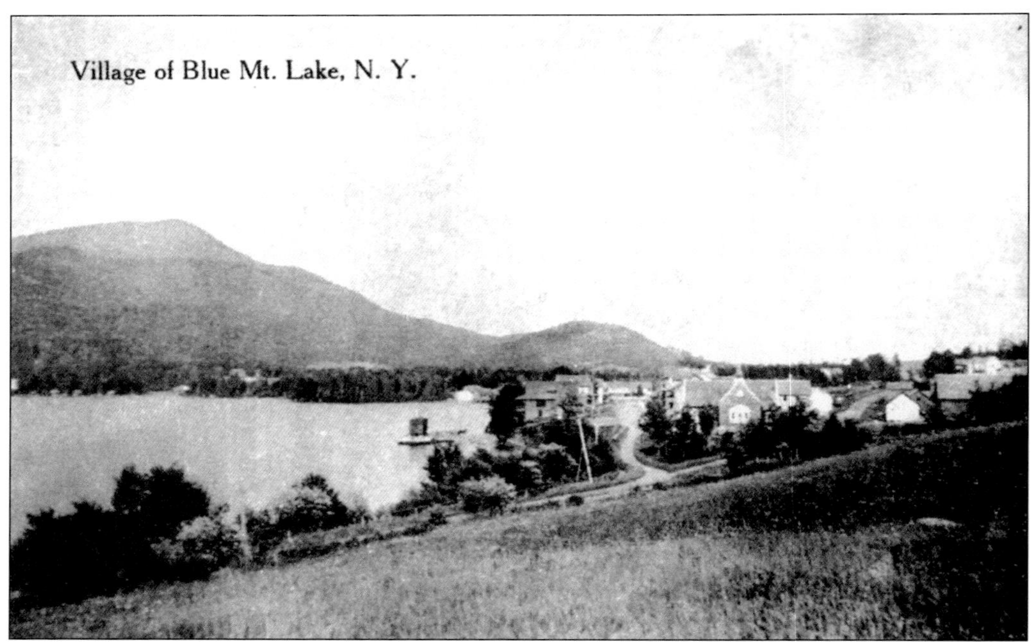

The hamlet of Blue Mountain Lake stands at an Adirondack crossroad where Route 30, the Adirondack Trail, meets Route 28. Blue Mountain Lake was once called Lake Janet after the wife of James DeKay, an early zoologist who explored the region. Blue Mountain Lake was settled in the 1850s, with Chauncey Hathorn being the first resident.

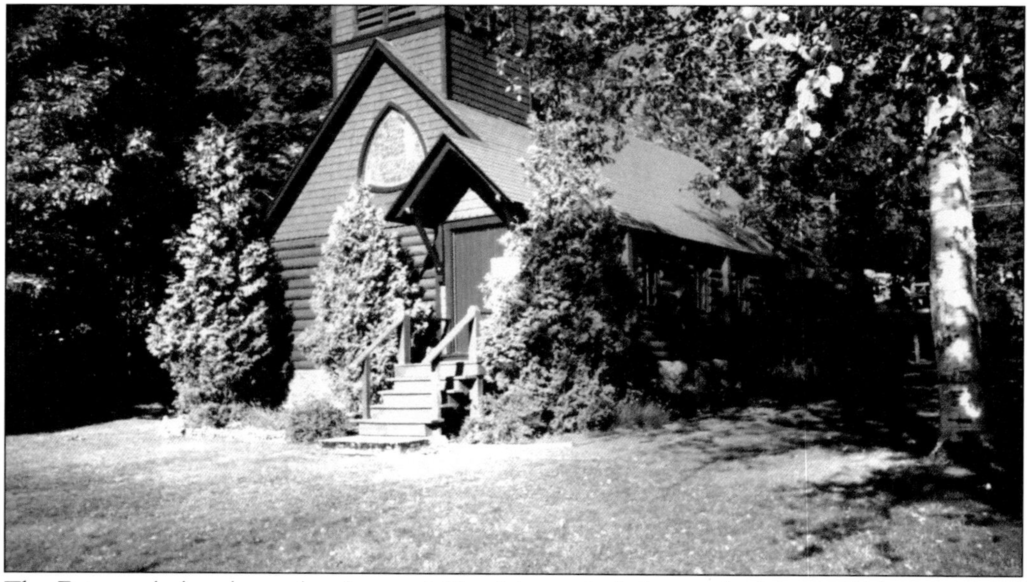

The Episcopal church on the shores of Blue Mountain Lake was built in 1885 by a group of parishioners who had been meeting since 1881. They first met in privately owned establishments and the public schoolhouse, a practice repeated in other Adirondack communities. Traveling to church services by boat was another practice common in the Adirondacks, with its many lakes. The church bell came from Troy in 1886 and was given by Lucy Norton, the wife of Levi Norton, the vice president.

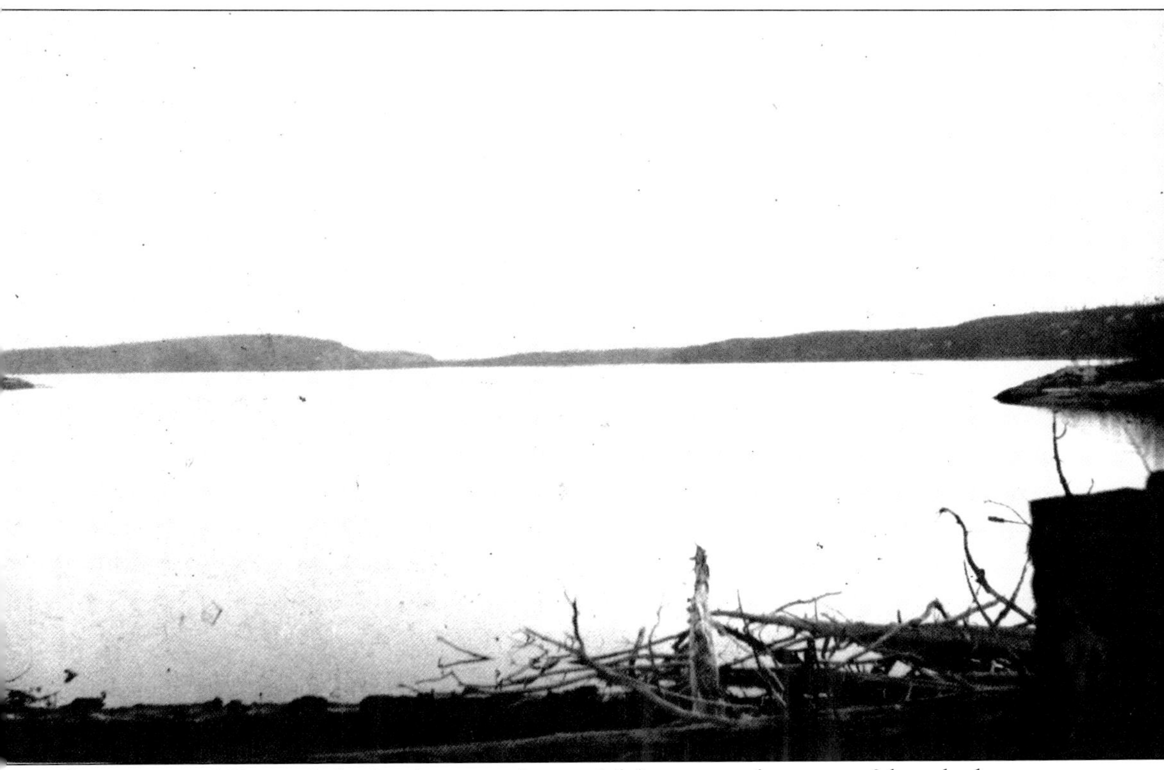

The naming of Tupper Lake has been a subject of debate over the years, although the name appears on some of the earliest Adirondack maps. One story tells of an early surveyor, possibly Benjamin Tupper, who passed through the area sometime before 1792. The Tupper Family Association of America lists surveyor Ansel Tupper, born in 1799, who was drowned in "Cranberry Lake, N.Y., afterwards called Tupper Lake." Another story refers to the Tupper family of Sandwich, Massachusetts. In the writings on the family, one author "maintained that the lakes, Great Tupper and Little Tupper, in the Adirondacks were a remembrance of the German homes of the Tuppers."

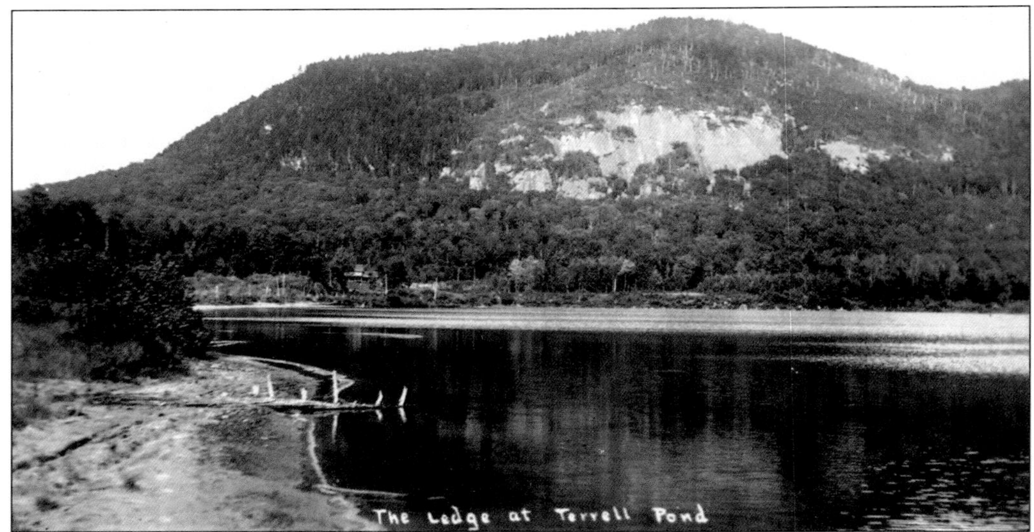

Fr. Michael Olivetti, pastor of a Whitehall church, bought part of Township 19 around Tirrell Pond and brought a colony of Irish immigrants to settle there, another practice that can be found repeated in other parts of the mountains. It was a short-lived settlement; there is oral tradition that tells of a disease, possibly diphtheria, spreading through the settlement. Today, it is a camping spot on the Northville–Lake Placid Trail.

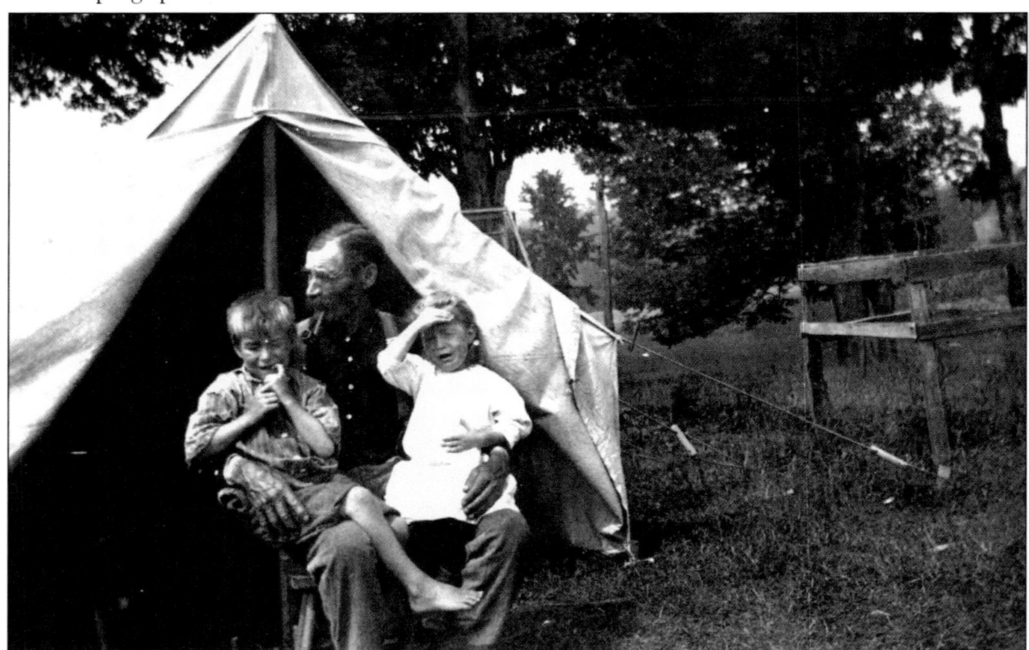

Most of the Adirondack settlements had a blacksmith to keep the horses shod and to make the tools, wagons, and sleighs the residents required. Charles Whitman, the blacksmith in Wells, was well-known for making cutters—sleighs to use behind the horses in the winter. He often entertained his grandchildren and great-grandchildren at his home. The tent in his backyard served as a playhouse for the children and a place to sleep outside on a hot summer night. During the hunting season, the big wall tents were used in the woods.

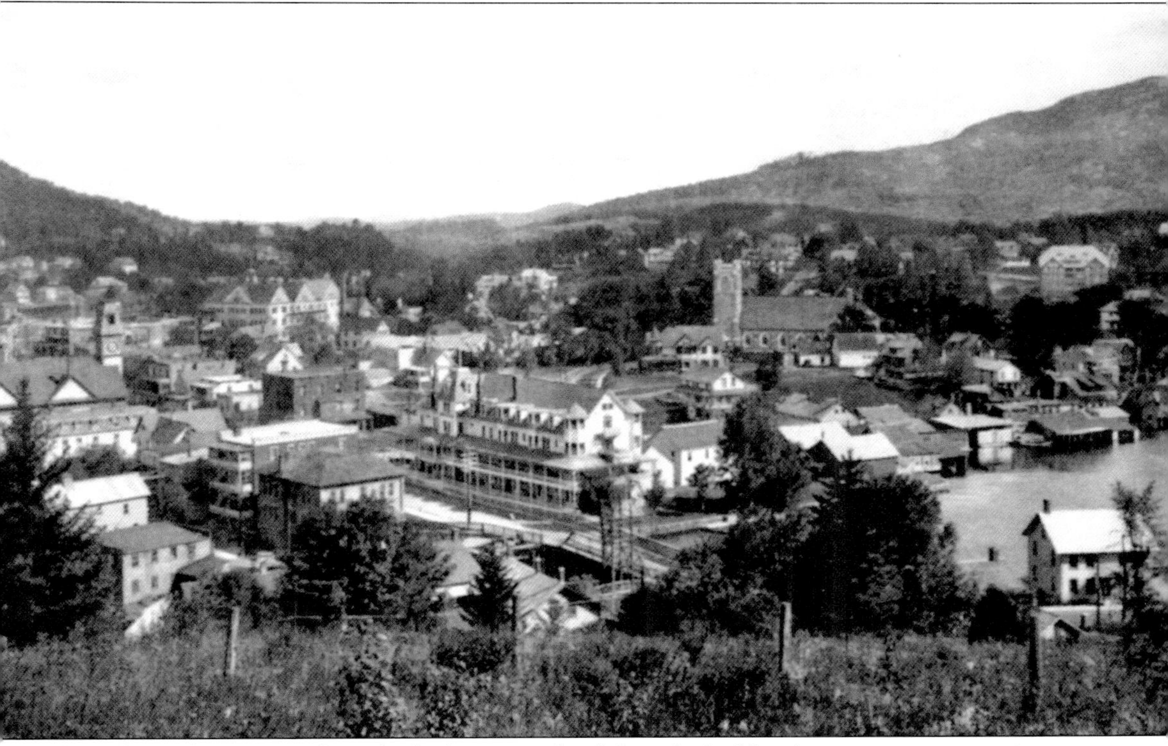

The village of Saranac Lake, "the little city in the Adirondacks," has been sponsoring a winter carnival for over 100 years, bringing thousands to enjoy the North Country winters. The original carnivals broke up the long snow season for those who came to Saranac's tuberculosis-cure cottages. The settlement got its start in 1819, when Jacob Moody, injured in a sawmill accident, came from Keene and built a log cabin on the site. It became the Adirondack's first incorporated village in 1892.

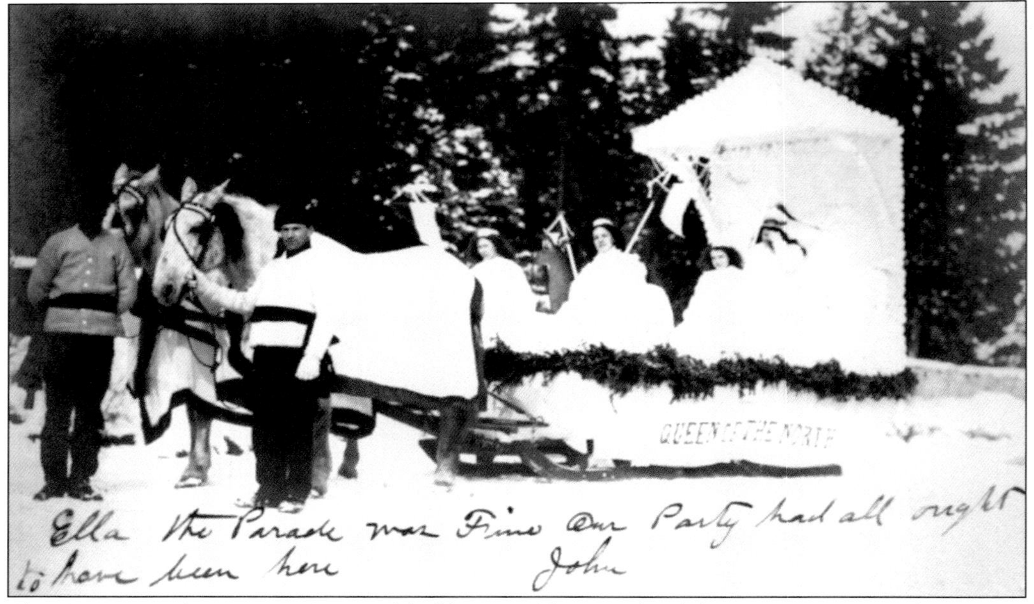

The Saranac Lake Winter Carnival held its 105th annual celebration in 2002. It has grown from a one-day festival to break the winter cabin fever to a nine-day festival. Parades, fireworks, and the giant ice palace attract thousands to Saranac Lake in February of each year. "Royalty" is coronated to serve during the celebration. The 1907 float holds the "Queen of the North" and her court.

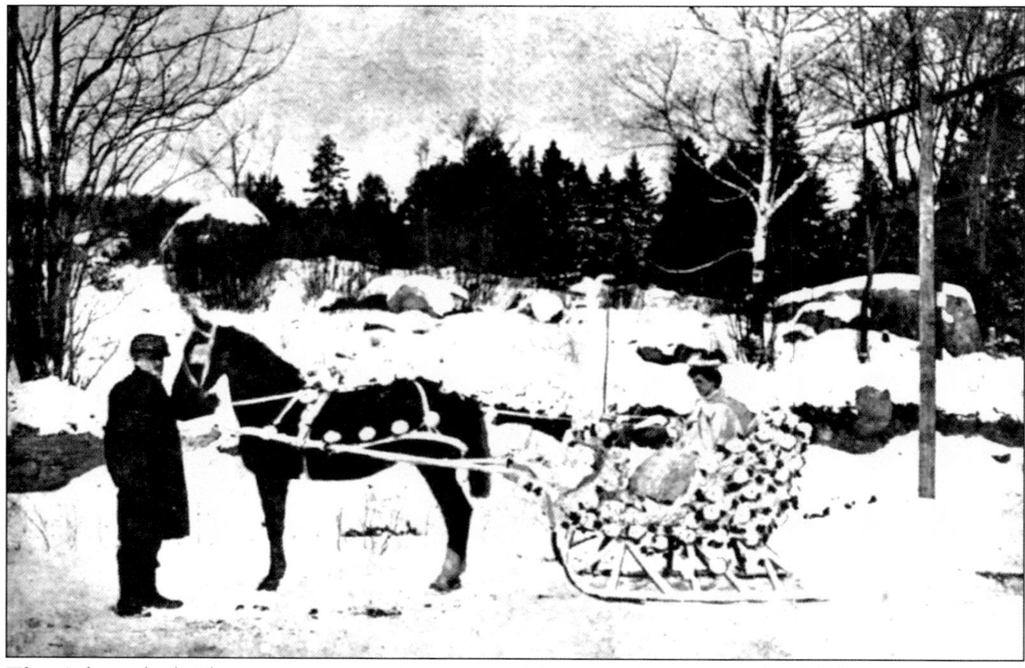

The Adirondack Pharmacy prepared a decorated horse and sleigh for the 1907 winter carnival parade. How did they keep the flowers from freezing in the cold North Country February weather? The carnival also included sports, music activities, dances, and dramatic productions.

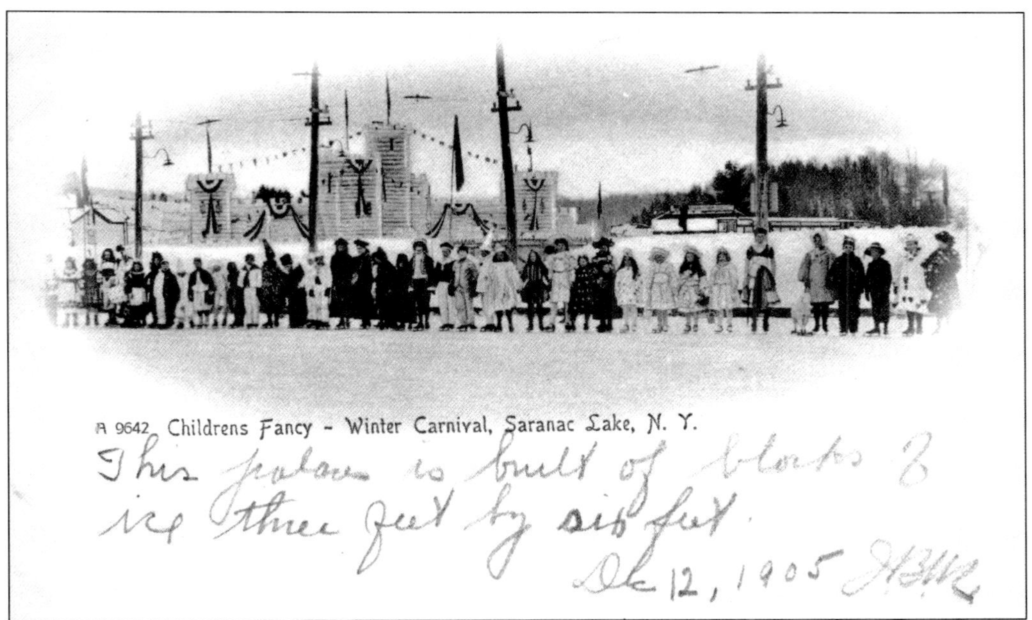

An architectural marvel, the ice palace at the Saranac Lake Winter Carnival is constructed with giant blocks of ice. The palace is large enough for the thousands of visitors to walk through and the colored lights add beauty to the crystallized ice. The 1905 ice palace can be seen behind the costumed children in this vintage postcard.

HELLO, VISITOR

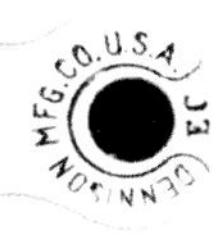

WELCOME TO OUR VILLAGE: Make yourself at home. This tag entitles you to park as long as you please in SARANAC LAKE. Do not mind the time limit with the exception of night parking from 1 to 6 A.M. Please keep away from corners, fire hydrants and safety zones.

Cordially, Thomas P. Ward, *Mayor,*
L. F. Kendall J. T. Stickney
S. Drutz A. W. Currier, *Trustees*
James Coughlin, *Chief of Police*
M. S. Johnson, *Village Manager*

(over)

Adirondack communities depend on the tourist dollar to feed the economy. The tag reproduced here was once used by the village of Saranac Lake to welcome visitors to the community. How many communities today can offer unlimited free parking?

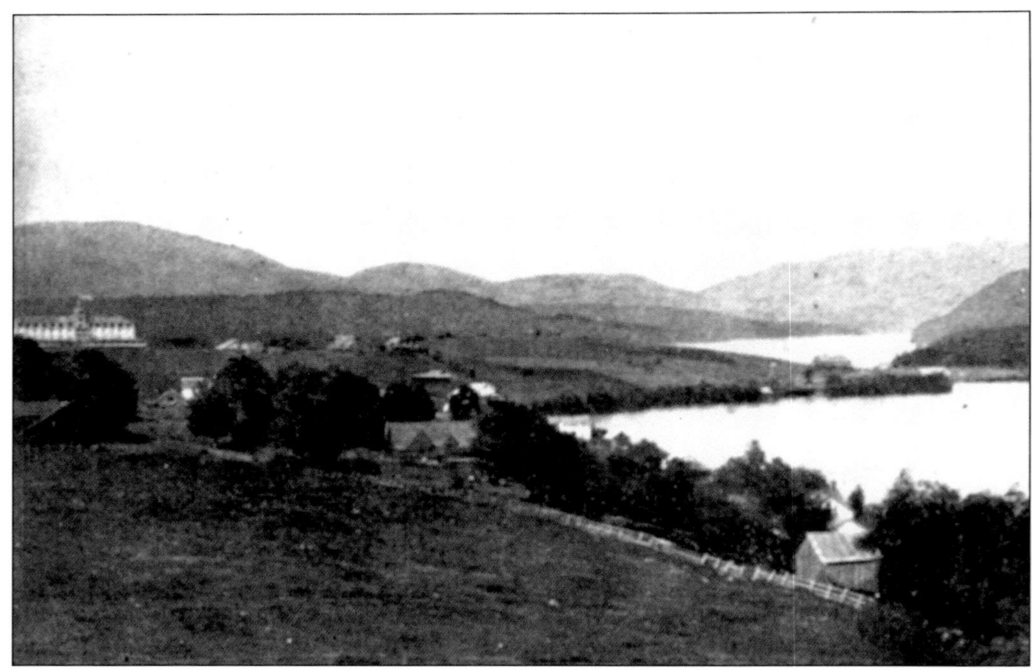

Lake Placid is known worldwide because of its fame as a winter sports center and tourist destination. Nestled in the surrounding mountainsides, with the little village sitting beside an Adirondack lake, it is one of the most picturesque scenes imaginable. In this 1908 photograph, one hotel and a few houses are the seeds for the growth that is to come later.

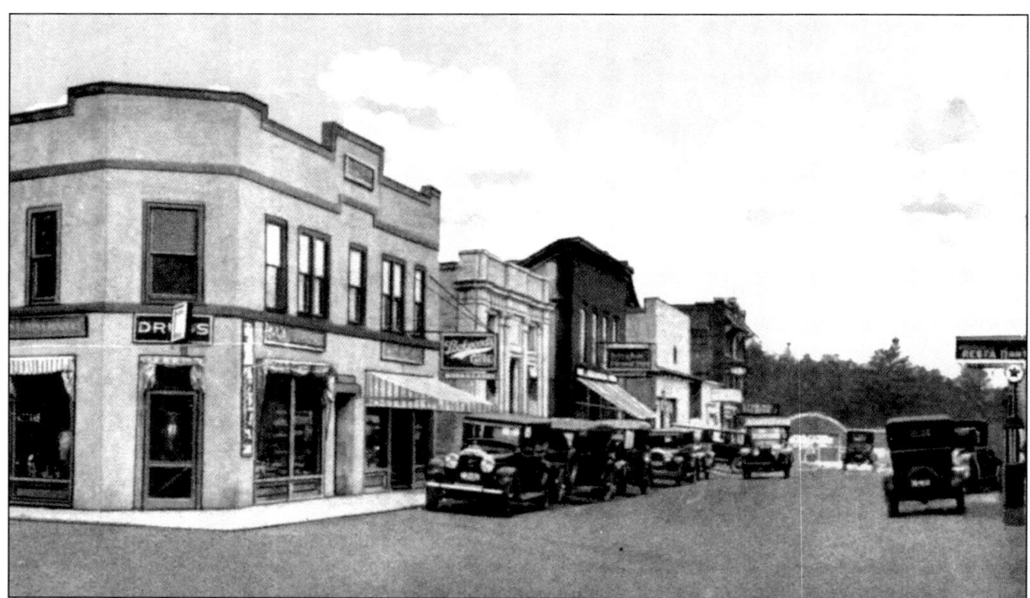

Old Forge ranks high on the list of popular Adirondack destinations, summer and winter. It has been known as the place where wilderness and civilization merge. Old Forge is the gateway to the Fulton Chain of Lakes, providing a wide choice for Adirondack visitors who come to the area. The Old Forge name comes from an unsuccessful attempt at mining iron at the site.

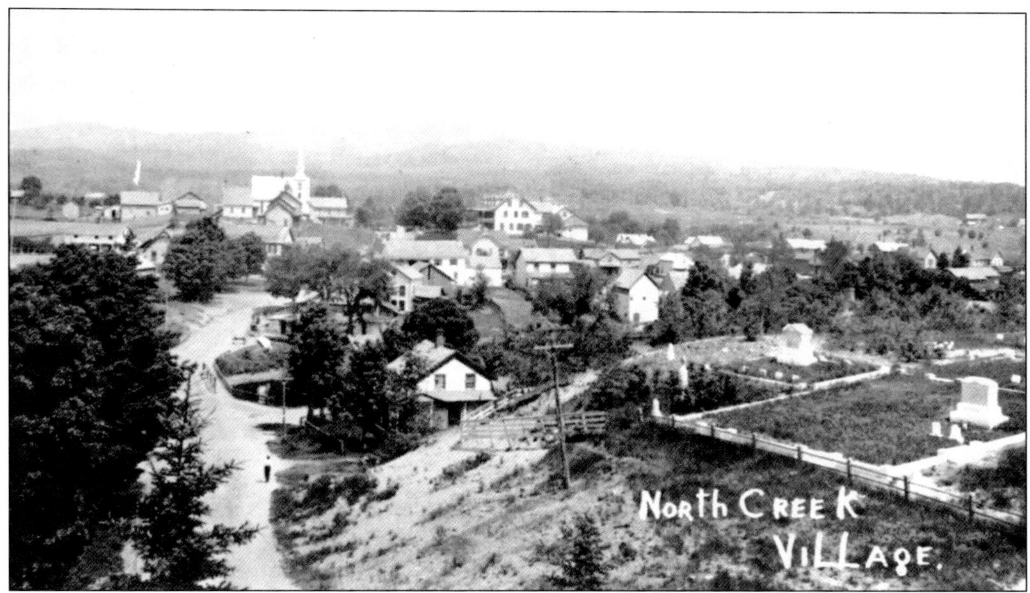

In the early days of skiing, snow trains made trips to the North Creek Gore Mountain ski bowl. The historic railroad station, where Theodore Roosevelt learned that he had become president of the United States, is back in use today. Historic North Creek's main street boasts one of the finest examples of the early shop-home combinations, in which the family lived upstairs over the store.

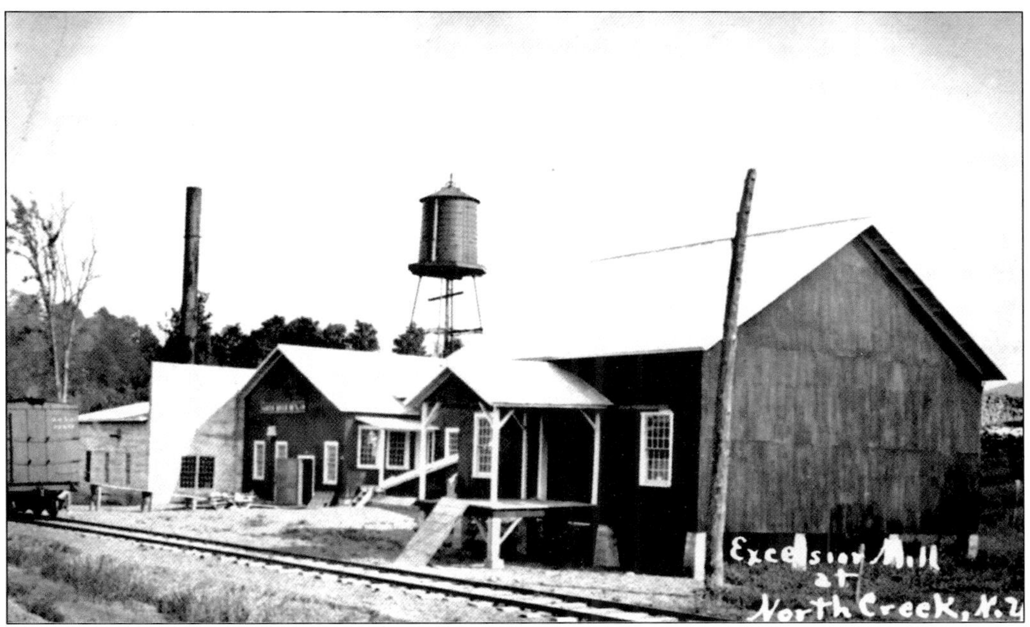

The Adirondack settlements depended on the forests for their early industries, and wood products topped the list. Potash, tanning, and pulpwood were among those industries. North Creek had an excelsior mill where wood was reduced to shavings for use in packing, stuffing, and the like. The railroad reached North Creek in 1871, providing the transportation for the products of the mill.

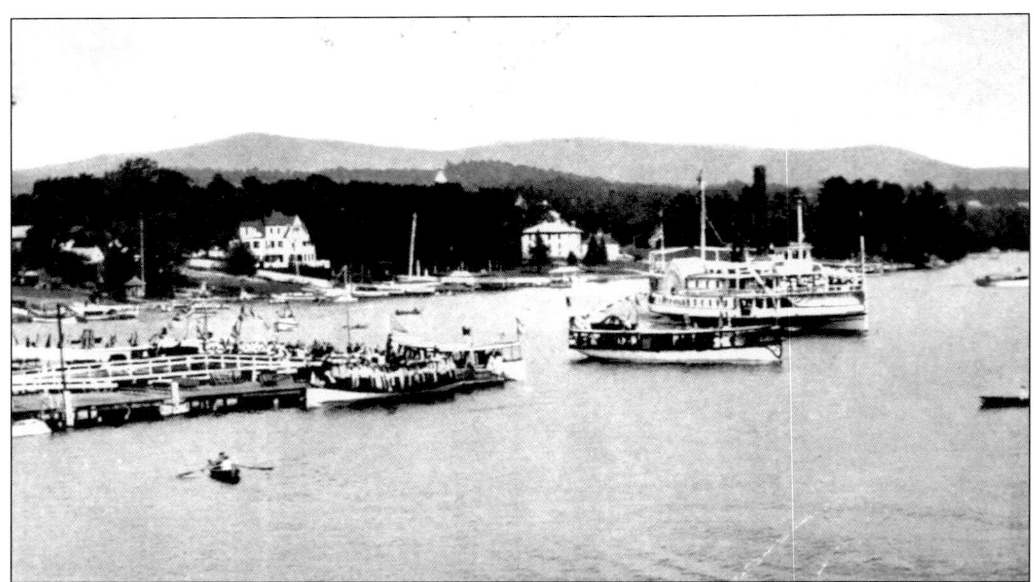

Lake George Village was once Caldwell, organized in 1810 in honor of James Caldwell, a prominent citizen. Lake George has a long history as an Adirondack resort and, as early as 1886, Frank Leslie's Magazine reported that "Lake George has become over-peopled!" An earlier 1857 magazine, *Putnam's Monthly*, had wrongly predicted that "The village never grows and has no occasion to grow!" Little did *Putnam's* know that Lake George would become a center for boating of all kinds and a popular summer resort.

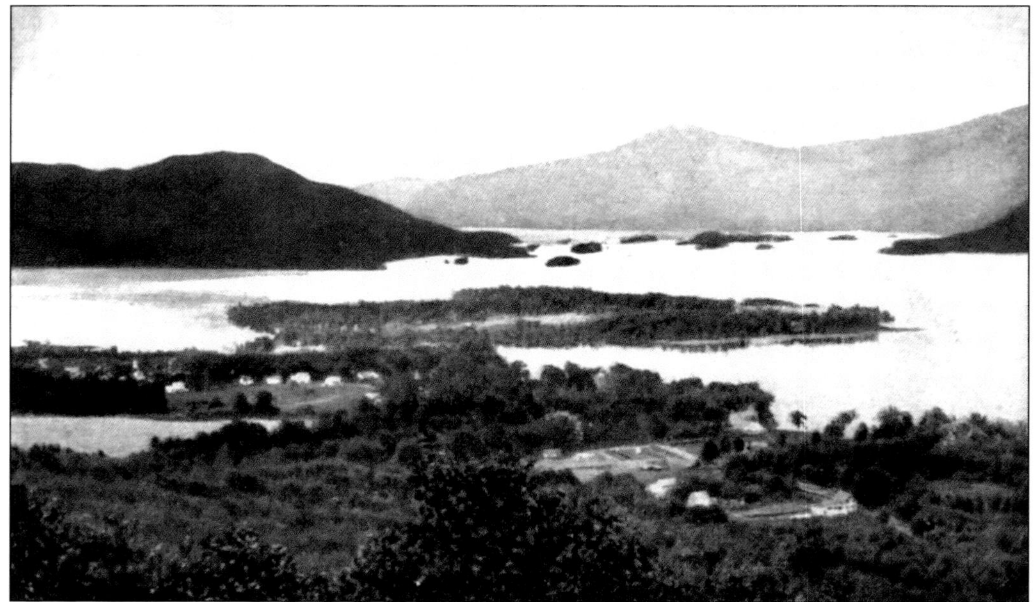

During the first decade of the 20th century boat rides became very popular on the Adirondack lakes. Lake George, a longtime tourist destination, has never lacked boats. Visitors can gain an appreciation of one of the world's most beautiful lakes by journeying through the island scenery by boat. Thomas Jefferson, while president, wrote to his daughter on a piece of Adirondack birch bark, saying, "Lake George is, without comparison, the most beautiful water I ever saw!"

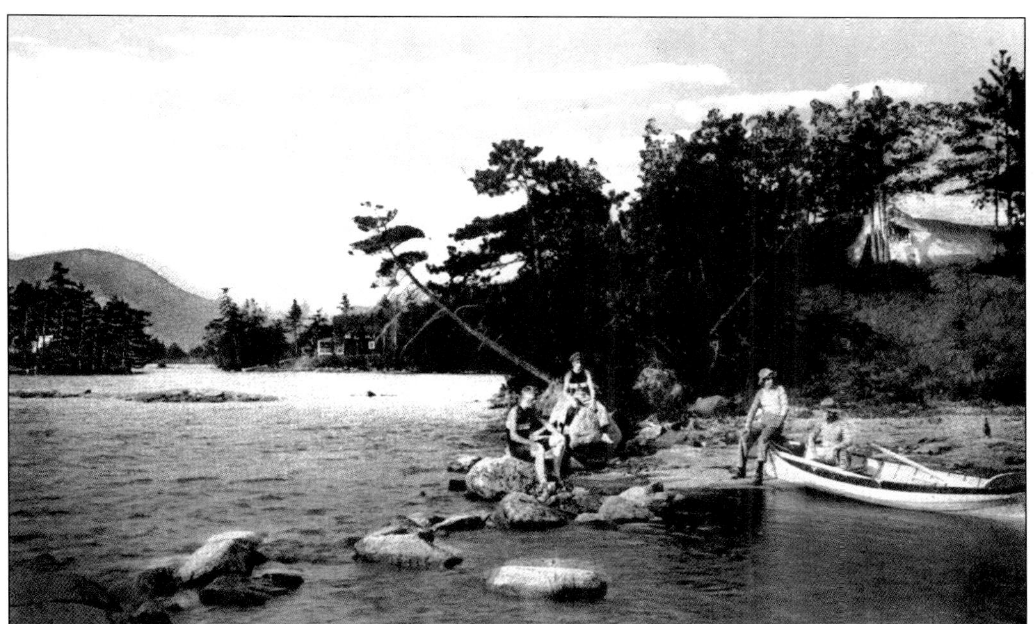

Lake George was left outside of the first proposed Adirondack Park in 1892, but it was included a year later when the "islands on Lake George in the County of Warren" were added. The 32-mile-long Lake George has a history that goes back to Fr. Issac Jogues's trip as a Mohawk prisoner in 1642. Father Jogue called it Lac du Sacrament in 1646, and it remained so for 109 years. It was later named by Sir William Johnson to honor King George.

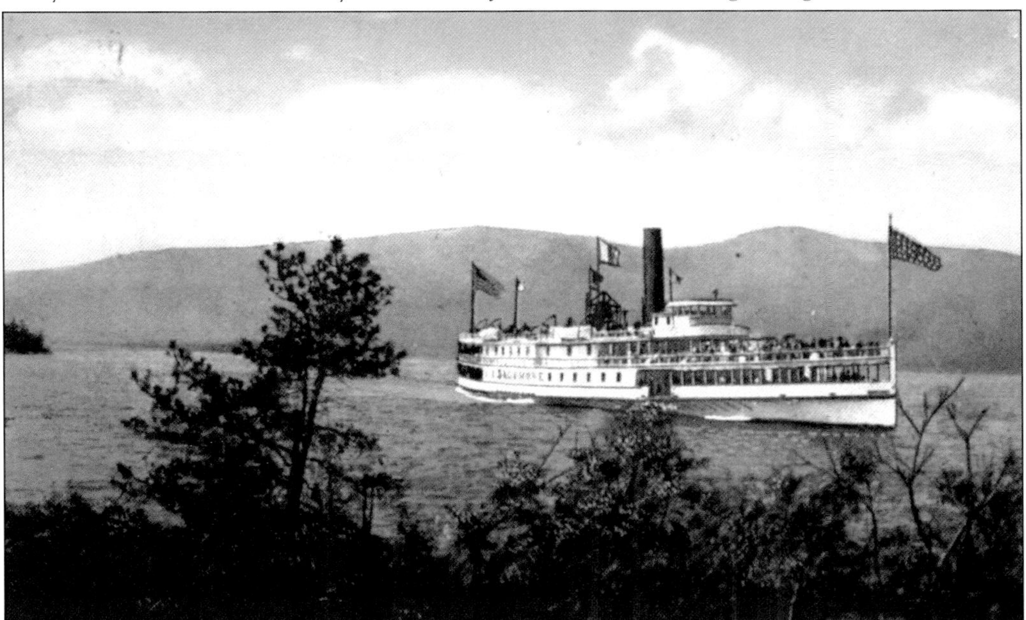

Pullman cars came directly to Lake George from New York City in the early days. Passengers could continue their journey on the lake steamers or stages. Lake George has never lacked for boats of all kinds. National championship powerboat races and regattas have been held on this "Queen of American Lakes."

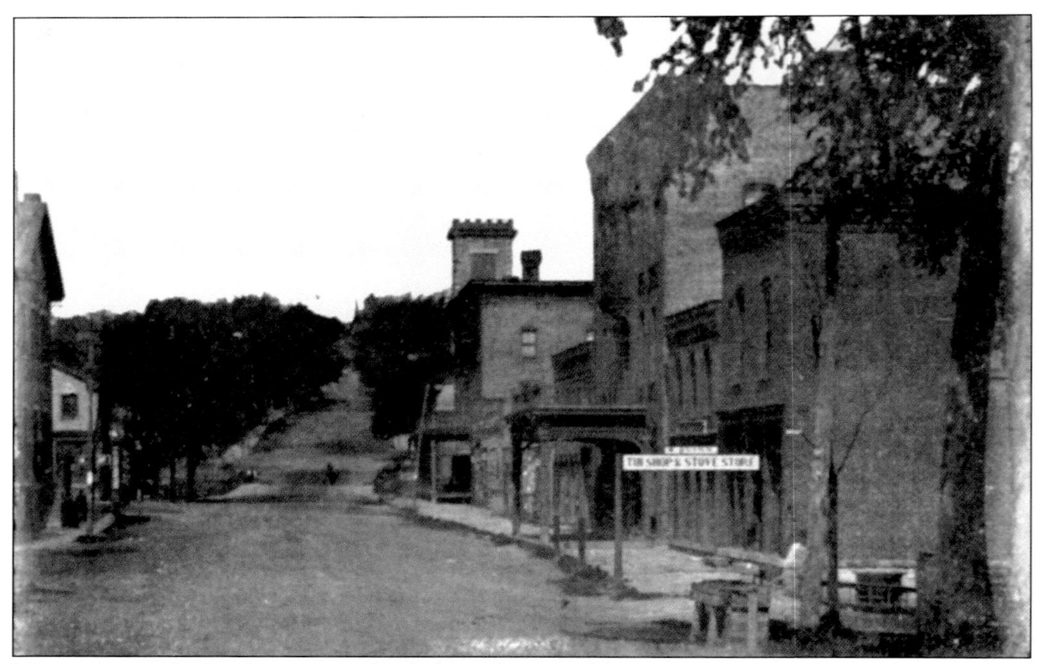

The immense hydraulic power afforded by the AuSable River at Keeseville made it a center of manufacturing beginning in 1808. Forges, a woolen factory, flour mills, a plaster mill, and a foundry were added to the wood-related enterprises in the mid-1800s. They made cut nails and other fabrics in two rolling mills. The production of horseshoe nails became successful in 1863, and twine, carpet warp, and wicking came into production shortly thereafter. Keeseville truly was a mill town.

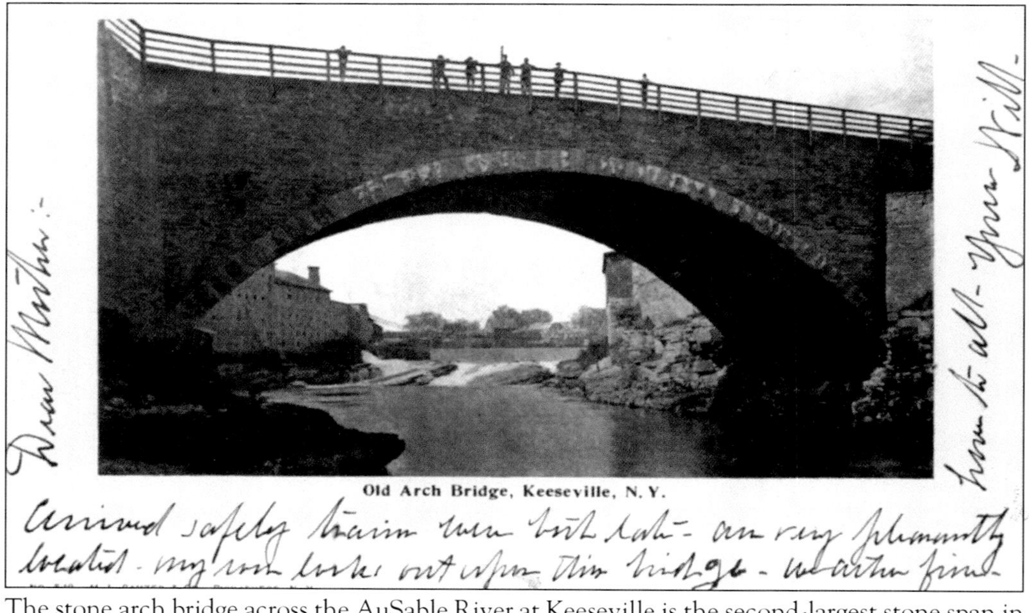

The stone arch bridge across the AuSable River at Keeseville is the second-largest stone span in America. The 110-foot-long single-arch bridge was built from local sandstone by master mason Solomon Townsend and 30 other men in 1843.

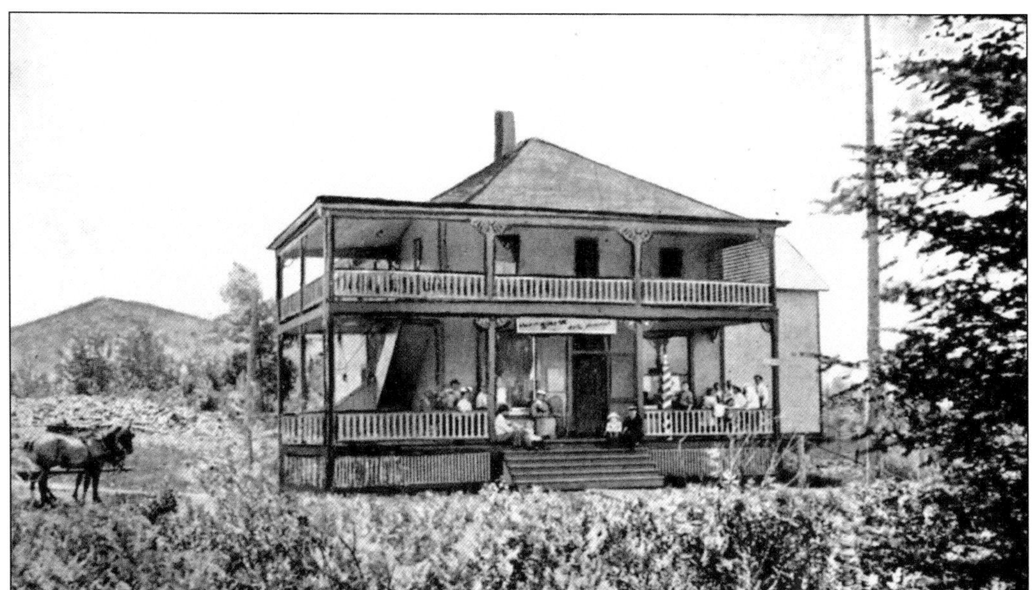

In 1909, when this photograph of Mountain View was taken, it was common practice to have mail delivered to the general store. Many times the letters were simply laid out on the counter or pickle barrel and picked up by the recipients when they came to town. J.W. Pond's general store served as the post office for the Mountain View area. Note that the store apparently ran a barbershop on the side.

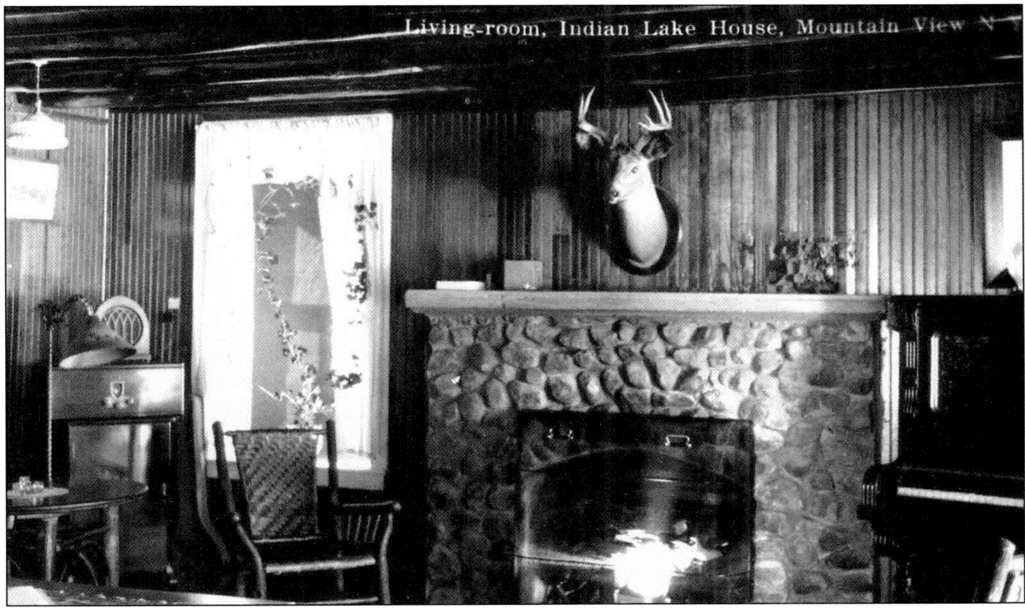

Mountain View in the Adirondacks is located on Route 27 near the northern boundary of the Adirondack Park adjacent to a small Indian Lake and Mountain View Lake. The interior of the Indian Lake House includes everything that is expected in an Adirondack lodge: a native stone fireplace with a mounted deer head, wainscoted walls, ceiling beams, rustic rocking chairs, a rustic table, ivy growing around the window, and a piano for evening entertainment.

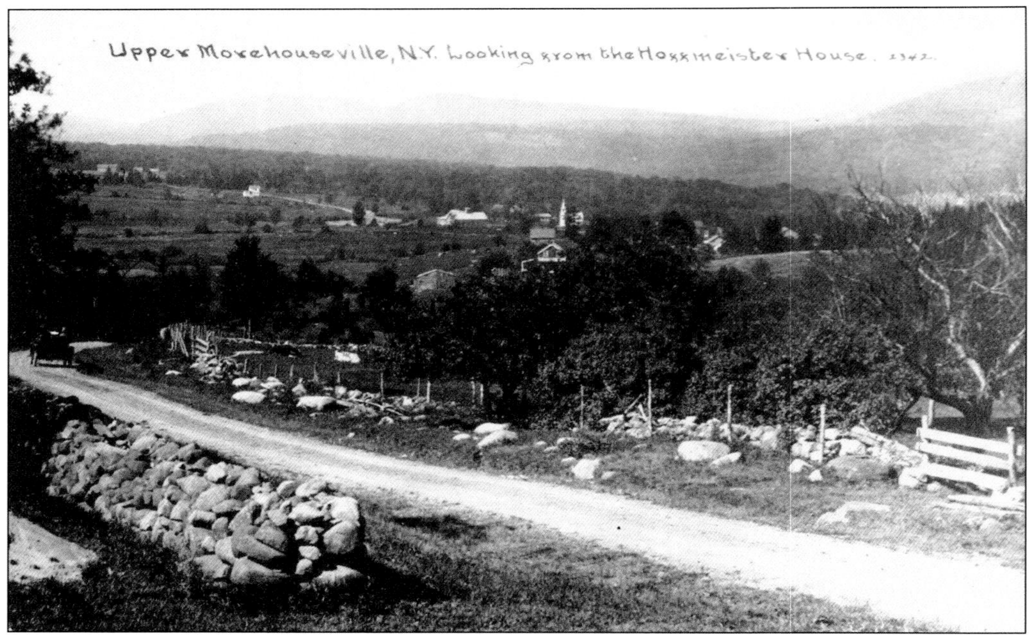

Andrew Morehouse, a New York City wholesale grocer, speculated on Adirondack lands and attempted an unsuccessful development in the 1830s. The town of Morehouseville was established by the state legislature in 1835. Morehouse was ahead of his time with his ideas on private land ownership, a court system, women voting, social security, and free schools. His tenants simply could not cope with the harsh weather of the Adirondack winters.

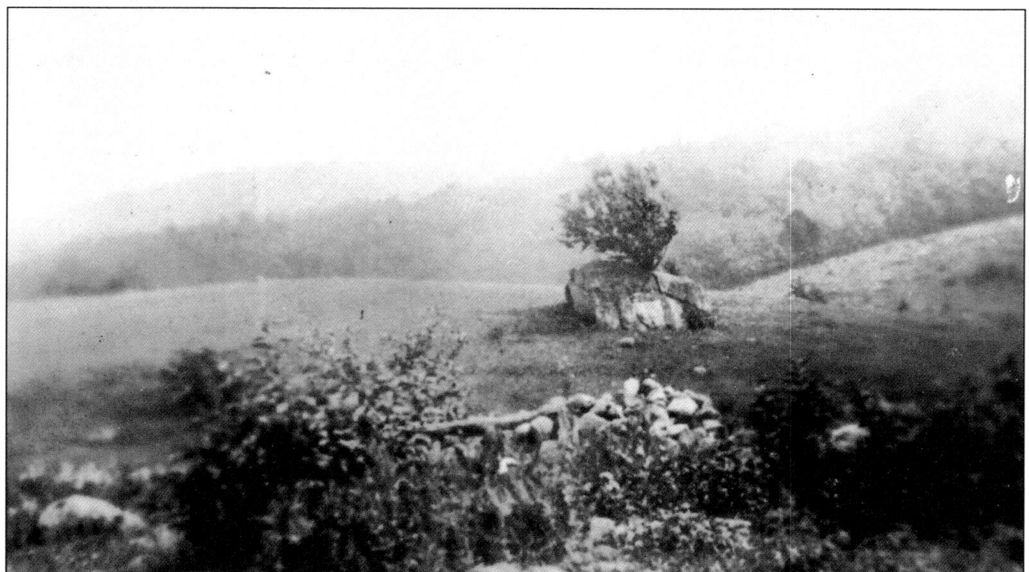

Hoffmeister is one of the least settled areas in the Adirondacks. This 1910 photograph, entitled "A Freak of Nature," shows a tree growing on the top of a large boulder. In the Adirondacks it is not uncommon to see a tree growing around a rock, with the roots extending down into the ground. Often children were asked whether the tree grew around the rock or the rock grew up out of the ground and push the tree up.

Five

HOTELS AND INNS

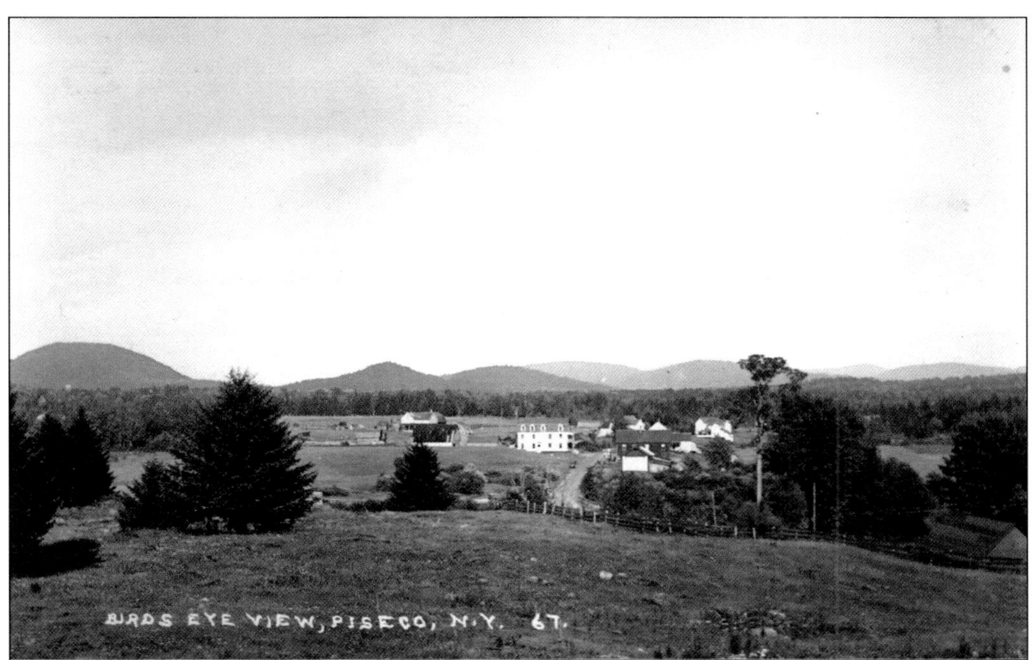

Sportsmen found the Piseco area in the early Adirondack days, and the Piseco Lake Trout Club of 1840 was one of the first sportsmen's clubs in the country. It is mentioned in George Bethune's 1847 edition of *Walton's Compleat Angler*. Andrew K. Morehouse laid out Piseco in the 1830s. Some say the name came from and old Indian named Pezeeko who lived on the shores of the Piseco Lake.

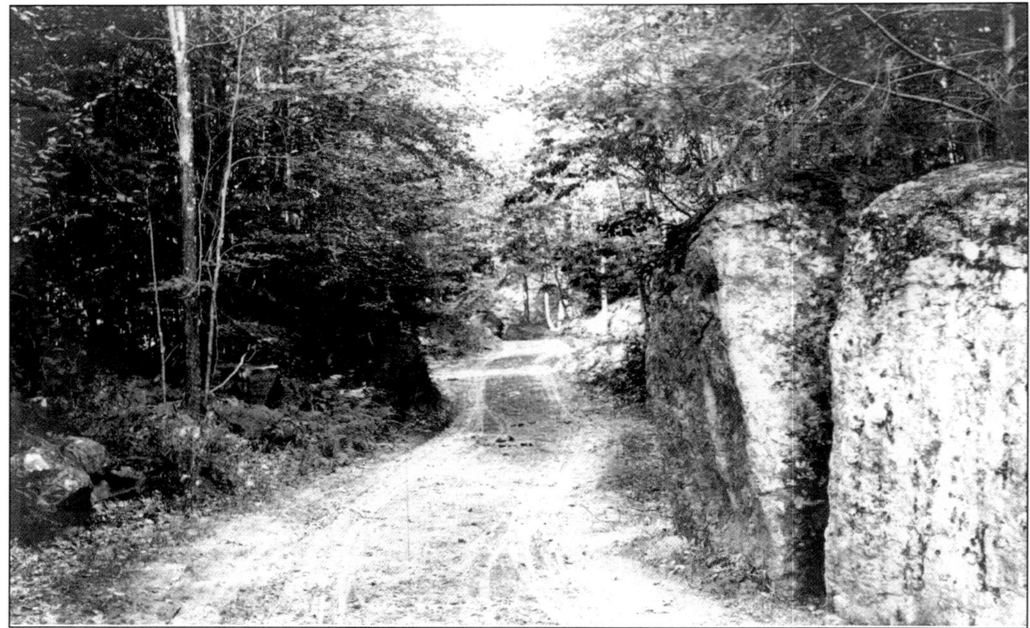

One of the most unique "hotels" in the Adirondacks is located on the old dirt road from Wells to Speculator through Gilmantown. "Bidwell's Hotel" saved the life of mail driver Charles Bidwell one stormy night. While driving his team and wagon to Speculator, Bidwell was stopped by a severe blizzard. He pulled into the wide split between the rocks (right) and slept the night out. He told his story the next day, and since then the storm shelter in the rocks has been known as Bidwell's Hotel.

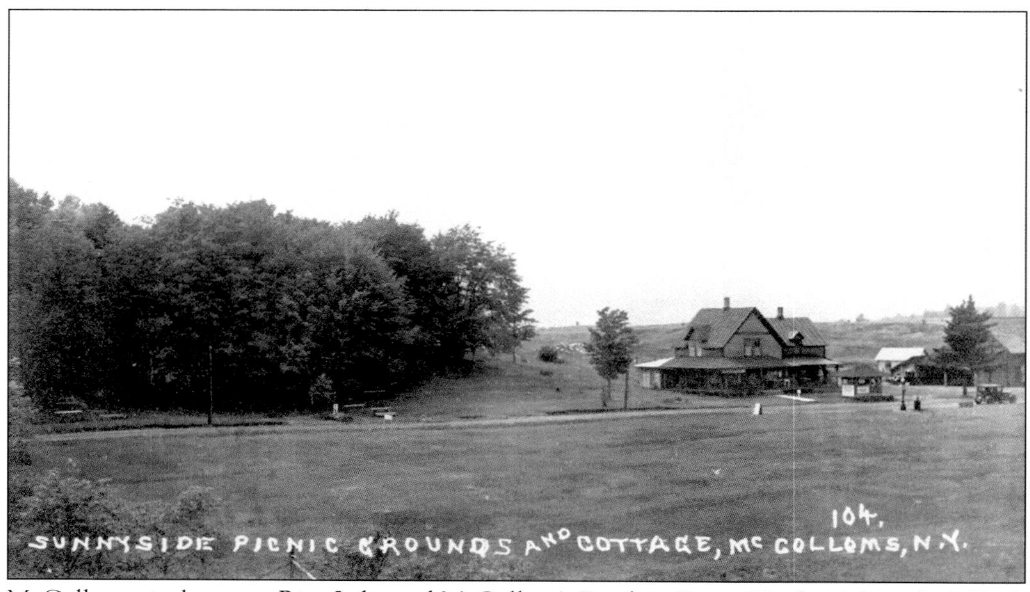

McColloms sits between Rice Lake and McCollom's Pond on Route 30, the Adirondack Trail, near the northern boundary of the Adirondack Park. In the 1920s, Sunnyside was a good place to spend the night and get a good breakfast. Gassing up the car after a long Adirondack trip could also be done at Sunnyside.

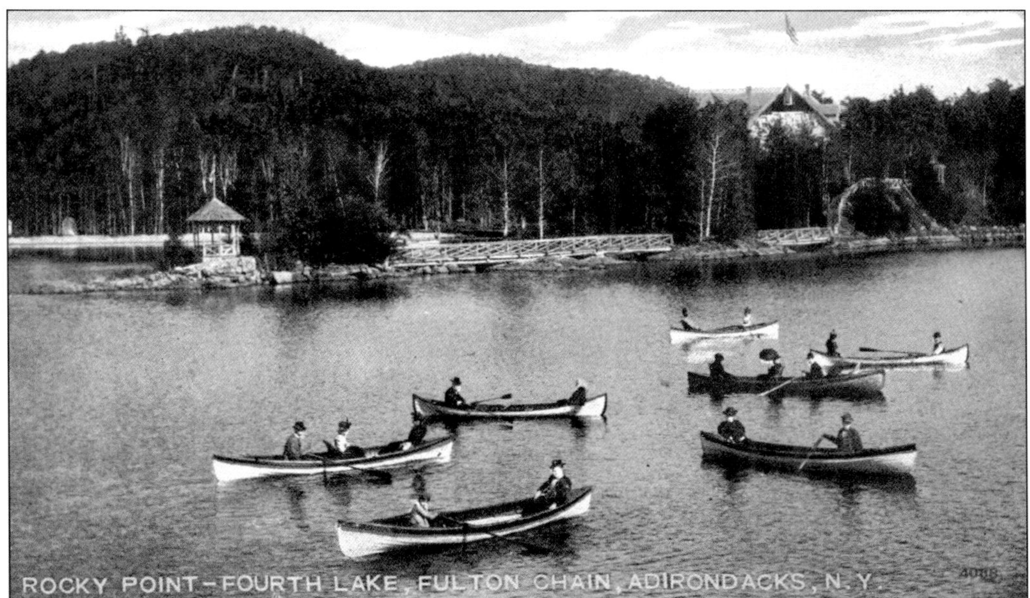

A.G. Delmarsh was the proprietor of the Rocky Point Inn at Inlet on Fourth Lake when weekly rates were $42 for a single. The attractive gabled hotel with cottages offered Adirondack seclusion on a rocky promontory stretching out into the bay at the head of Fourth Lake. Wide verandas with rustic rocking chairs helped provide the guests with a restful and pleasant stay.

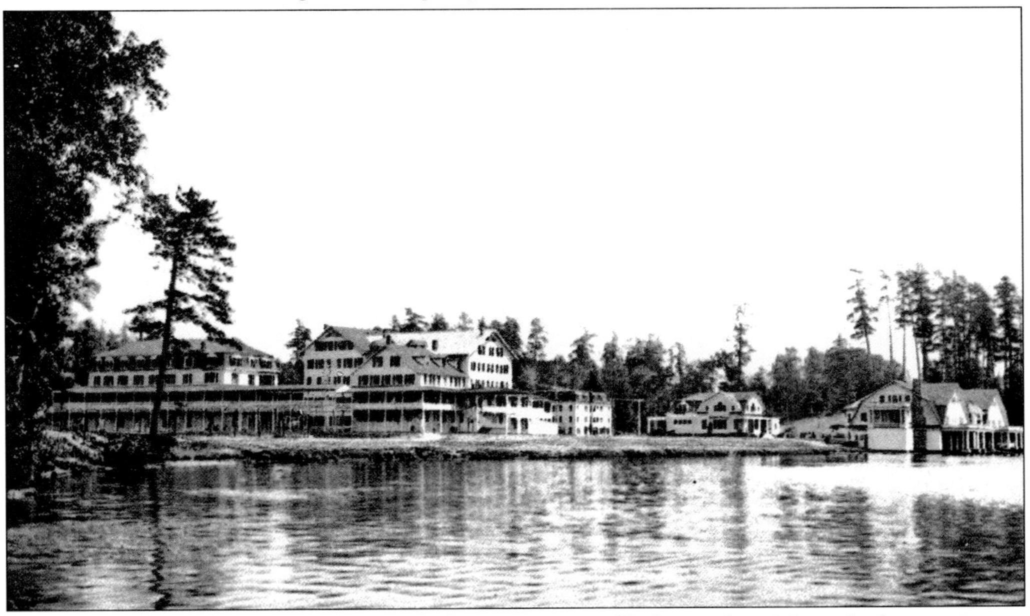

Paul Smith is an unparalleled Adirondack success story. He began his Adirondack experiences as a young guide in the 1840s and ended his career with a 100-room resort hotel, a railroad, a real estate company, a lumber company, a stage line, and his own post office. Today, his legacy is the Adirondack's four-year Paul Smith's College. Smith had a unique sense of humor and many Adirondack sayings are attributed to him, including the famous explanation as to why the mosquitoes did not bite him: "They bite the outsiders first and save the natives for later!"

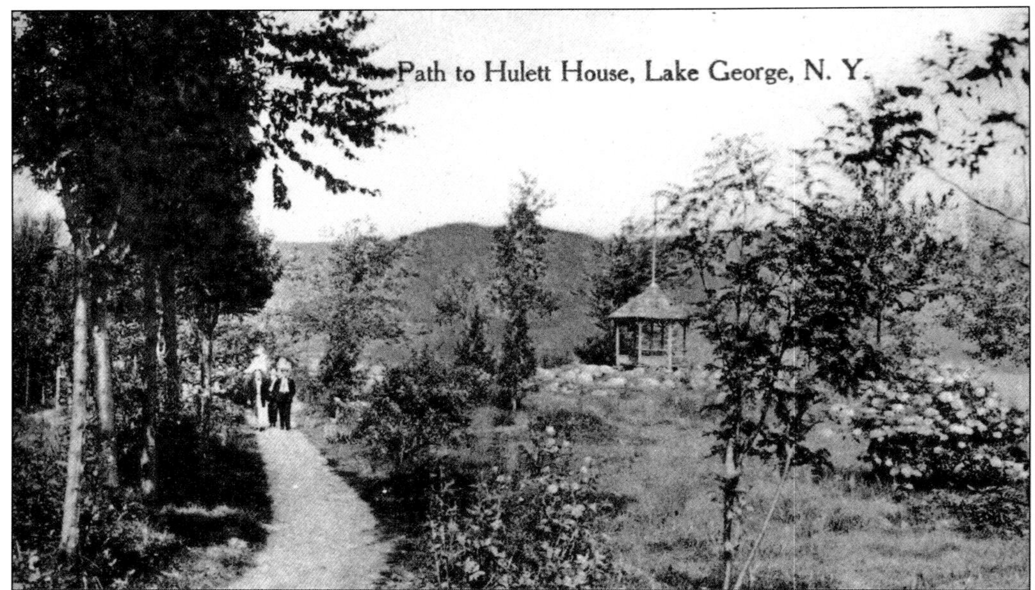

"Remember the advantageous location of the Hulett House; located midway on the lake near the islands and the best fishing grounds, with hundreds of acres of forest land to tramp through; our motor launches, canvas-covered canoes, boats, etc., our safe sandy beach and best of fresh water bathing, our daily program of social entertainment; Catholic and Protestant churches, and above all, the beautiful panoramic view obtained from every window in the hotel."—*A Summer Paradise*, Delaware and Hudson Railroad Booklet, 1924.

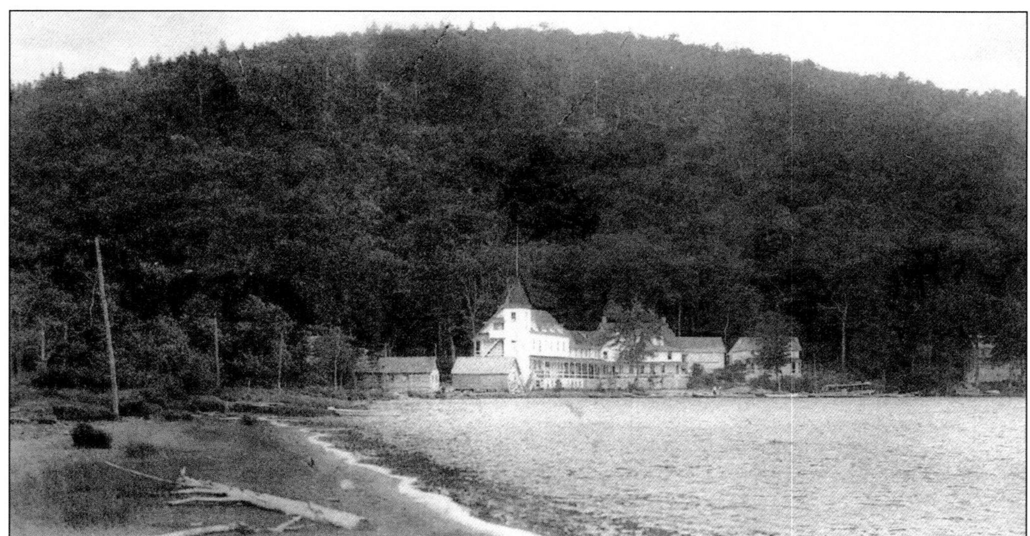

The Canada Lake Hotel was built on Canada Lake in the late 1880s by James Fulton. "Free from hay fever" was in its advertising. The hotel offered several boating choices and attracted guests from all over. The three-story building burned in a tragic fire in October 1914.

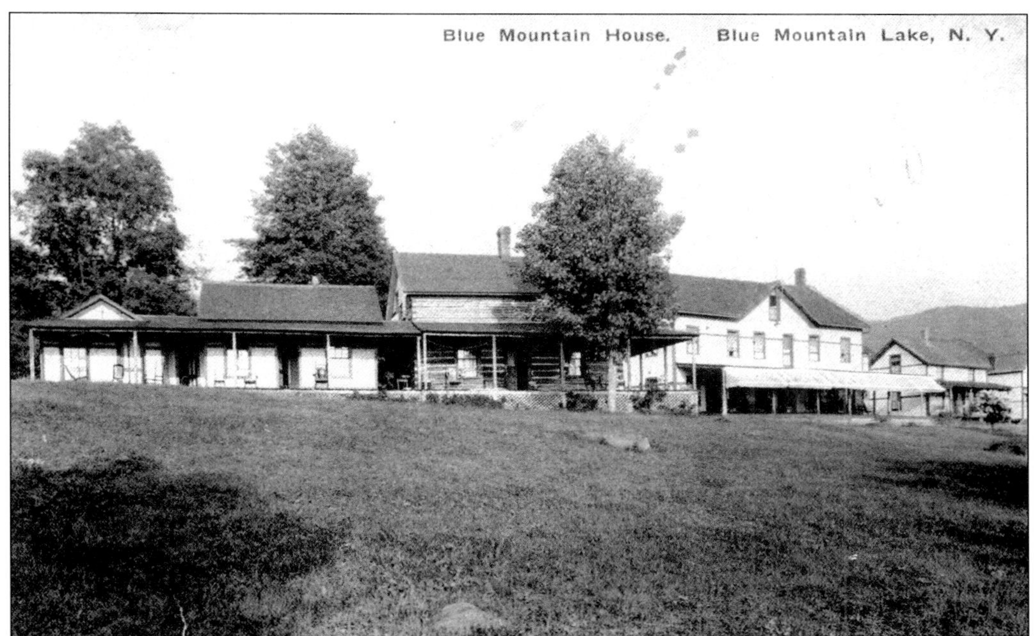

M. Tyler Merwin built the log section of his Blue Mountain House in 1874. An additional cottage was built in 1876, and the place could then accommodate 40 guests. After a fire in 1880, a three-story frame building was constructed, which Merwin ran until 1935, taking 80 to 100 guests. Merwin had his own farm to supply honey and fresh cream. William Wessels bought the business in 1935 and sold it to the Adirondack Historical Association in 1954 for the construction of the Adirondack Museum.

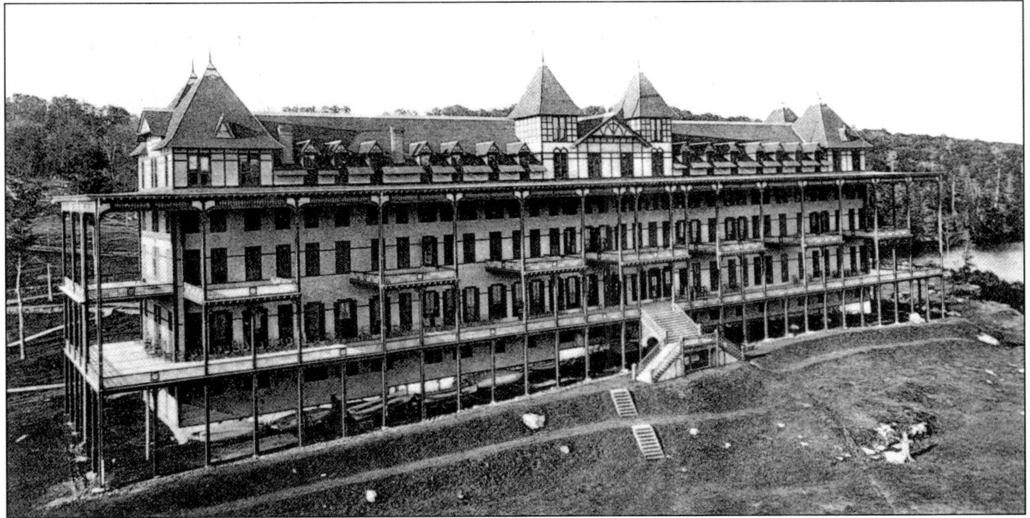

The fabulous Prospect House on Blue Mountain Lake had a decline in business in the 1890s and that dip combined with the 1893 financial panic caused owner Frederick Durant to mortgage the place to his brother, Howard Durant. Howard took over and, in order to improve its reputation, changed the name to Hotel Utowana in 1900. New owners took over and an outbreak of typhoid fever struck the hotel in 1903 causing it to close forever. The hotel was torn down in 1915.

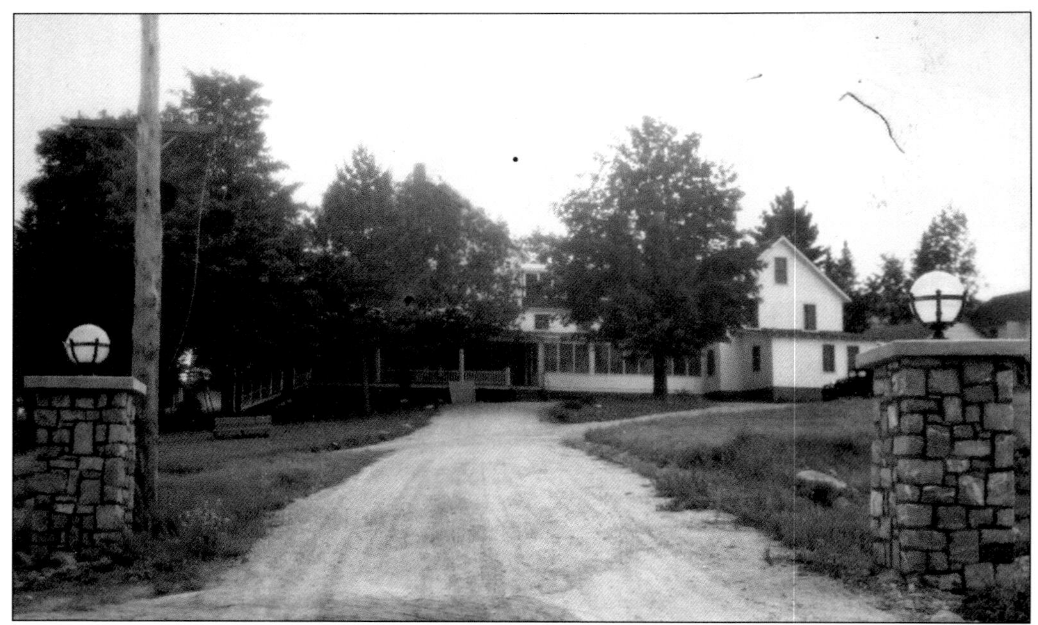

The Hotel Sabael opened early in the 1890s in Indian Lake as the Locke House. The hotel was an attractive social center with a golf course and tennis courts. In addition, the hotel provided horses and held formal dances for its guests. At some point after 1936, the business was sold to the O'Toole family, and the name was changed to the Hotel Sabael. Others took over the management and it became Indian Lake Lodge and eventually Air-O-Tel. The hotel burned down in 1962 in a blaze fought by six fire companies.

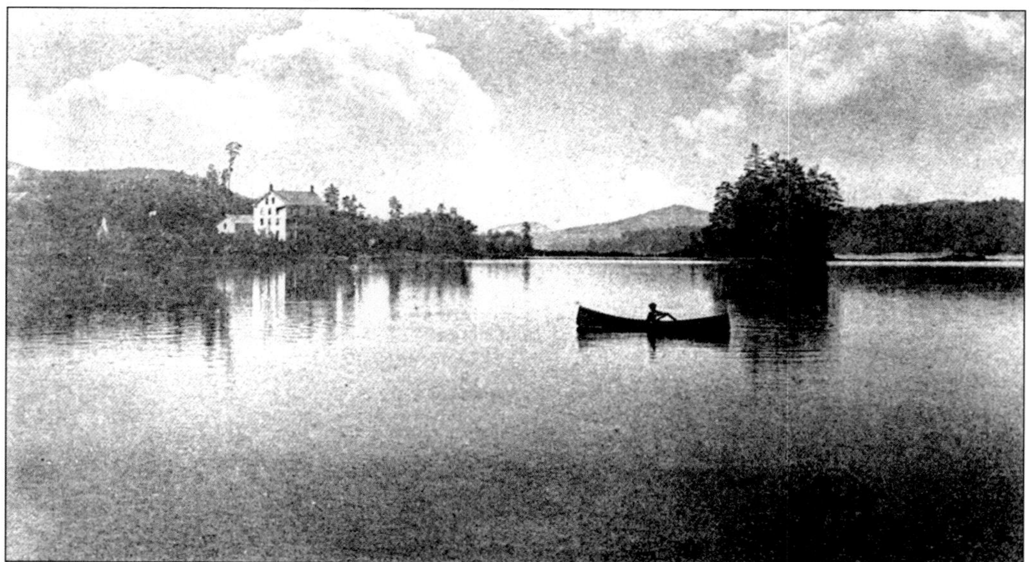

The Lake House was built by Cyrus Kellogg on the shores of Long Lake about a half-mile from the village in 1879. After Cyrus Kellogg's unexpected death at age 60 during the same year, his widow, Christine Kellogg, was forced to operate the 35-guest hotel. She sold it in 1893 and it went through several other owners, a pattern often observed with Adirondack hostelries. William Helms, 80, and his partner, Theron Smith, 63, were running the hotel in 1905.

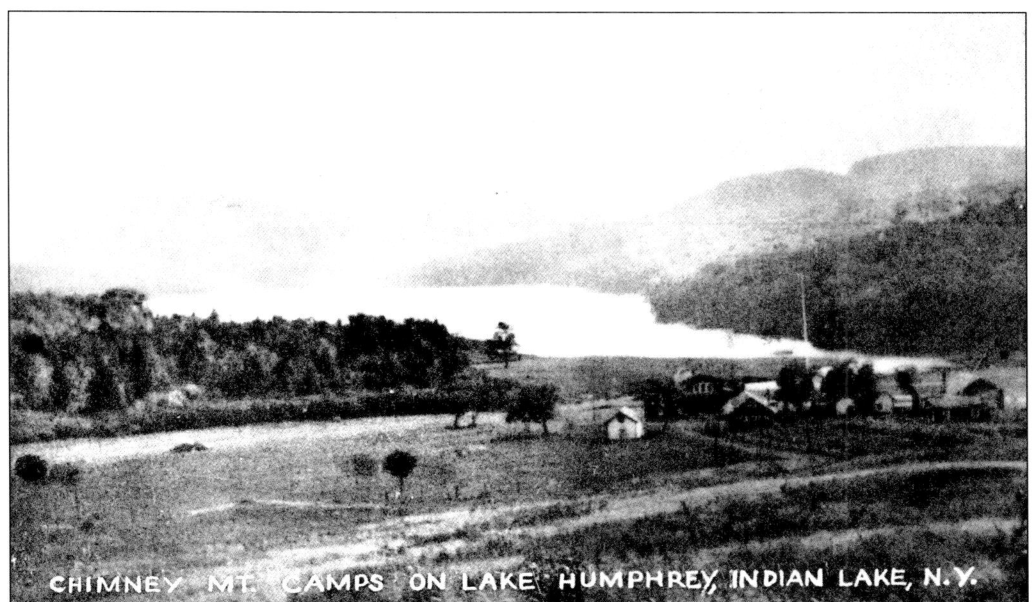

The Chimney Mountain House and Cottages, built *c.* 1920, were open during the summer and winter. They were built on Lake Humphrey on a 300-acre farm site. Early owners included Harland and Gretchen Fish and Douglas Fish. Nearby Chimney Mountain, with its large sandstone towers and deep crevices in the mountainsides, has long been a popular hiking destination.

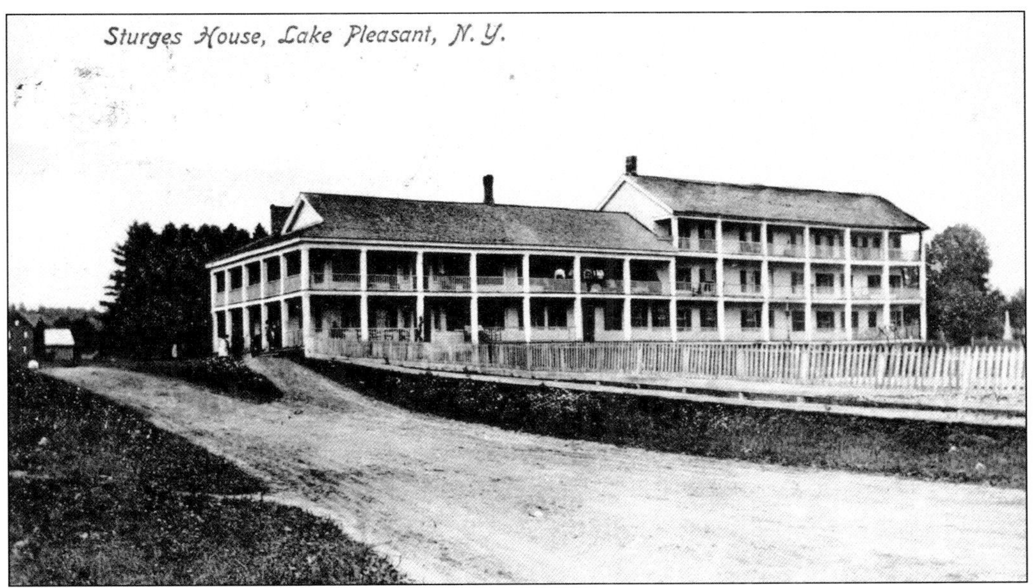

Dave Sturges started out as an Adirondack guide in the mid-1800s, went to work in the sawmill to earn money for lumber, and built an inn at Newton's Corners, later Speculator, in 1858. The post office moved into the hotel in 1872. Sturges operated his hotel for over 50 years. During World War II, the Sturges House met the same fate as that of many other Adirondack hotels: it burned in a disastrous fire.

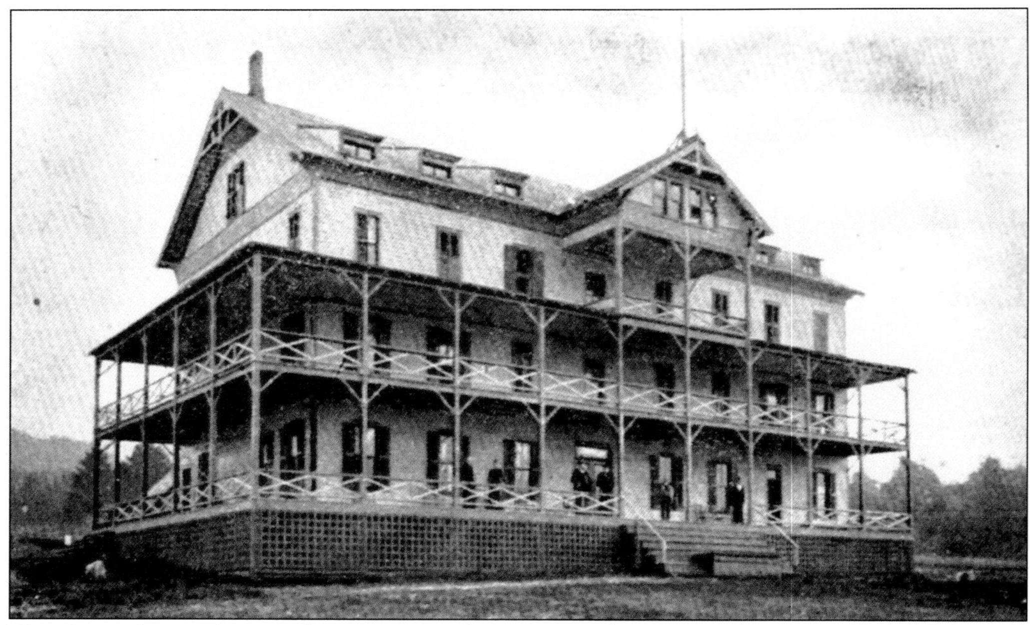

The Sacandaga Lake Hotel was not on the Great Sacandaga Lake; it was situated between Lake Pleasant and the other Sacandaga Lake in Hamilton County. The hotel overlooked both lakes, a real advantage when the breezes kept the mosquitoes away. J. Thomas Sterns was the proprietor in the 1890s.

Sacandaga Lake Hotel,

EASY OF ACCESS VIA FONDA, JOHNSTOWN & GLOVERSVILLE RAILROAD, AND STAGE FROM NORTHVILLE.

LAKE PLEASANT, HAMILTON CO., N. Y.

AN IDEAL ADIRONDACK RETREAT.

"FAR FROM THE MADDING CROWD."

For the Fisherman. With its numerous near and well-stocked Lakes and Mountain Brooks of gamy Trout, and 18 miles of Boating.

For the Hunter. With its nearby feeding grounds and runways for Deer, and delightful open woodcock and partridge shooting.

For the Health Seeker. With its altitude of 2,000 feet; pure, bracing air; grand scenery, and exhilarating vigor of the primitive woods.

The Finest Family Resort in this section of the Woods.

Large, Airy Rooms; Grand Views; Pure Air and Water.

J. THOS. STEARNS, Proprietor.

Most of the Adirondack resort destinations advertised the advantages of vacationing in the Adirondacks. The fishing, the hunting, and the health-giving features are the top three on the Sacandaga Lake Hotel list. Catering to families was a common practice, especially when father had to leave during the week to go to work while mother and the children stayed in the Adirondacks.

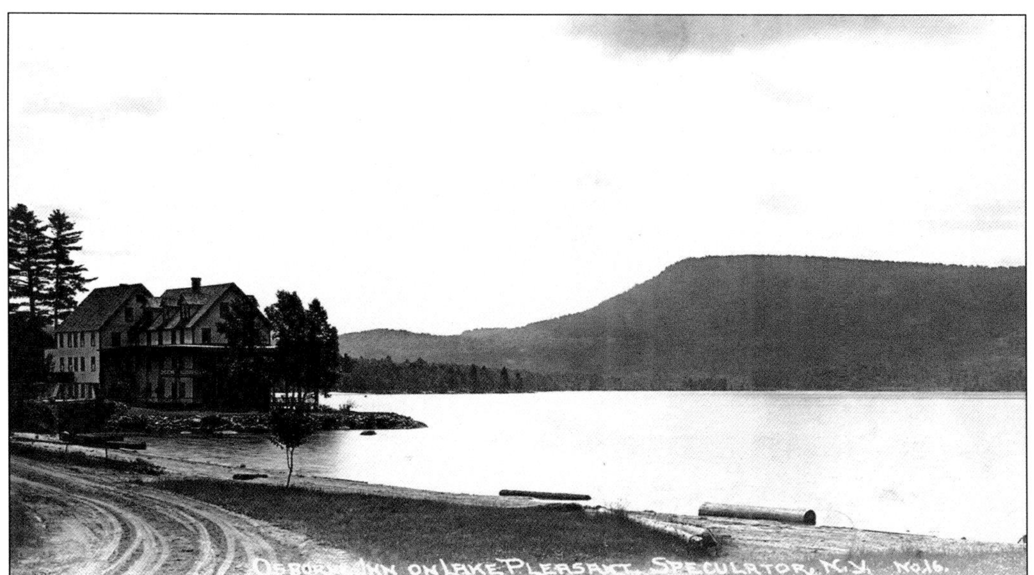

A 1926 advertisement in a national magazine reads, "The Osborne Hotels, Speculator, Tunney is training here." This refers to the training camp of Gene Tunney, who made the Osborne Inn his headquarters because of his World War I friendship with Bill Osborne, son of the owners. Max Schmeling and Max Baer also trained there in the 1930s.

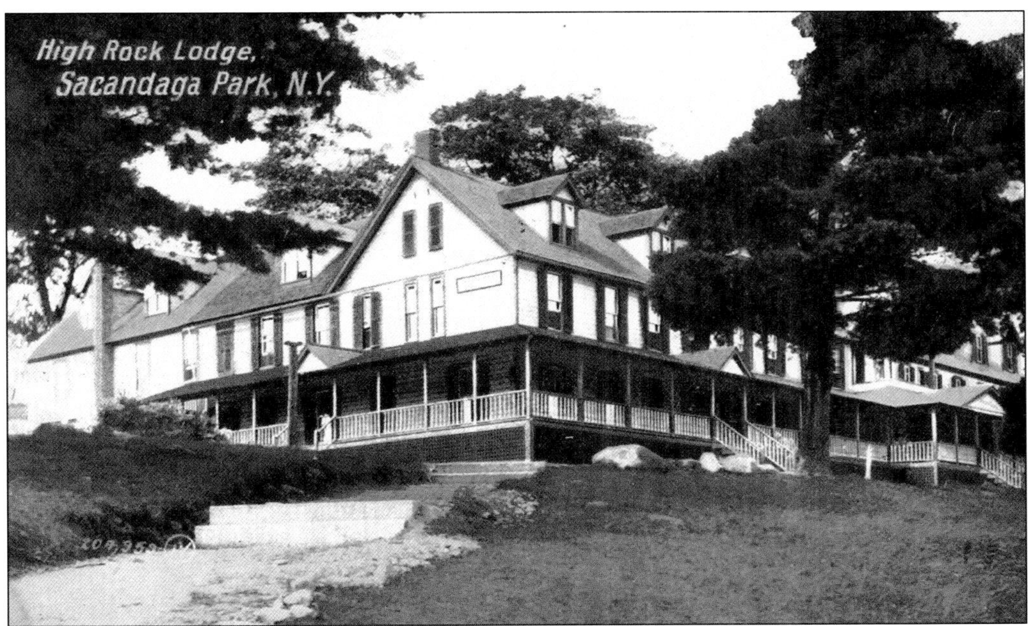

High Rock Lodge, near Sacandaga Park, was another choice for celebrities. Many well-known actors who were performing at Sacandaga Park stayed at the lodge, including Groucho Marx. The lodge was built in 1901 by James Hull for a Mr. Buckingham, who operated a farmhouse-inn. Mildred C. Dawes operated the three-story, 54-room building as a summer hotel and restaurant from the 1940s until it burned on August 22, 1951.

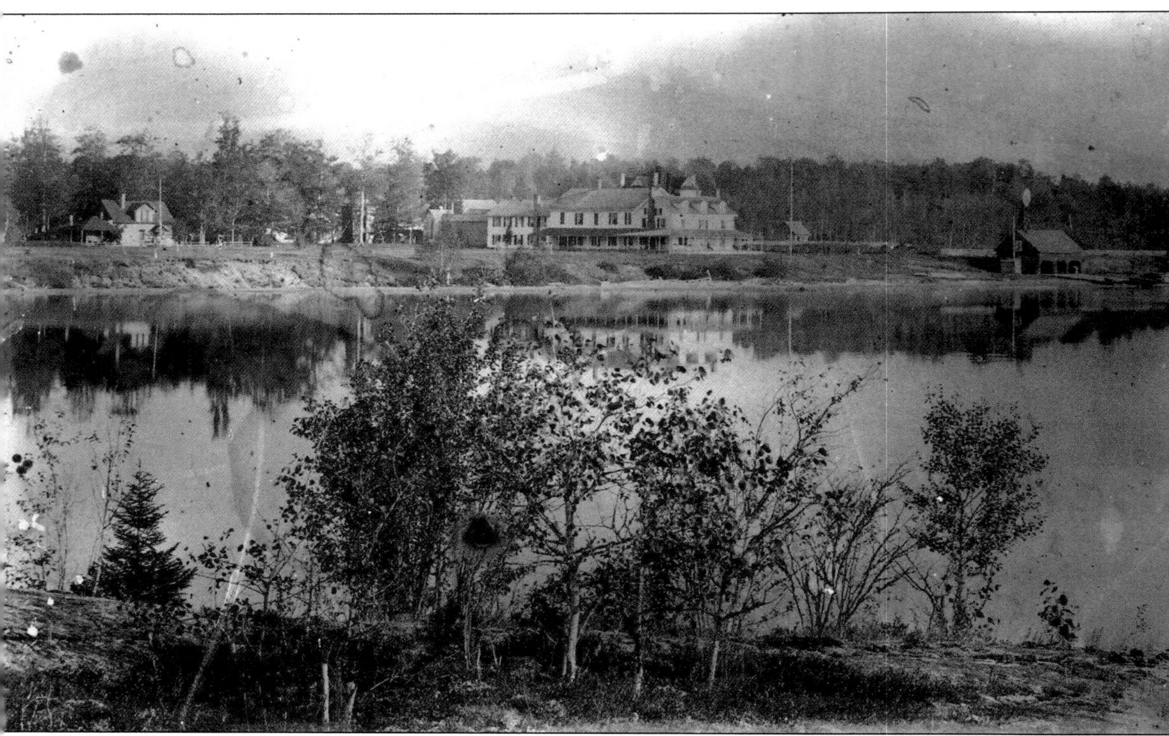

The Saranac Inn, originally called the Prospect House, is located on the Upper Saranac Lake. In Stoddard's 1892 *The Adirondacks Guidebook*, the inn advertises boats, guides, fishing tackle, supplies, and camp outfits furnished at the house in "The Country of Fish and Game and Healthful Recreation." The inn was "a favorite spot with ex-President and Mrs. Cleveland and headquarters during their visits to the woods." The Prospect House was "a clean white building with a thrifty look about it that speaks volumes in its favor," according to Stoddard's 1875 *Adirondacks Illustrated Guidebook*.

Six

FAMOUS ADIRONDACKERS, GUIDES, AND SPORTS

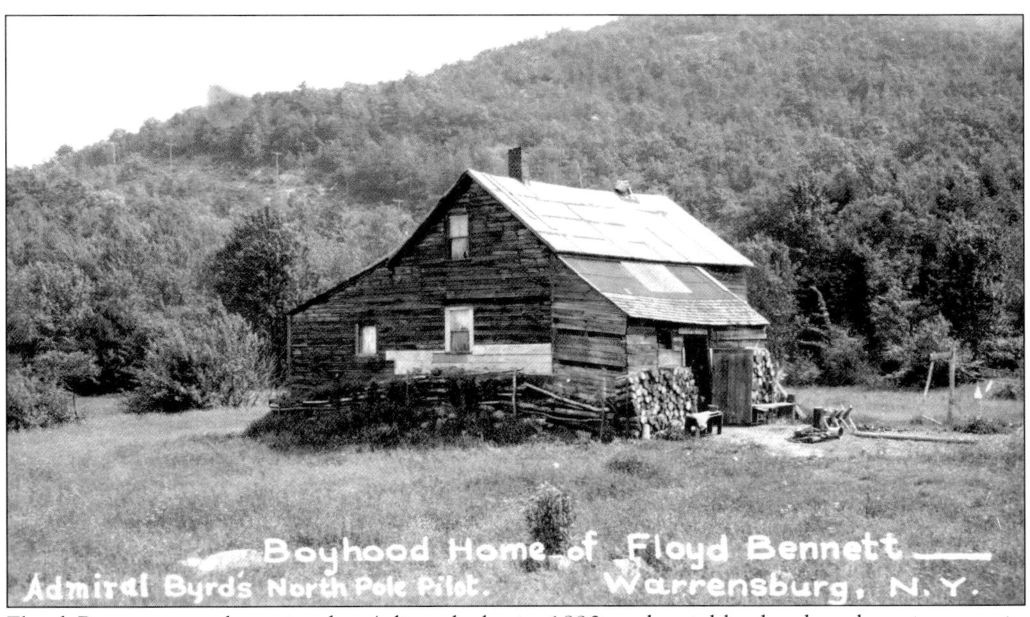

Floyd Bennett was born in the Adirondacks in 1890 and quickly developed an interest in mechanics after the invention of the automobile. He went into the auto repair business and joined the U.S. Navy in World War I. He dived into airplane mechanics, which led to his becoming a pilot. Bennett joined up with Adm. Richard Byrd and they flew to the North Pole in 1926. Bennett Field and Bennett Park are named in his memory.

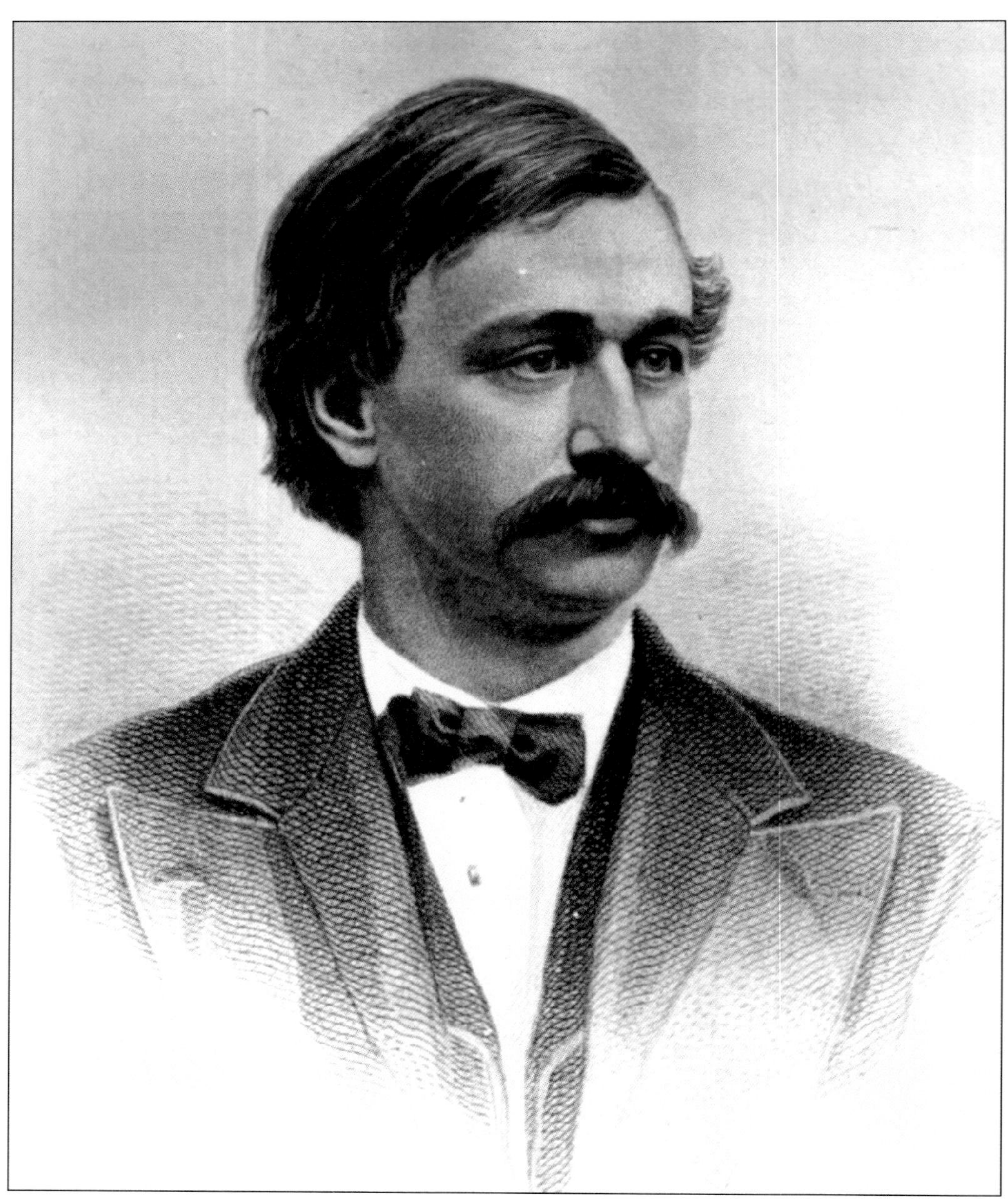

The Reverend William Henry Harrison "Adirondack" Murray's book *Adventures in the Wilderness or Camp Life in the Adirondacks* is said to have "kindled a thousand campfires." Written in 1869, it caused a rush of tourists to the promise of renewed health and enjoyment in New York's great wilderness. Murray, of Boston's prestigious Park Street Church, found the Adirondacks in 1866 and made many vacation trips to "marvelous Adirondack country." Although he preached many sermons on the value of getting out into the out-of-doors and reminded parishioners that Jesus was an outdoor man, there were some who said he should spend more time with his church duties and less time camping in the Adirondacks. Murray's many books of Adirondack tales were highly popular in their day and are still read by today's Adirondackers.

Mart Moody was known as the Mark Twain of the Adirondacks because he loved to tell stories. He was an Adirondack guide who guided many noted Americans including Pres. Grover Cleveland. Moody and his wife, Minerva, operated the Tupper Lake House, where he often had a captive audience for his Adirondack tales. One of his stories about an encounter with two Adirondack black bears ends with "They et me up, of course!"

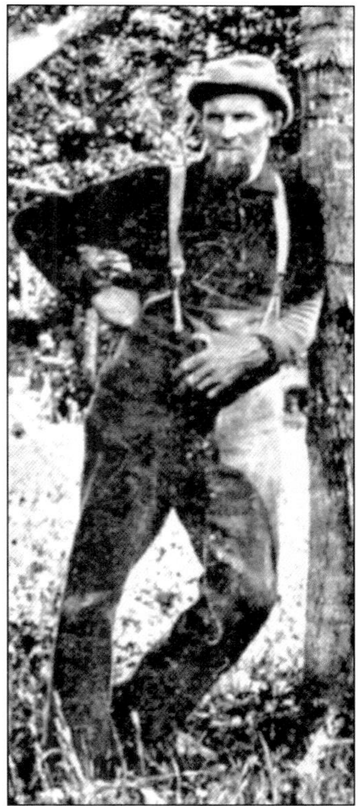

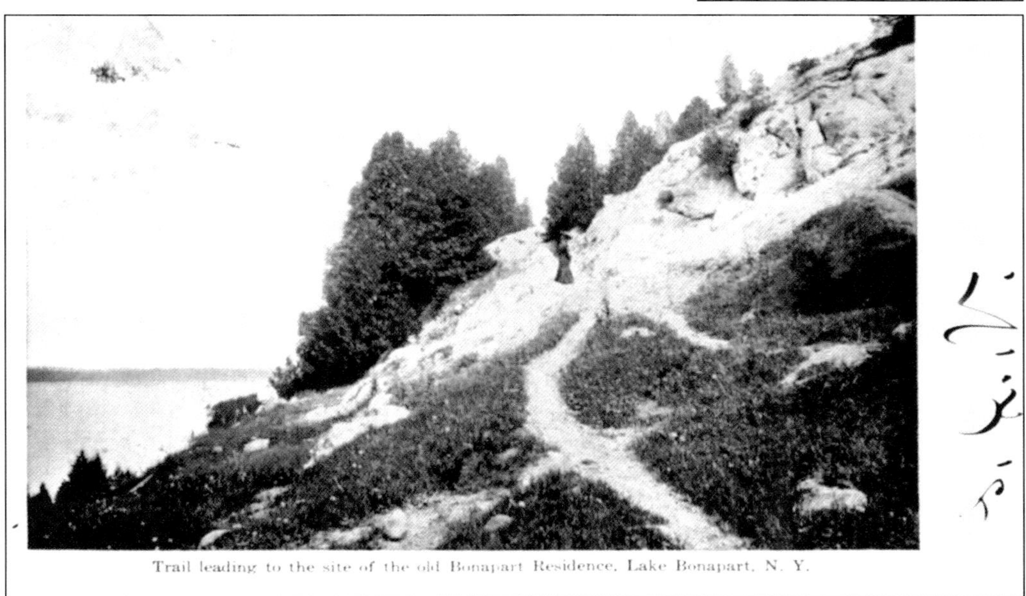

Trail leading to the site of the old Bonapart Residence, Lake Bonapart, N. Y.

Emperor Napoleon Bonaparte's big brother, King Joseph of Spain, came to America in 1815 and settled in New Jersey. He had speculated on some 150,000 acres of land on the western slopes of the Adirondacks where he built a log fortress in the woods and a lodge on Lake Bonaparte. King Joseph traveled through the Adirondacks in a six-horse coach and used a six-oared gondola on the waters.

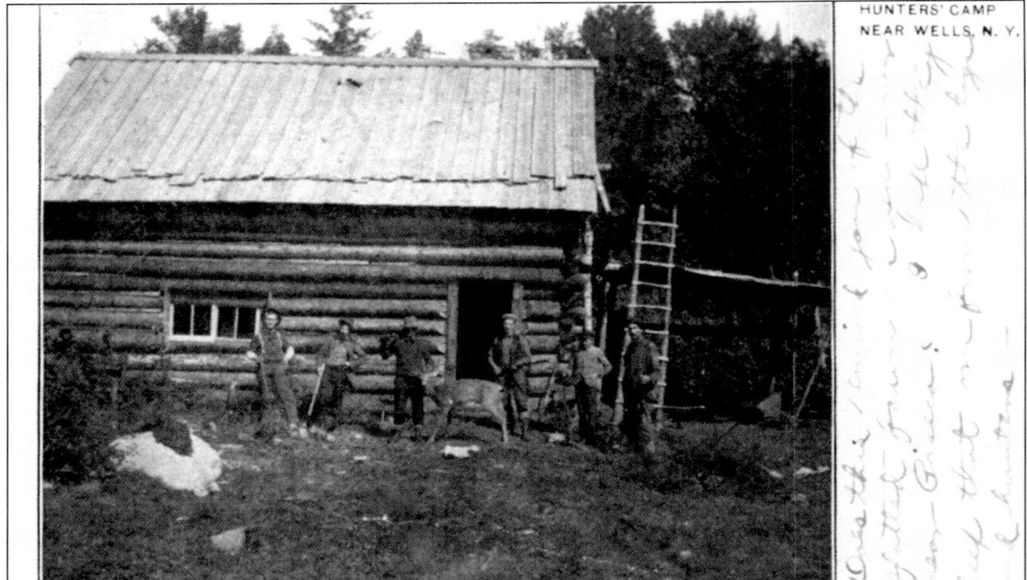

Some of the camps operated by the Adirondack guides ended up on state land, and it became the job of the conservation department to have them removed or to burn them down. Once the camps were gone, the guides had to depend on large wall tents and stoves for their clients, often transporting them into the woodland territory with horses. At this hunter's camp, an orphan deer has joined the group.

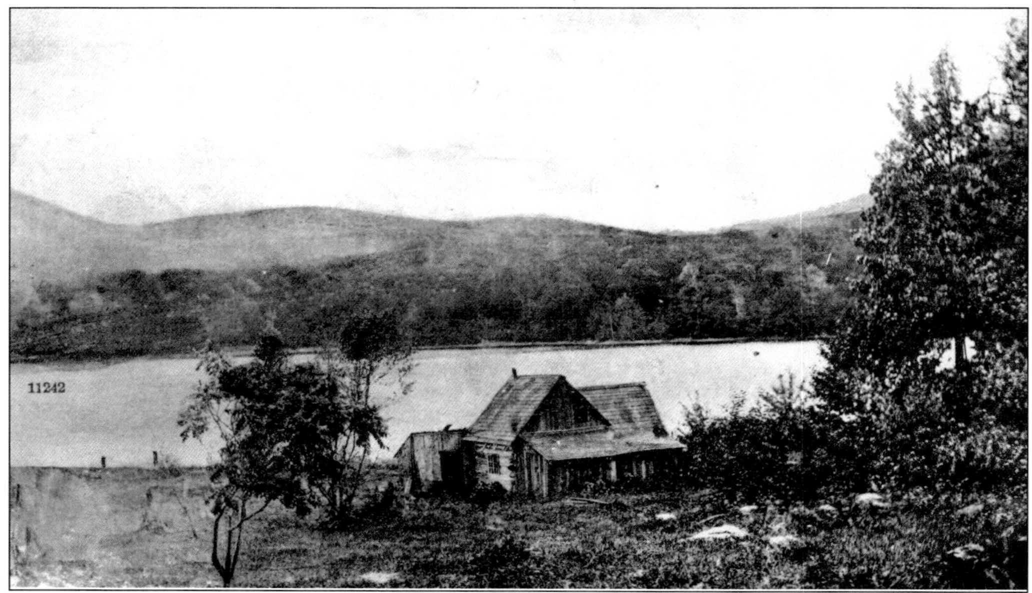

The old hermit's camp on Gilman Lake, originally one of the 40 Mud Lakes found in the Adirondacks, was the home of Willard Letson. Regarded as a hermit, Letson did some guiding in the Adirondacks and worked as a handyman at the Klondike Hotel at the head of the lake. The landlady of the hotel and her boyfriend got mixed up in a jealousy situation and the boyfriend killed Letson in May 1906. The murderer got a life sentence, and the hotel burned down the following September.

Sam Dunakin held the honor of being "the oldest guide on the Fulton Chain of lakes." He had a camp on Fourth Lake, where he lived most of his life, having served a few years in the Civil War. He occasionally took boarders at his Fourth Lake Camp. In the early 1900s he was making bear-paw snowshoes, a style of snowshoe highly useful in the snowy Adirondack winters.

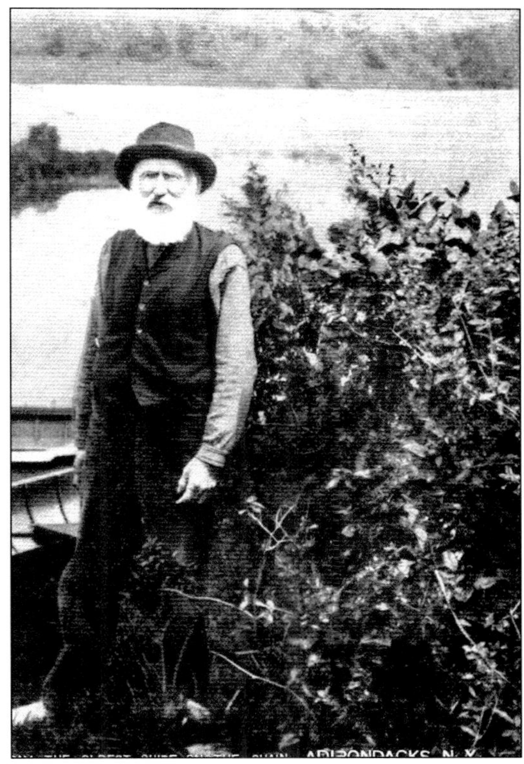

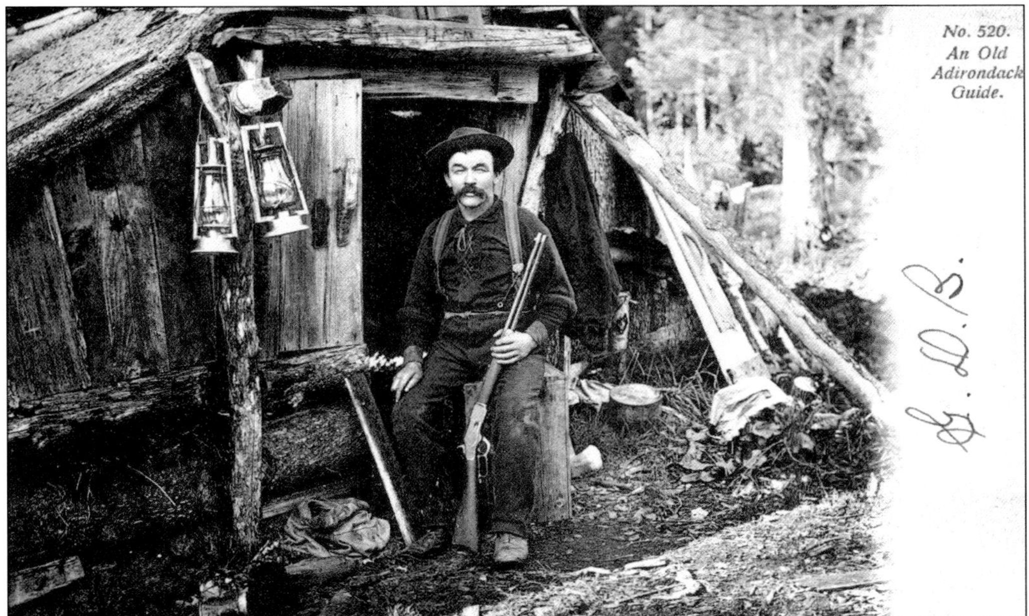

Louis Seymour, known as "French Louie," arrived in the Adirondacks in 1869. He built his guide's cabin at Lewey Lake and later moved to West Canada Lake country. He welcomed visitors and, when he took his deer hides to Speculator, he spent time with the local children. He kept pet snakes in his cabin to put in his garden each year to keep down the rodents.

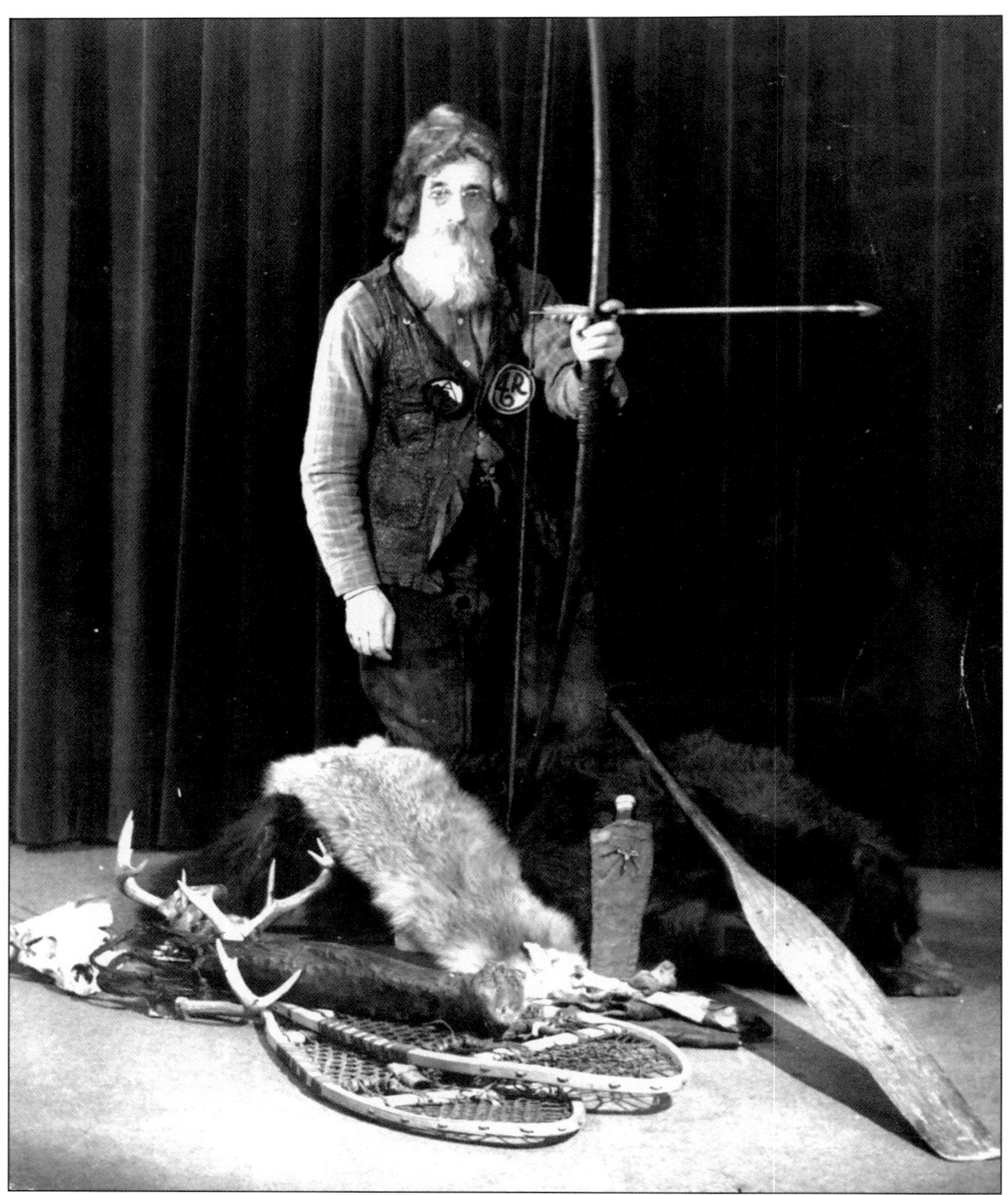

Noah John Rondeau is perhaps the most famous of the Adirondack hermits. He lived alone for roughly 30 years on the Cold River, 19 miles from the nearest settlement. Rondeau was born in 1883 and lived in the Adirondack wilderness most of his adult life. He spent nearly one entire year alone with the exception of 10 days and set a record by keeping his wood fire going for 138 continuous days during one rough winter. In later years, the conservation department brought him out of the woods to appear at sportsmen shows, where he once befriended a little girl. He wrote her a benediction: I pray Jehovah, God Almighty, and his son, Jesus Christ, that they will so bless you and yours that you will escape the plagues to come, and be ready for God's Kingdom which is near at hand.

The statue of Nicholas Stoner, Adirondack guide, stands at Caroga Lake to keep a watchful eye on the scorekeeping of the golfers on the local golf course. Stoner, Fulton County's folk hero, served in both the American Revolution and the War of 1812. As one of the first Adirondack guides, he guided surveyors, hunters, and fishermen into the forested Adirondacks in the early 1800s. According to New York historian Jeptha Simms, Stoner could "kindle a fire, climb a tree, cook a dinner, shoot a deer, hook a trout, or scent an animal quicker than any other man."

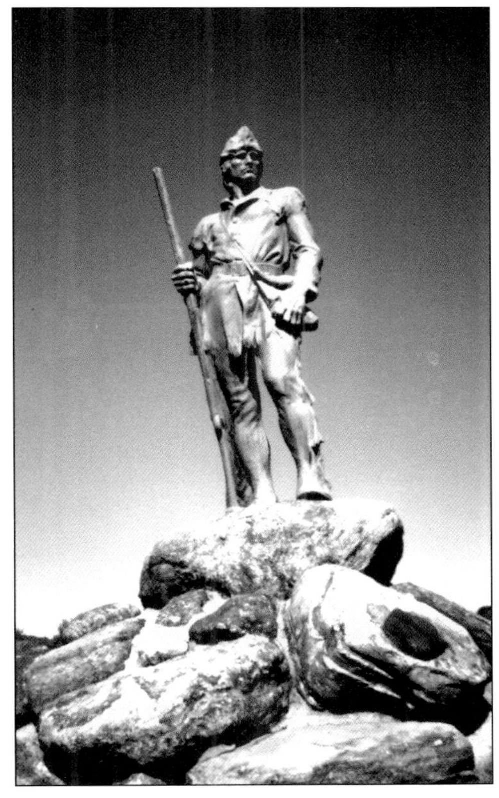

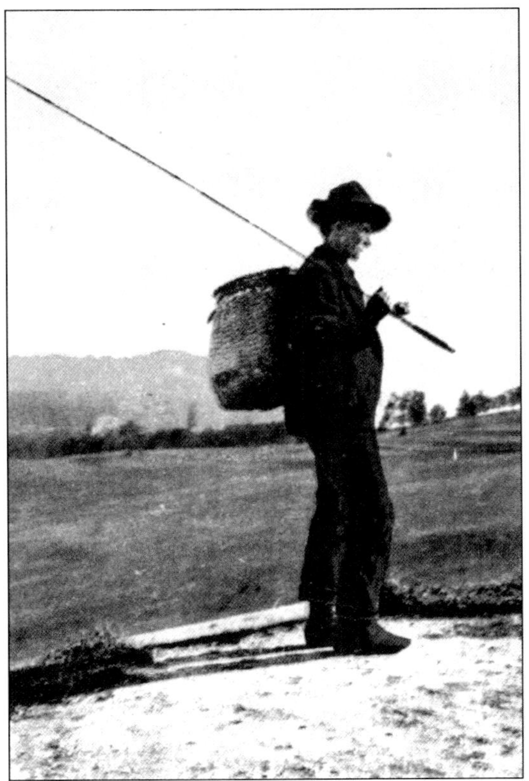

Sam Barton was a noted Adirondack guide in Lake Placid and AuSable Forks. He served in several Civil War battles. He guided many who came to the Adirondack Mountains at a time when the resorts were catching on with the traveling public. Barton was one of the original members of the Adirondack Guides Association, founded in 1891.

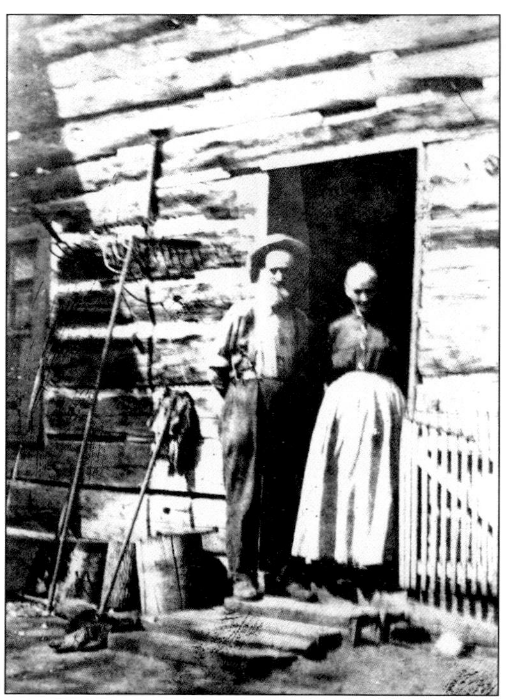

Oliver Wesley Whitman built his log cabin back in the woods on the West Hill above Wells. There he lived with his Irish bride, Annie, and their family. He guided hunting parties, tended his garden, raised bees, and did many other chores to survive in the wilds. These chores included gathering forest products like ginseng and spruce gum and tapping maple trees for sap. Whitman also kept a daily journal from 1882 to 1920, detailing his life in the Adirondacks.

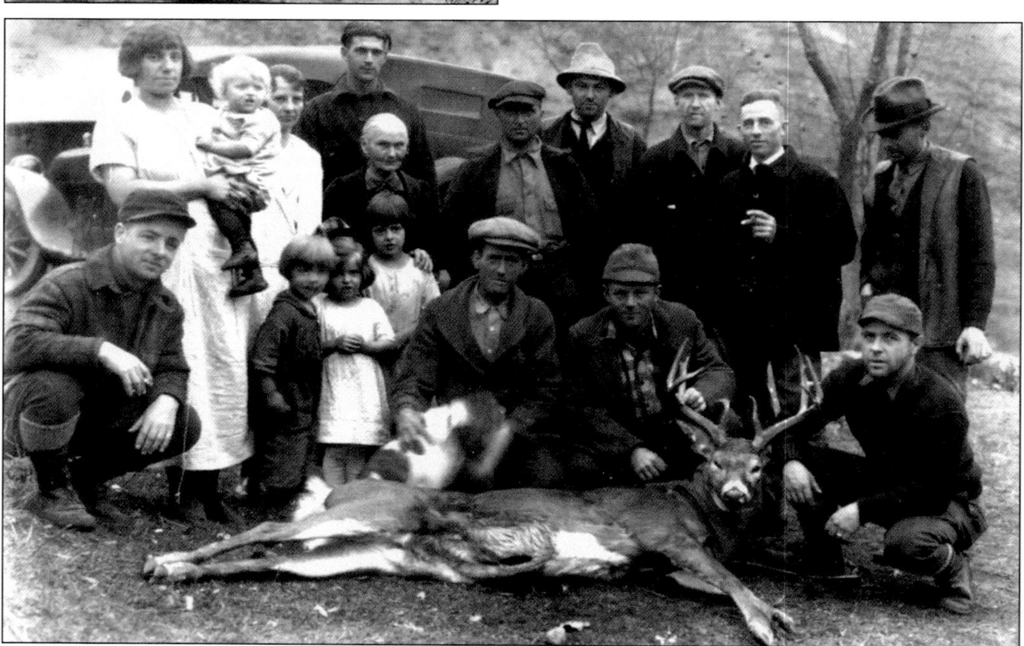

Oliver Henry Whitman (center, trying to hold the dog still) was a well-known southern Adirondack guide. His hunting parties from the capital district of New York always met with success. His mother, wife, and children joined him in this photograph of one of his hunting parties. Whitman once invented a broken shell extractor to remove bullets from a gun, and it was produced commercially for many years. He often turned to the woods for reducing stress and would state, "I wandered and I pondered!"

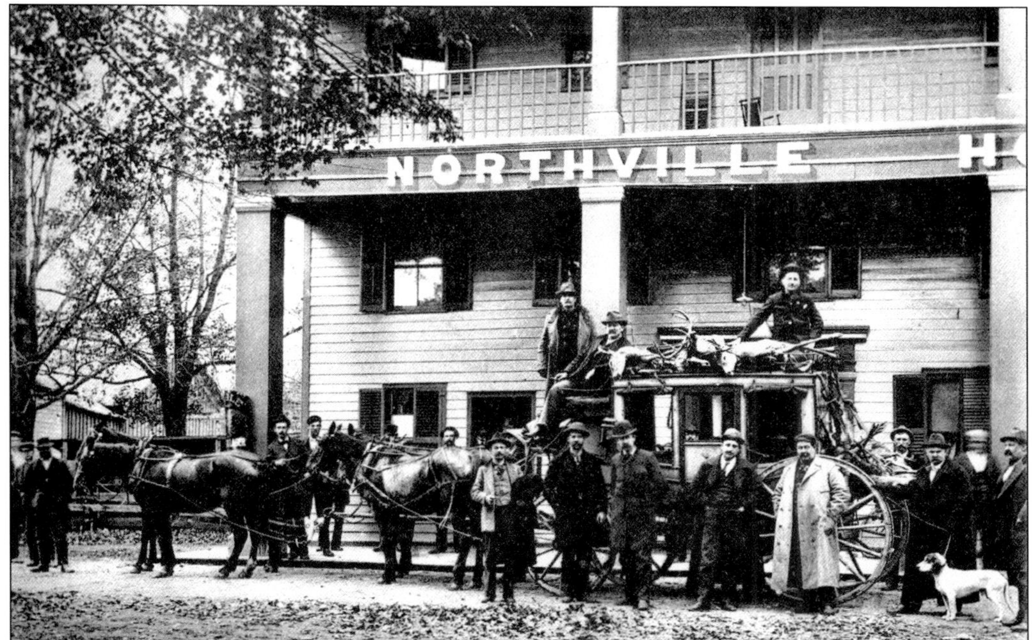

It was not uncommon to have hunting parties pass through the Adirondack hamlets during the hunting season. Some came by train to the Northville Station, the southern gateway to the mountains. When they returned, the stage with their deer would transport them to Northville to spend the night in a hotel, and then they would catch the train the next day.

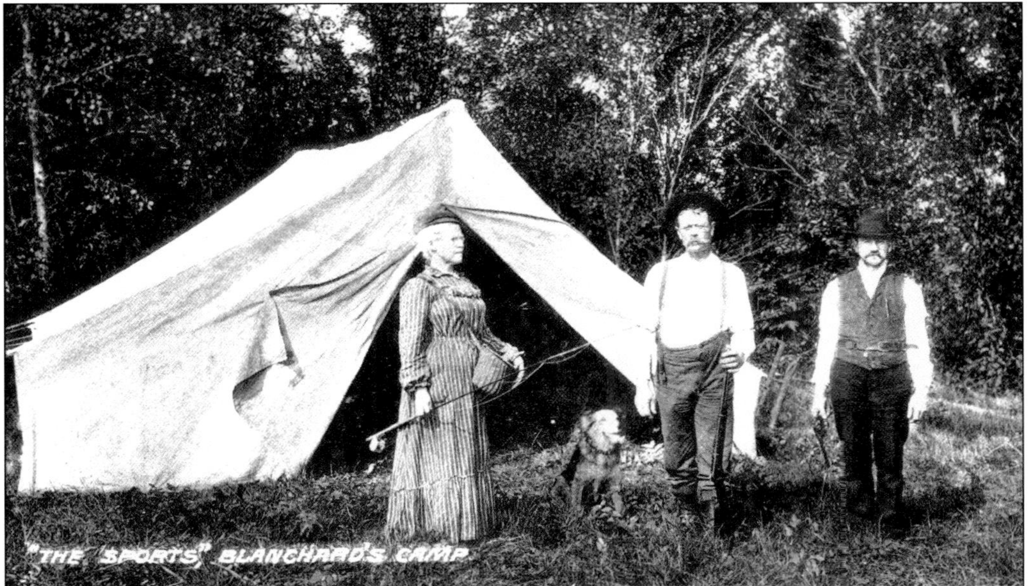

City folk who came to the Adirondack Mountains to camp, hike, hunt, and fish were called "sports." They usually hired local residents to guide them during their trips. Many stayed at the cabins or tent camps of the guides and returned year after year. As time went on, more and more women found the Adirondacks to their liking and chose to join the men in their woodland pursuits.

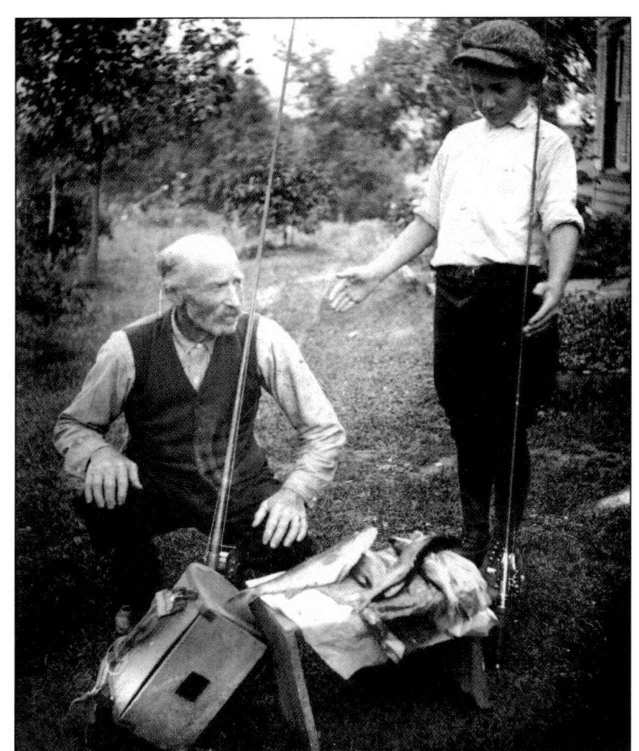

William Greenslete, a graduate of the Rome (New York) school for deaf mutes, opened a barbershop in Wells in 1893. In business for a long time, he also did photography work, repaired watches and clocks, fixed bicycles, and mended shoes and umbrellas. In these 1917 photographs, he and his son, Andrew, are reenacting the Adirondack fish story of "How big was the fish?"

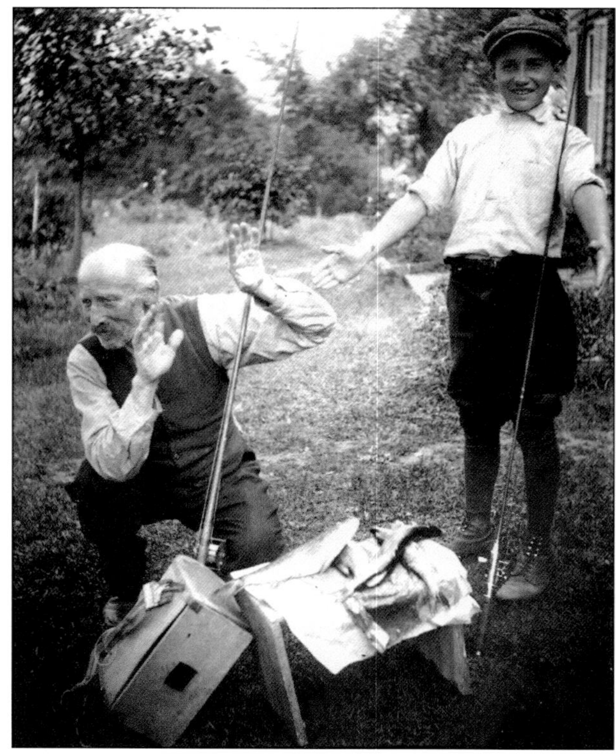

Seven

Adirondack Transportation

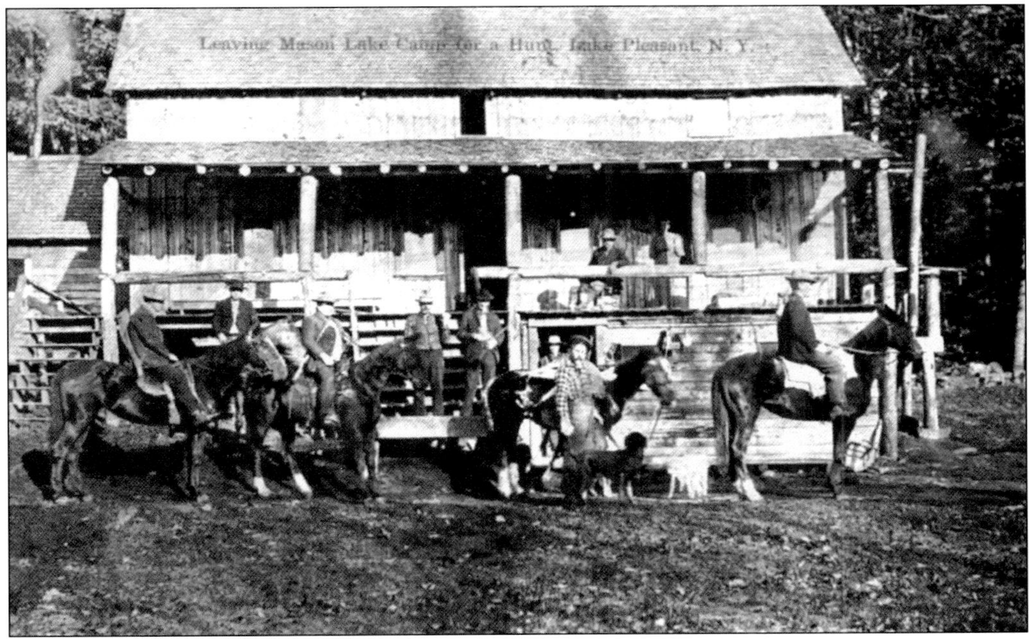

At this hunting camp at Mason Lake near Speculator the hunters look ready for an old West hunt. Horses and dogs were used in the early Adirondack days when it was legal to chase deer and bear with hunting dogs. The sports can be seen in their fancy jackets, and the guides are wearing their flannel shirts. The woman on the porch may have been the camp cook.

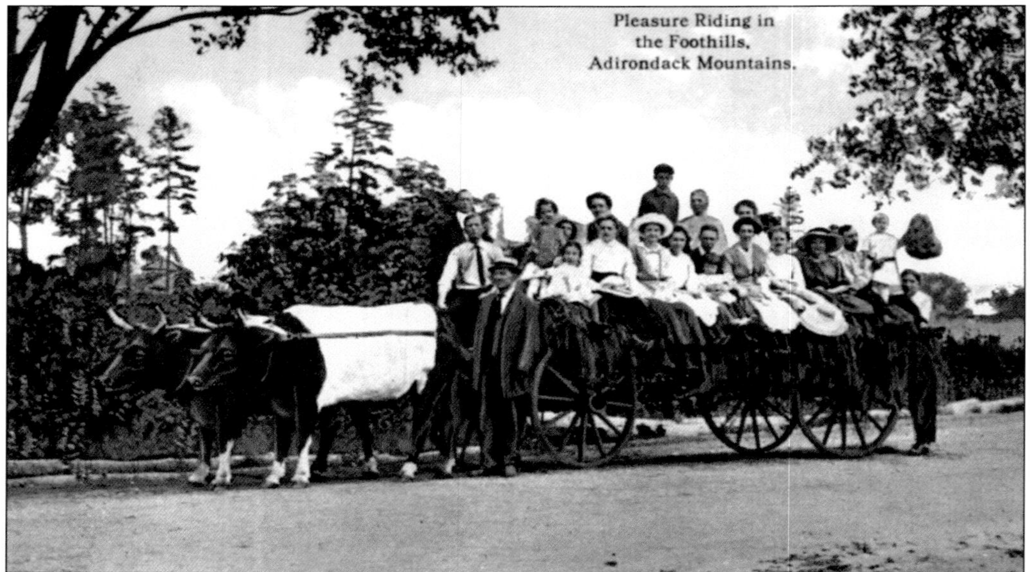

Oxen pull a wagon filled with a church or school group on a hayride. The ox was the workhorse of the Adirondacks. Oxen were often stronger than horses and did not spook as skittish horses did. The oxen did not require expensive harnesses, as they could be hitched to the load with an ox yoke hewed from an Adirondack log. In the mid-1800s, 360 working oxen were reported in Hamilton County alone.

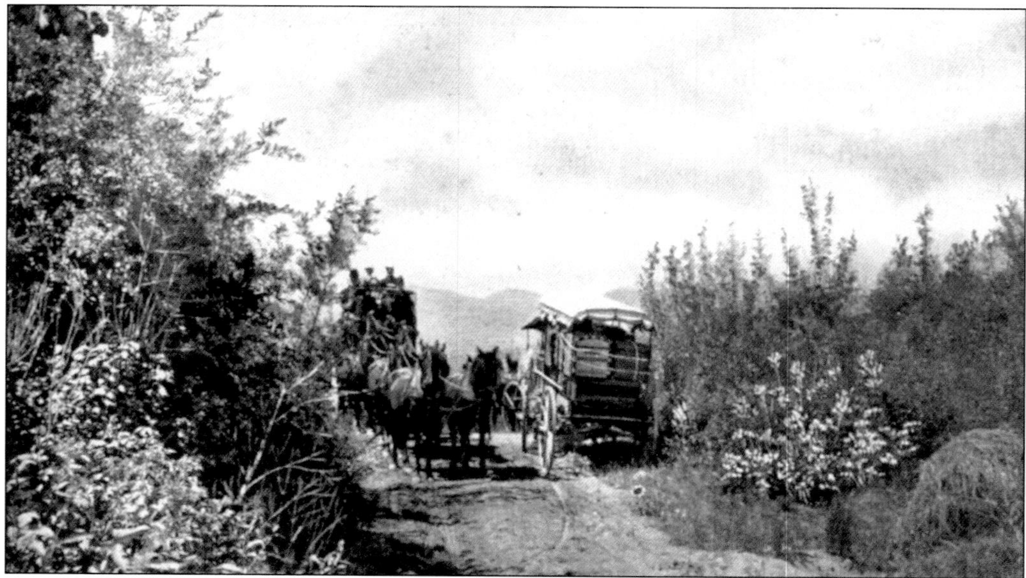

From c. 1855 to the beginning of the 20th century, everything in the Adirondacks depended on the stagecoach lines. People, parcels, medicine, mail, and news traveled on the horse-drawn coaches. An 1880 advertisement from the Adirondack Company's Railroad publicized reaching the "Adirondack Wilderness via Six-Horse Concord Coaches from Saratoga, North Creek, and Riverside." When the stagecoach met with a wagon on the narrow Adirondack roads, it took some careful maneuvering to get by. According to Adirondack historian Arthur Donaldson, there were no fatal accidents during the stagecoach years.

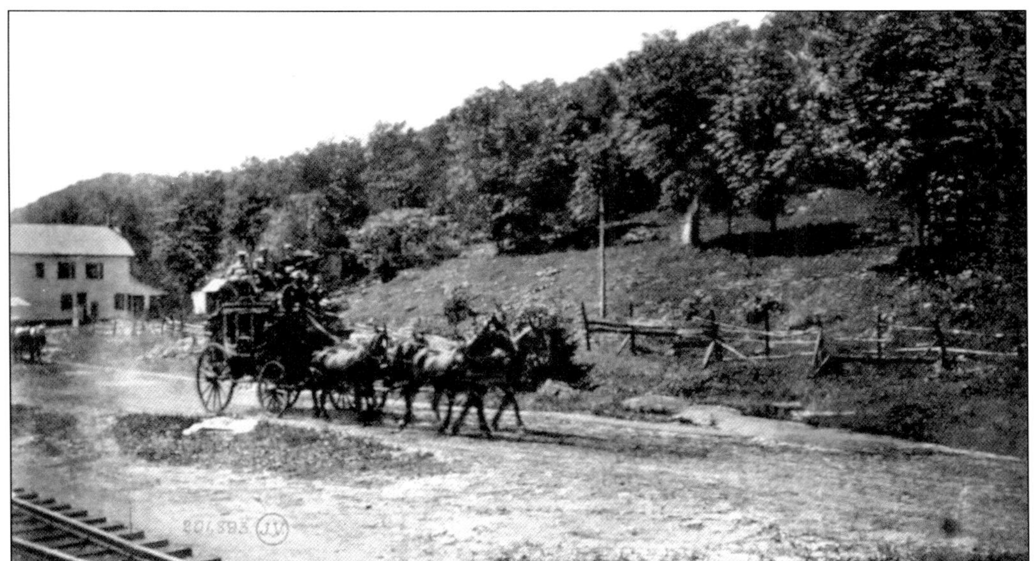

The Schroon Lake Stage picked up passengers at the Riverside Station for the seven-mile trip to Schroon Lake resorts. According to Phillip Smith Sr.'s *History of Riparius*, George Leavitt and C. Thurman Leland opened the stage line from the railroad station at Riverside to Schroon Lake and Pottersville before 1873. They used Concord coaches, which held 24 passengers, pulled by four horses.

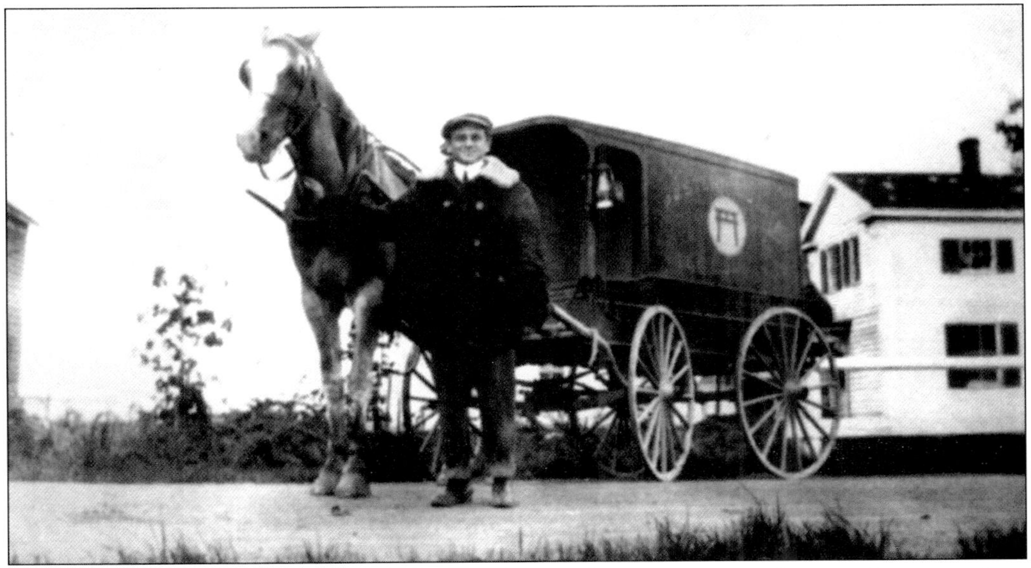

The early Adirondack settlers often depended upon the itinerant peddler to bring them their needs. The peddlers traveled from town to town with their wagons filled with a variety of goods. Peddlers also spread the news of the day. A. Cashinsky peddled seasonal goods in the early 1900s in the Adirondacks. S. Brooks sold ladies' and men's furnishings. Alex Duheme peddled apples. They delivered laundry, ice, and milk to the Adirondack homes. The Jewel-T man (pictured) had a variety of cooking products including the "best vanilla" in the world. Peddlers often stayed overnight at the last home they visited that day; it did not take them long to learn which homes served the best food.

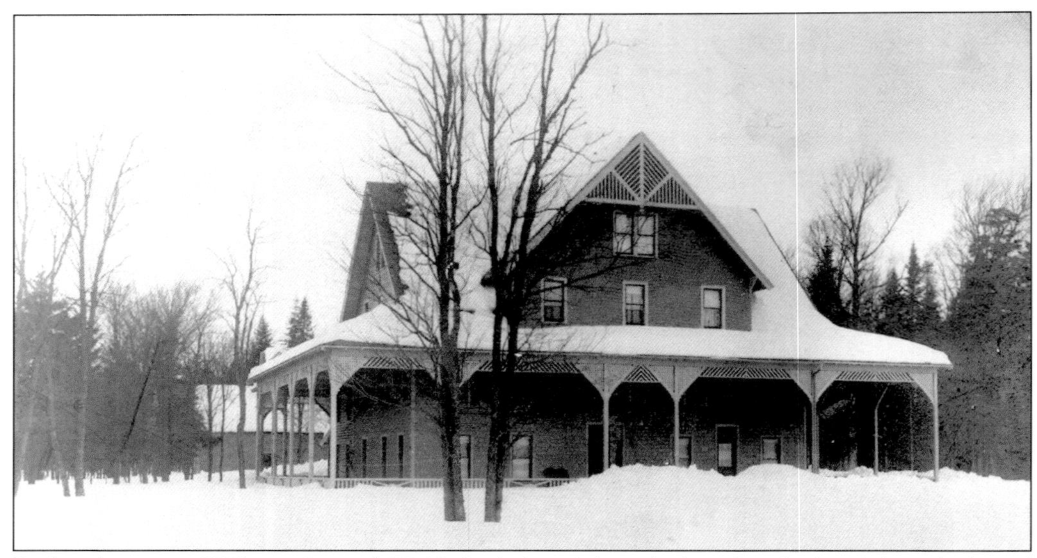

Railroad tycoon William Seward Webb built his Adirondack railroad, the Adirondack and St. Lawrence Railroad, in 1891–1892. He owned a large 225-square-mile Adirondack estate and had his own railroad station, Keepawa, on his property. Later, he consolidated several rail lines into the Mohawk and Malone Railroad and sold it to the New York Central Railroad. The Adirondack rail line, abandoned off and on over the years, has been reopened for train trips through the Adirondacks and to Lake Placid. The Beaver River Hotel (pictured) was on the Mohawk and Malone line. The line was needed since the only way to get to roadless Beaver River was by boat.

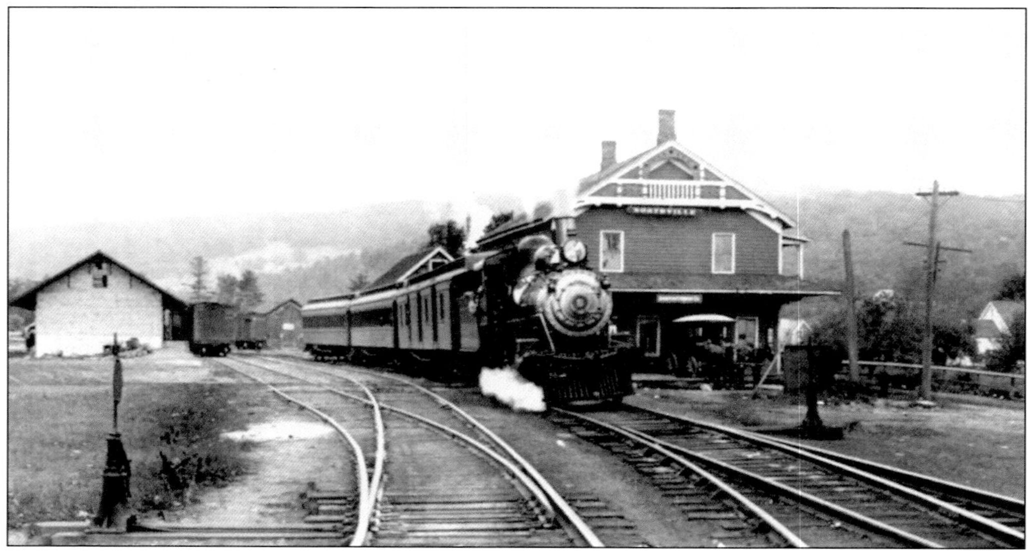

Coming from the south, the Northville Station of the Fonda, Johnstown, and Gloversville Railroad was the last stop before the Adirondacks. At the station, which opened in 1875, travelers boarded stagecoaches to continue their journey into the Adirondacks. Other passengers disembarked at Sacandaga Park, an amusement park just south of the Northville Station. The railroad connected with the New York Central at Fonda (see Images of America: *The Fonda, Johnstown & Gloversville Railroad*, by Randy Decker).

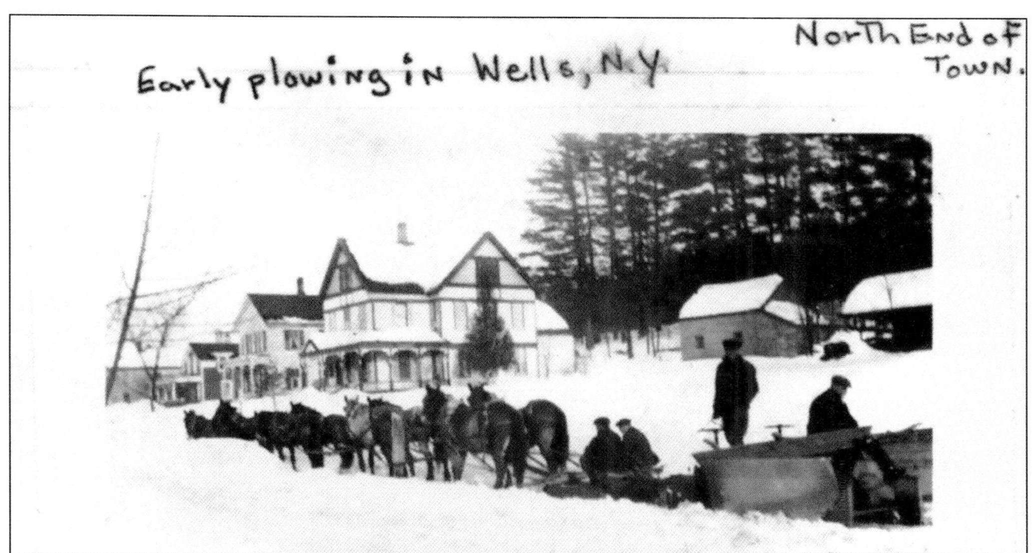

Early plowing in the Adirondacks often required four or more teams to push aside the deep Adirondack snow. A "Michigan rig," operated by a team of road workers, pushed the snow off to the sides of the roads. However, the roads were not completely cleared; snow and ice were left for use by cutters and sleighs.

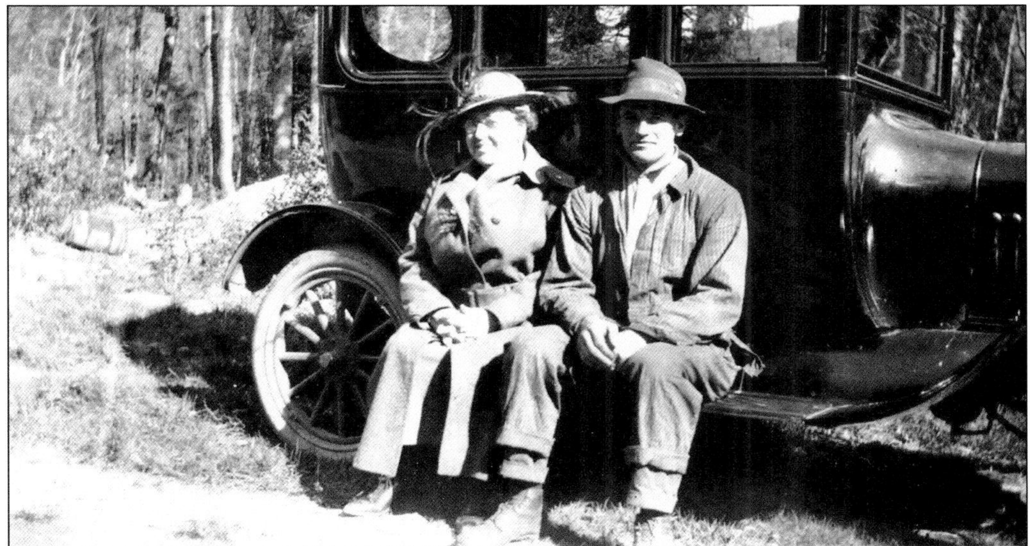

Mary and Orra Buyce stop to view the scenery in this early road trip. The invention and use of the automobile might possibly have been the greatest single factor in opening up the Adirondacks to the general population. Once the automobile entered the Adirondacks, American travelers could journey to the wilderness and stay at the roadside campsites and hotels that followed. In July 1902, Mr. and Mrs. Herbert Sackett honeymooned at the Lower Saranac Lake and Paul Smith's Hotel. They drove a horseless carriage, probably the first to be seen in the Adirondacks. Auto travel in the early Adirondacks was not easy, with broken springs, backing up the hills to keep the gas flowing, flat tires, and deep mud and ruts in the roads. After some people were hit by "fast-moving vehicles," speed limits of 10 to 20 miles per hour were established in the Adirondack communities.

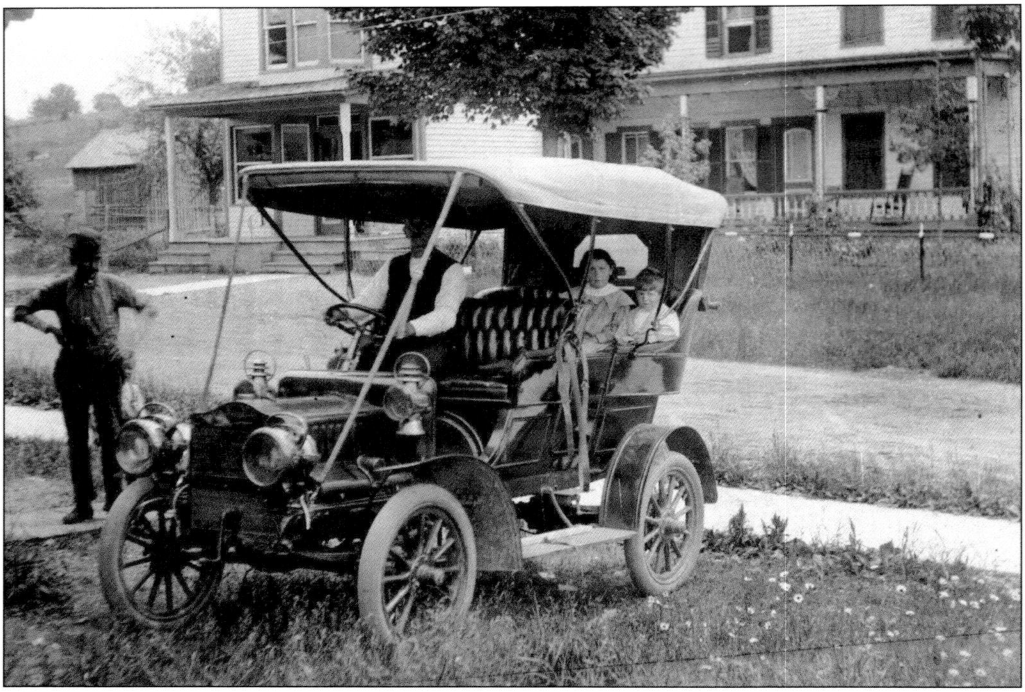

The main road, today's Route 30 running through Wells, was still a dirt road when this automobile was in use *c.* 1912. The driver of the car, Myron Buyce, successfully operated a dry goods and grocery store, built in 1895, which can be seen across the street. Notice the crank on the front used to start the car. These cranks were occasionally the cause of a broken arm when they kicked back.

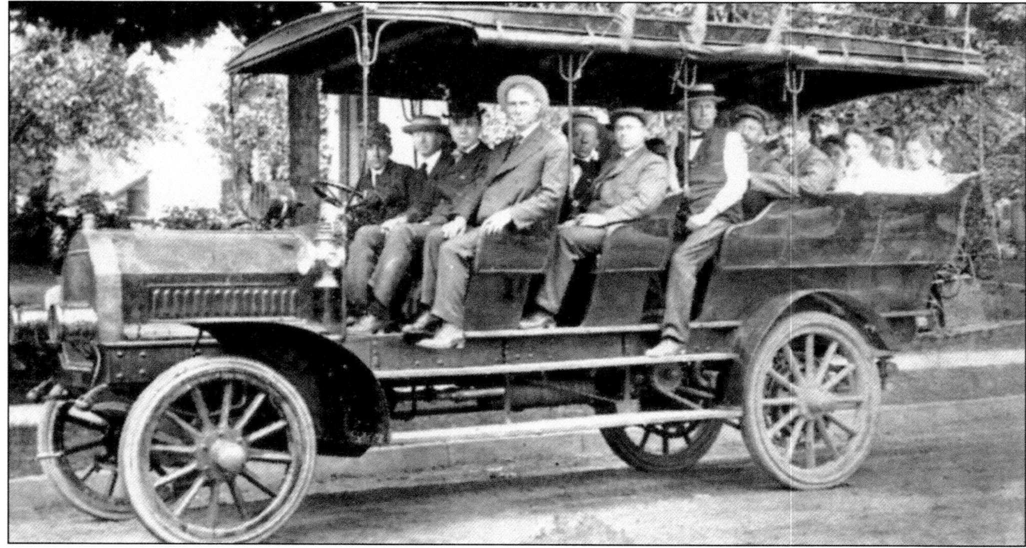

John Ostrander and Ed Call bought an automobile stage in 1907. The stage could hold about the same number of passengers as the old Concord coaches, about 24 people. Unfortunately, Adirondack roads were too narrow and too rough for an automobile stage and the business did not last long.

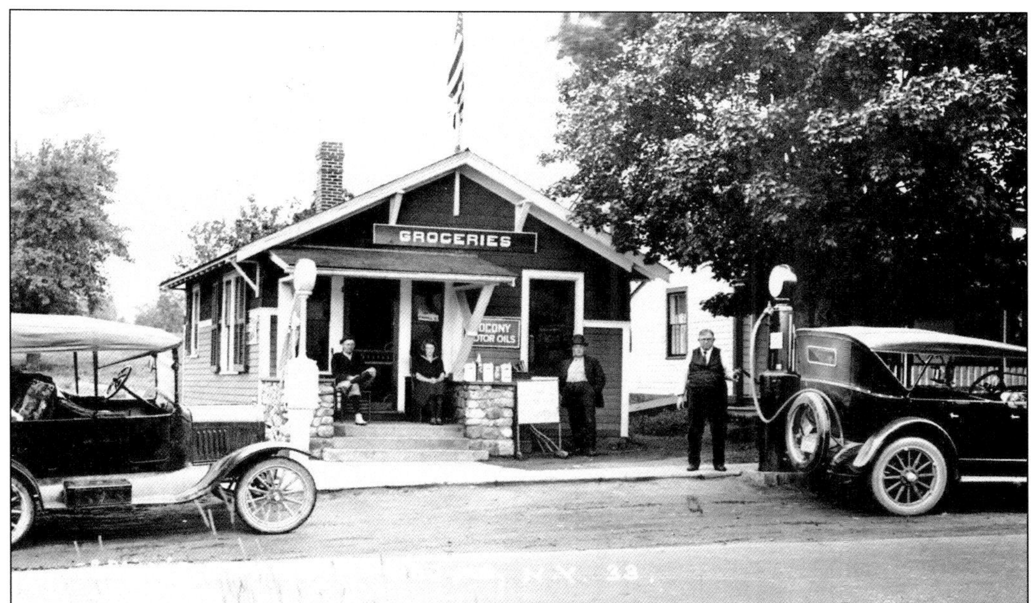

Spain's store in Newcomb featured Socony gas in its hand-cranked gas pumps. Adirondack gas stations were supplied from the Standard Oil Company of New York's distribution center near the railroad station in Northville. With the advent of the automobile, Adirondack touring became popular in spite of the "element of risk and uncertainty in automobile travel." Fortunately, the Adirondack garages advertised "Tourists treated same as home folks!"

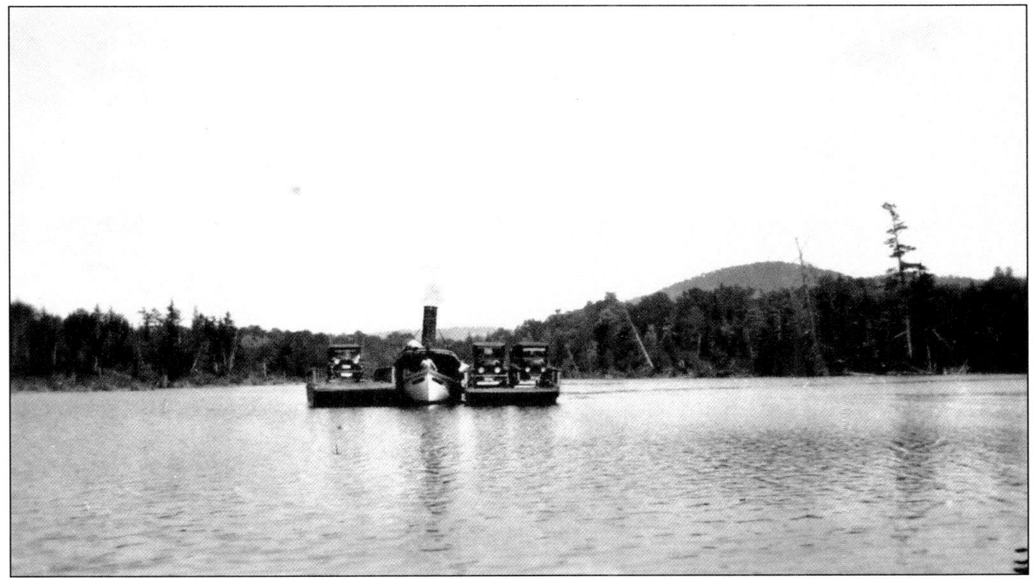

When automobiles came into use, getting them across the Adirondack lakes called for the use of ferryboats. To transport these automobiles across Raquette Lake, two barges attached to the sides of a small steamboat were required. Some brought in cars to be left at their camps for use on the Adirondack back roads during the summer season.

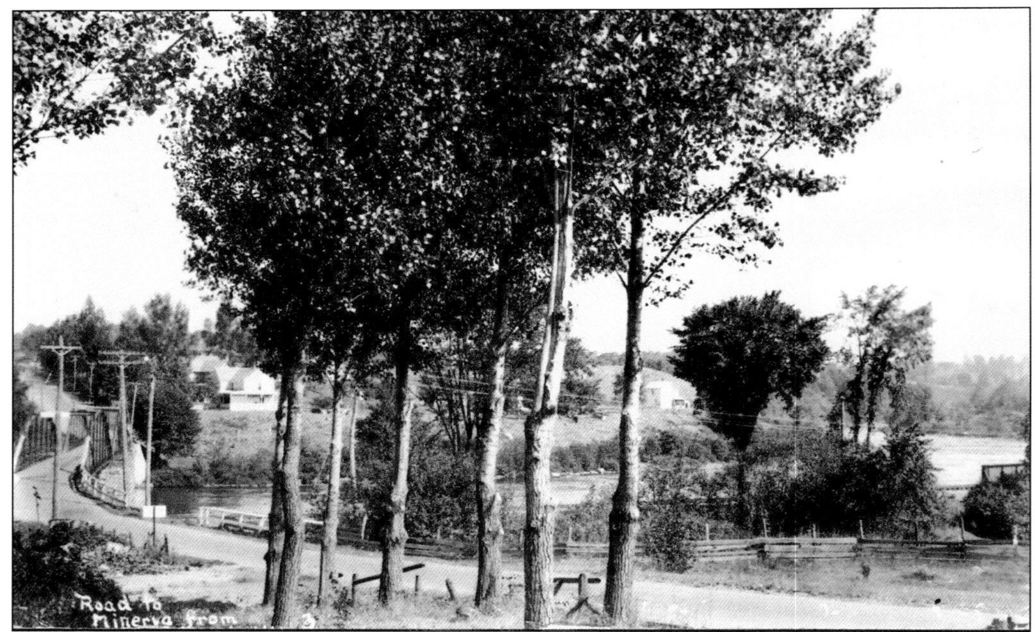

The road to Minerva is one of the most picturesque highways in the Adirondacks. In the fall of the year, it is a breathtaking drive to view the autumn foliage. This scenic view is from an early 1900s postcard. Note the little bridge, the wooden guardrails and fences, and the upper Hudson River flowing to the ocean. The telephone poles with their strings of wire indicate that electricity had come to this part of the Adirondacks.

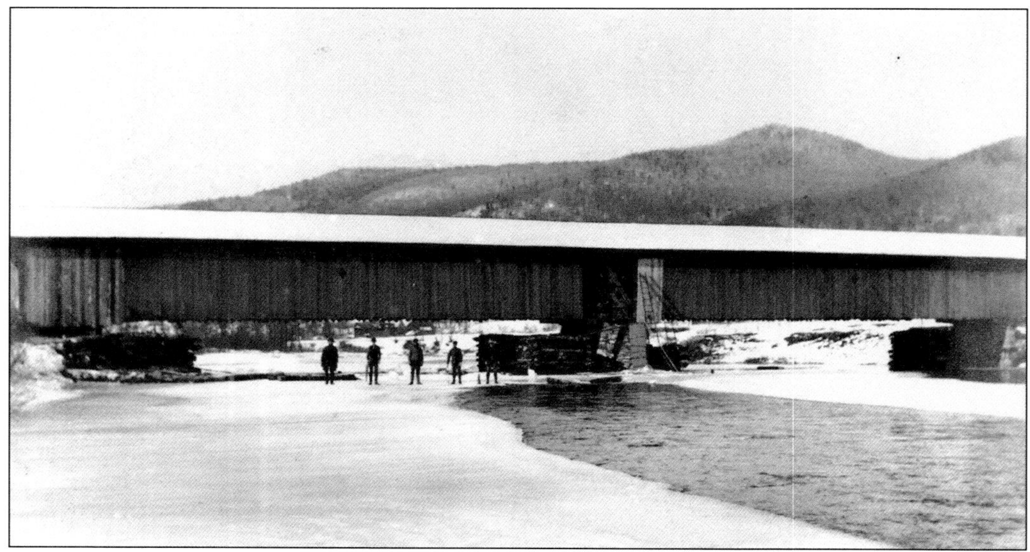

The covered bridge across the Sacandaga River at Wells served the travelers well for 63 years. Built in 1866 at the cost of $3,000, it replaced an older wooden bridge at the site. A new bridge of concrete and steel was built across the river in 1929. Shown here in 1886, the bridge was raised two feet and new piers of stone were put in. The old log piers are still seen standing beside the stone piers in the photograph. In 1892, the record shows that those who crossed the bridge "on a trot" were fined $2.

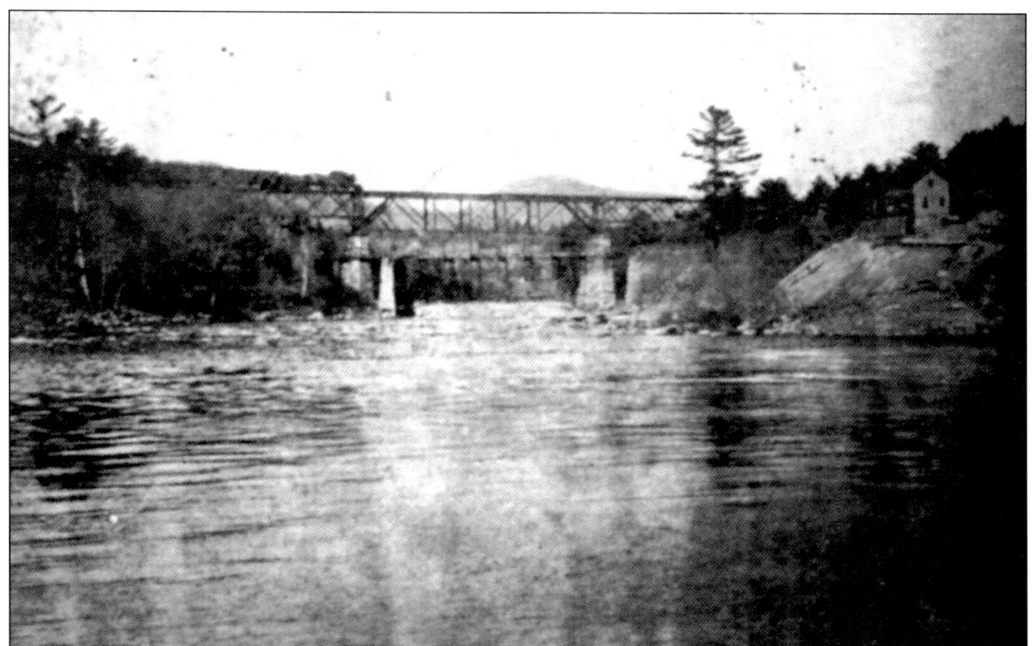

The Bow Bridge, barely visible in front of the railroad trestle, was built across the Sacandaga at Hadley in 1885. The bridge was built on the abutments of an 1813 covered bridge, which had burned. Closed to traffic in 1993, it is an extremely rare (only one of two in the United States) mid-deck lenticular, or parabolic, truss bridge. Efforts are being made to save it from being dismantled.

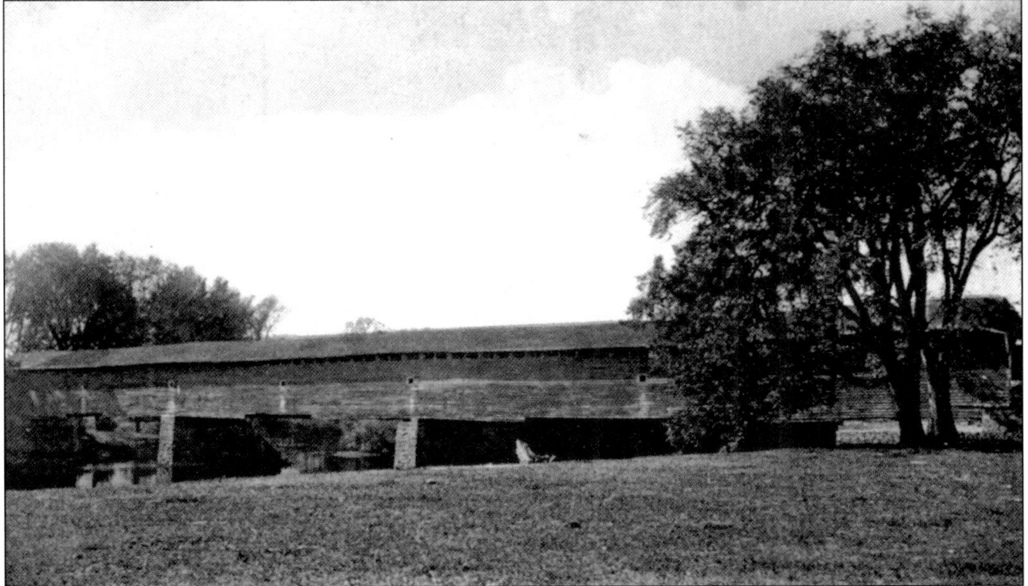

The largest and only two-lane bridge across the Sacandaga River was built by Daniel Stewart at Fish House in 1814. When a dam on the river created the Sacandaga Reservoir in 1930, the fast-rising water raised the Fish House bridge off its piers and destroyed it before it could be saved. The bridge lumber was salvaged for many uses by those who "helped themselves."

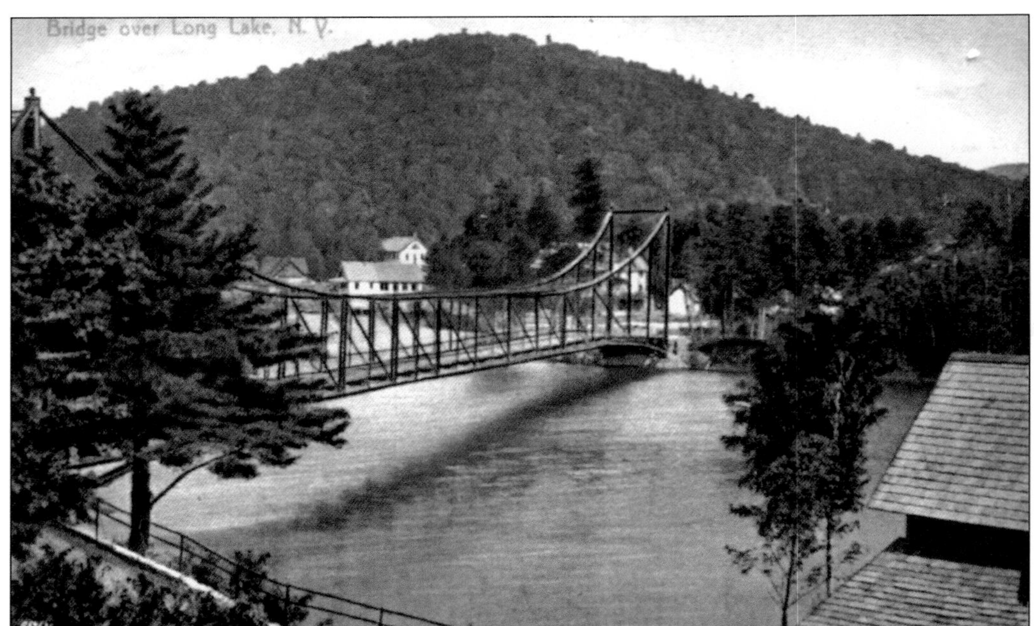

In 1901, an iron bridge was built across Long Lake, and it served the community for the next 38 years. The bridge had a 545-foot span and required 540 feet of planking. The cost of the bridge, built by businessman Patrick Moynehan, was under $35,000. By 1937, the bridge became too small to handle the increased traffic, so it became a one-way bridge. The state replaced it with a new steel bridge in 1938. The original float bridge on the site had been neglected and the elements had destroyed it by 1900, when a ferry took over. Voters desired a new iron bridge, which led to the building of the bridge in the photograph.

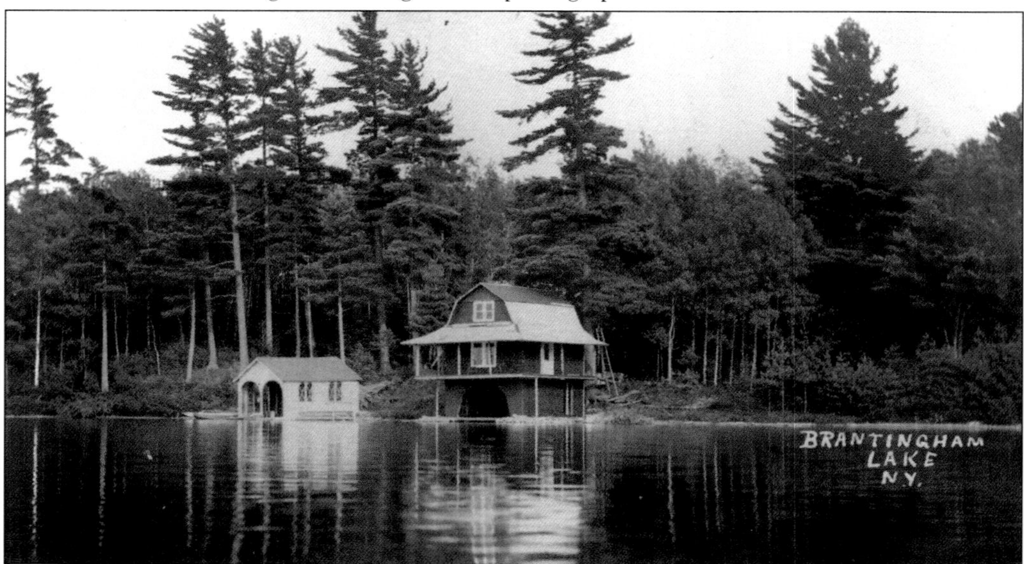

These two structures on Brantingham Lake serve as boathouses. Built right at the water's edge, they allow boats to be driven directly in to shelter. The upper story of the larger building served as living quarters for the camp owners. New regulations govern the building of boathouses on Adirondack waters today.

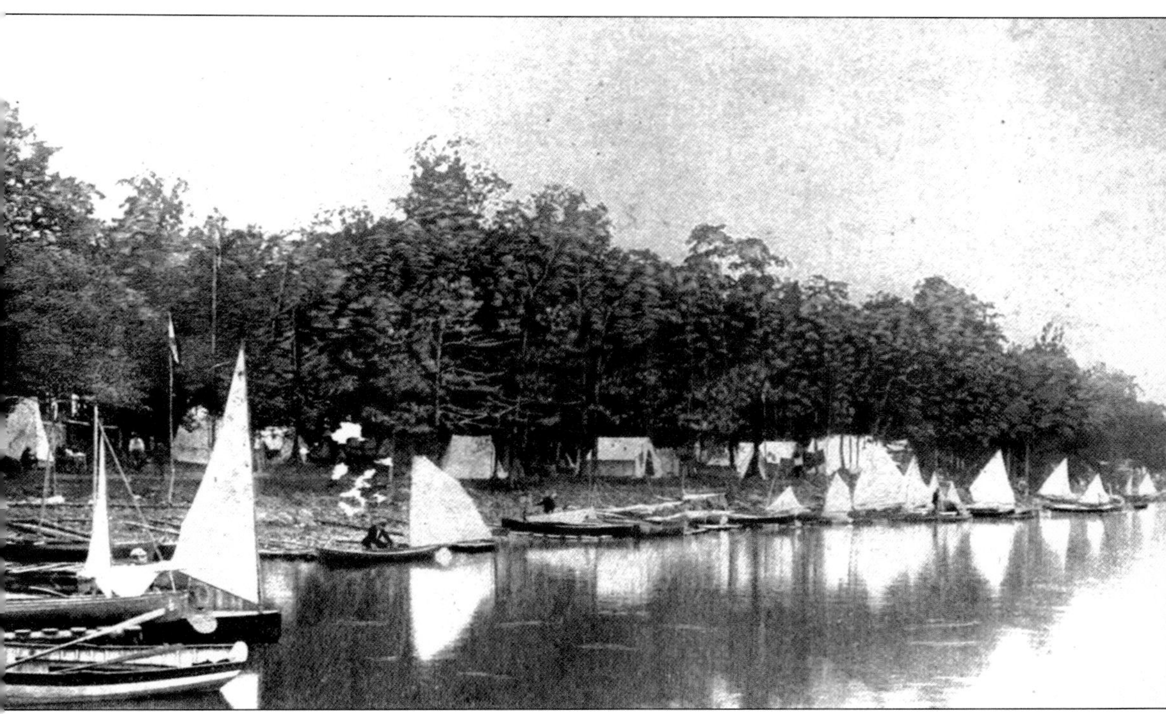

The Adirondack guide boats are closely connected to the history of the Adirondacks, but the canoe played an equally important role on Adirondack waterways. Native Americans and early explorers used canoes on Adirondack waters long before the New York Canoe Club was founded in 1870 by William L. Alden, reintroducing canoeing to the United States. *Harper's Magazine* featured a Lake George canoe article in 1880, and the American Canoe Association was founded there the same year. Today's canoeists have a wide choice of canoeing waters in the Adirondacks.

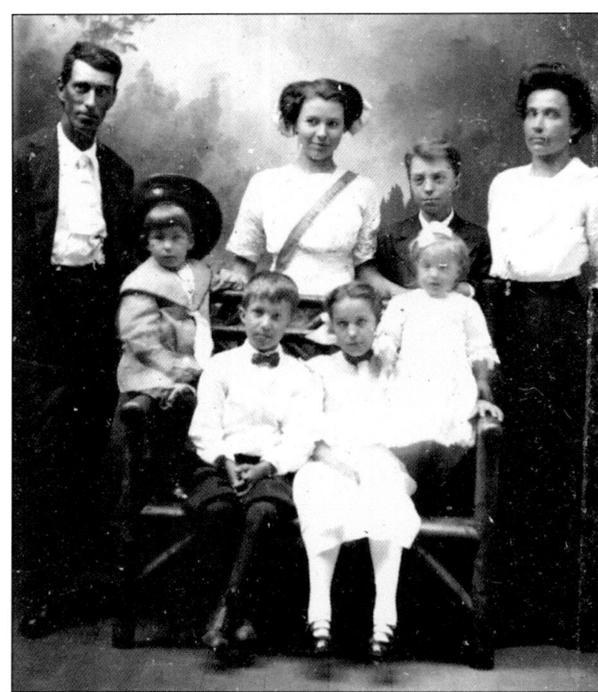

Families and organizations held their outings and picnics at amusement parks near the population centers in and around the Adirondacks. One such park, the Sacandaga Park owned by the Fonda, Johnstown & Gloversville Railroad, hosted groups from the nearby cities until 1930. The John Whitman family (pictured) traveled by train from Mayfield in August 1906 to enjoy a day at the amusement park. The photograph gallery was a popular attraction at the park as it provided a record of the outing.

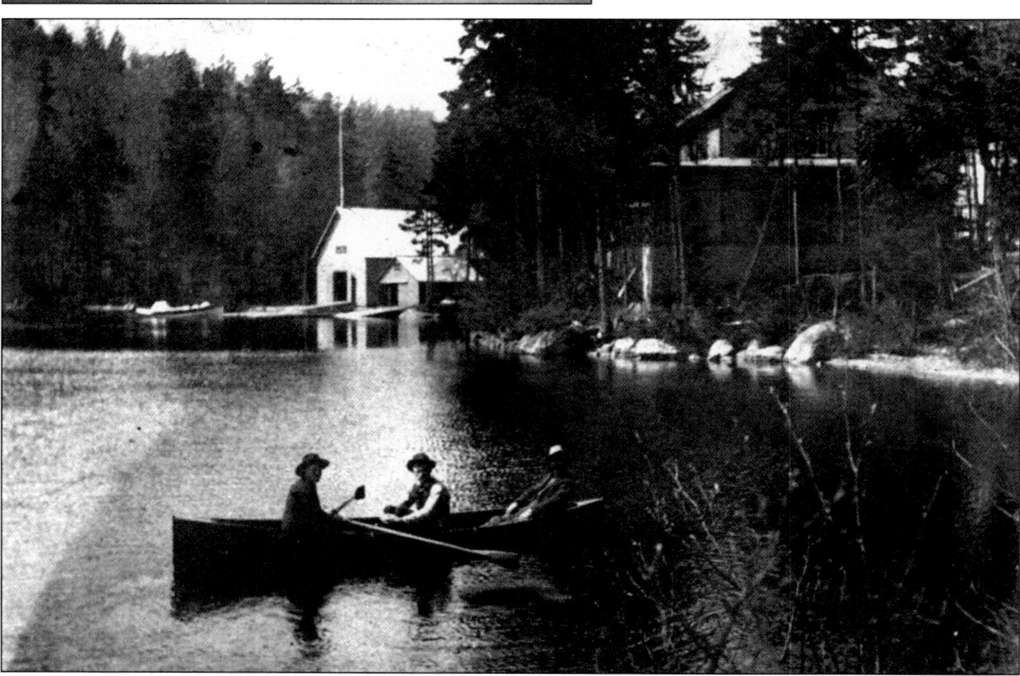

The sturdy Adirondack guide boats were in wide use on the Adirondack lakes beginning in the mid-1800s. They could easily hold three passengers and could be rowed from the end seat or the middle seat. There were two separate sets of oarlocks to hold the long guide boat oars. Rare, antique guide boats made by some of the famous builders are in great demand and bring high prices today.

Eight

Animals, Places, and Pastimes

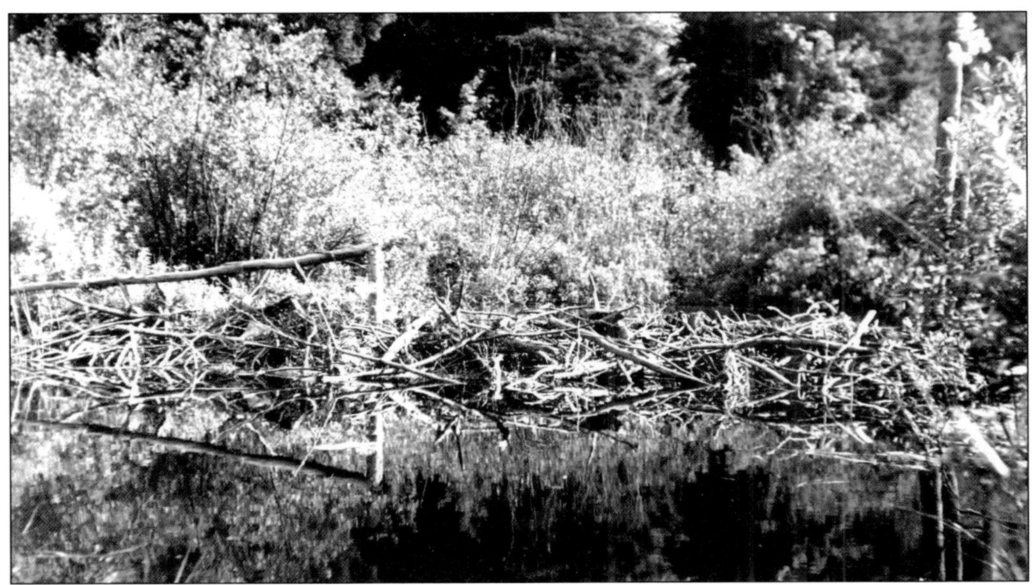

Beaver, native to Adirondack country, attracted the 17th-century trappers and hunters who sought their hides for the lucrative European market. Wars were fought over the beaver trade, and man's greed had wiped out the Adirondack beaver by the beginning of the 20th century. Beaver were brought back to the Adirondacks from Yellowstone Park, the Midwest, and Canada, and they have repopulated the Adirondacks. Beaver dams (pictured) can be seen throughout the Adirondacks.

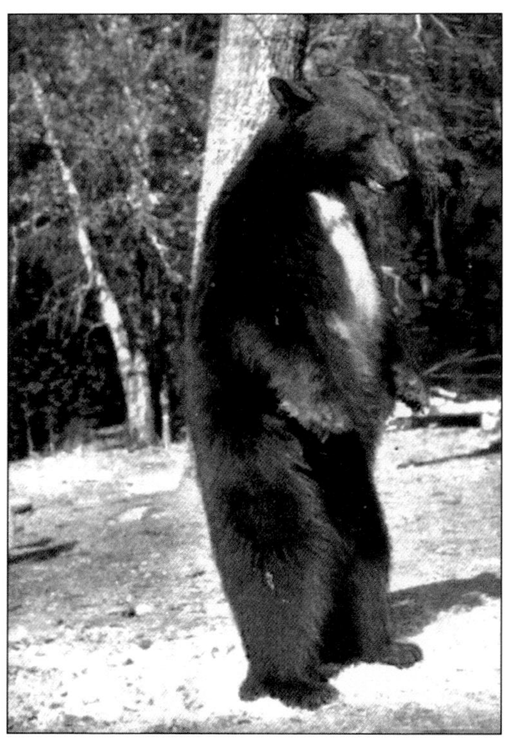

The Adirondack black bear survives well in the Adirondacks. Some estimates put the population at 8,000, although the species was near extermination in 1903. Some bears become "worldly wise" and raid camps and campsites for food. They are not aggressive unless their food or their cubs are interfered with. Adirondack bears have been the subjects of many Adirondack campfire stories dating back as far as the mid-1800s.

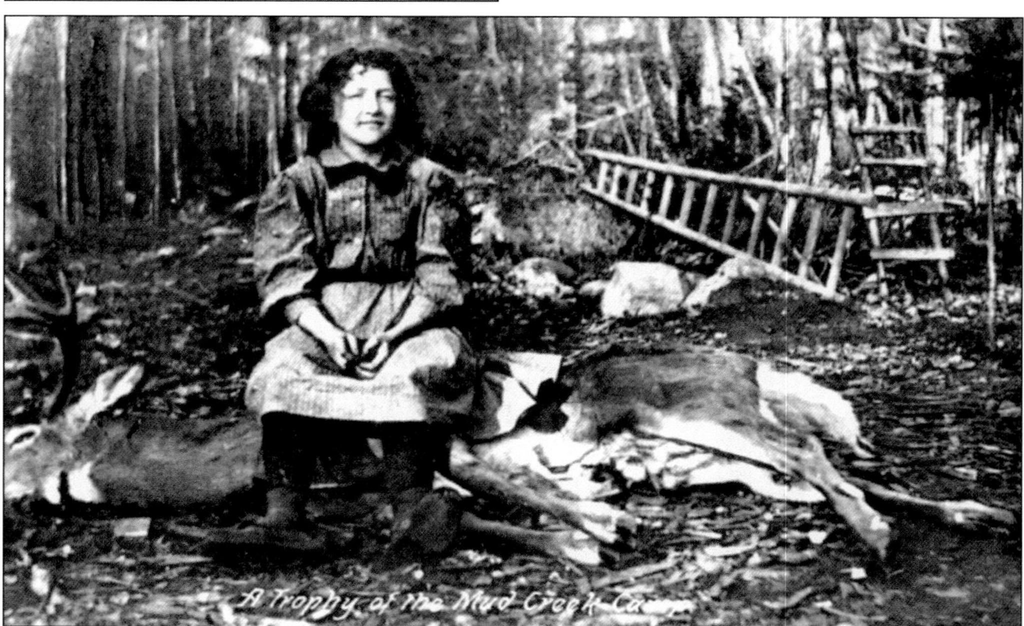

The taking of an Adirondack white-tailed deer was a part of life for those who grew up in the Adirondacks. Children accepted the annual hunt along with other needed pursuits such as planting the gardens or picking berries or searching out beehives for honey. It provided food for the family to get through the winter. This girl is all dressed up to pose with the deer taken at the Mud Lake Camp.

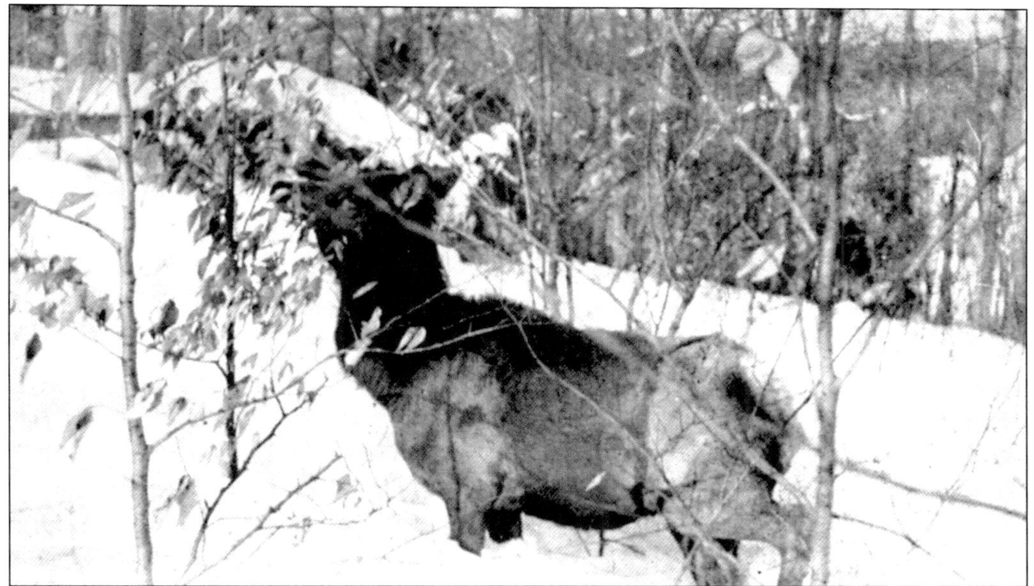

Oral history tells of herds of elk that once roamed the southern Adirondacks. Early hunters and trappers reported moose and elk in the Adirondacks. Swedish naturalist Peter Kalm reported elk in the mid-1700s near Lake George. Since the 1890s, several attempts have been made to reintroduce the elk to the Adirondacks, but none have met with success. Much like the moose, the elk may make a comeback when times are right.

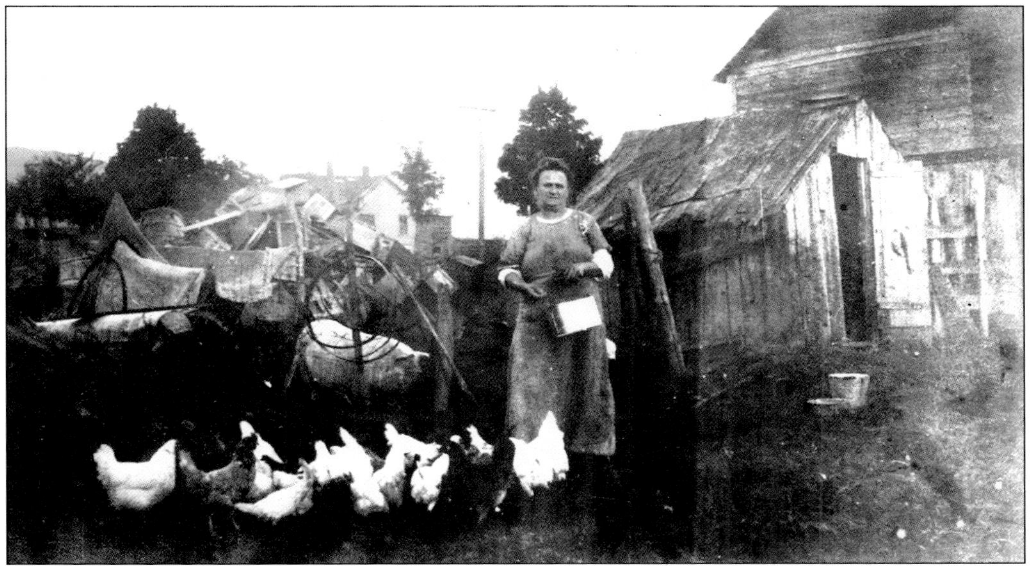

No one knows how many chickens lived inside the Adirondack Blueline (the original line drawn on a map to mark the boundary of Adirondack Park) in days gone by. Occasional references in the written history mention large chicken coops and some hotel's raising chickens to serve in their dining halls. Most settlers kept a small flock of chickens for eggs and chicken dinners. Oliver Whitman fed his chickens small fish, and when he served Sunday dinner, those "chickens tasted just like fish." Mrs. Sweet of Northville had this flock of some two dozen chickens to feed her children.

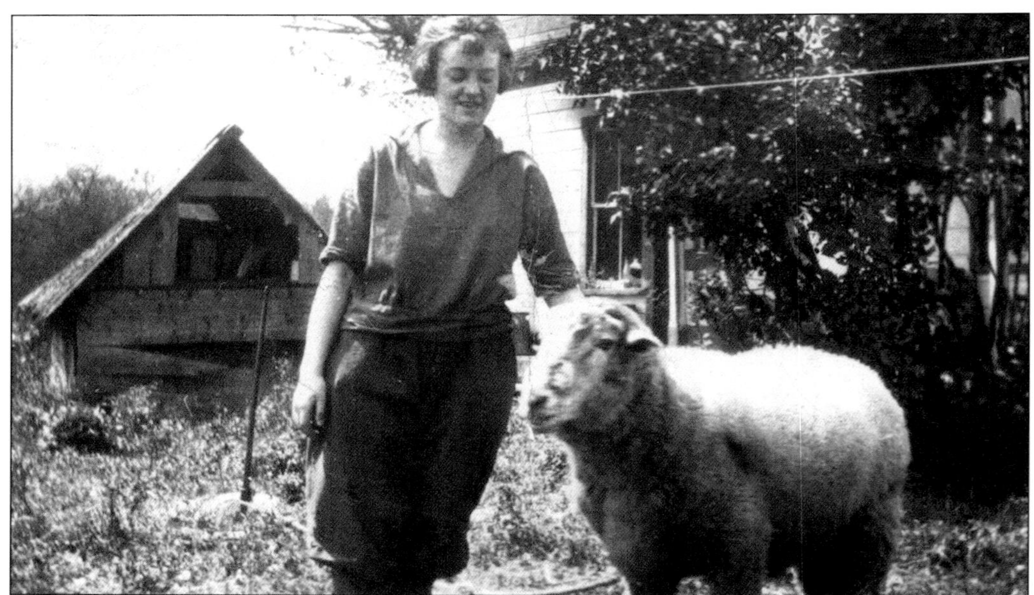

Many find it hard to believe that there were once more than one million sheep in the 12 Adirondack counties. The 1845 census confirms that million-plus total. Raising sheep provided wool for home use and for sale, as well as food for the family. Sheep tallow was used for making candles and soap, and for waterproofing Adirondack boots. Great Adirondack estates, including Hudnut's Fox Lair and Pruyn's Santanoni, raised prize sheep.

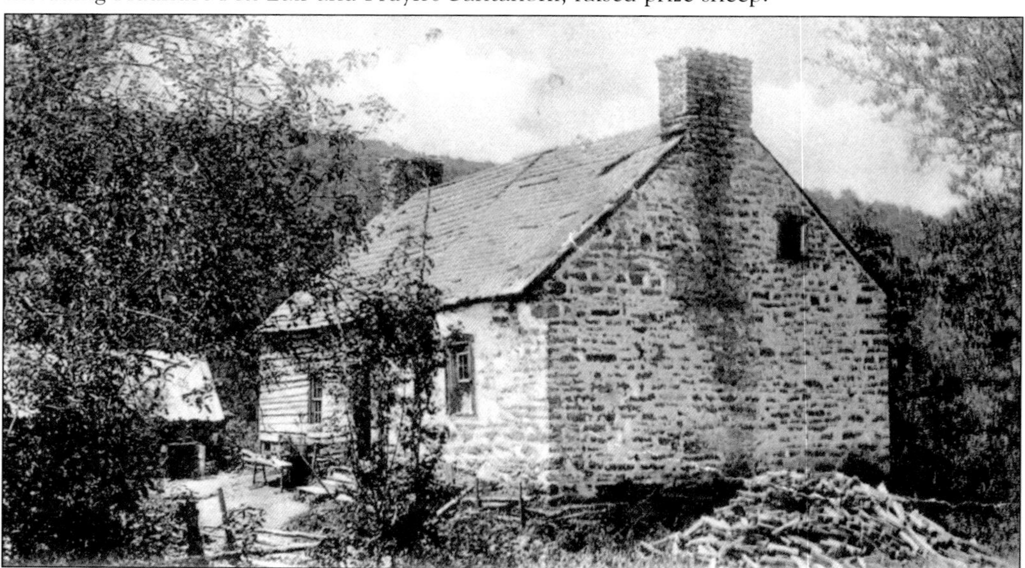

Some people can remember seeing the ruins of an old stone house on Route 30, the Adirondack Trail. Pictures of it appeared on old postcards and photographs for sale in local stores. The photographs were labeled "Old Eglin House, Wellstown Road," "1775-built by David Isdell, fell down 1930, Hope, NY," "Old house on road to Speculator," and "On the way to Wells." David Isdell bought the land in 1801 and built a house of stone with an escape tunnel for protection against marauders. Unfortunately, his youngest daughter was supposedly taken while picking berries and was never heard from again. One story told of her dying in an Indian village.

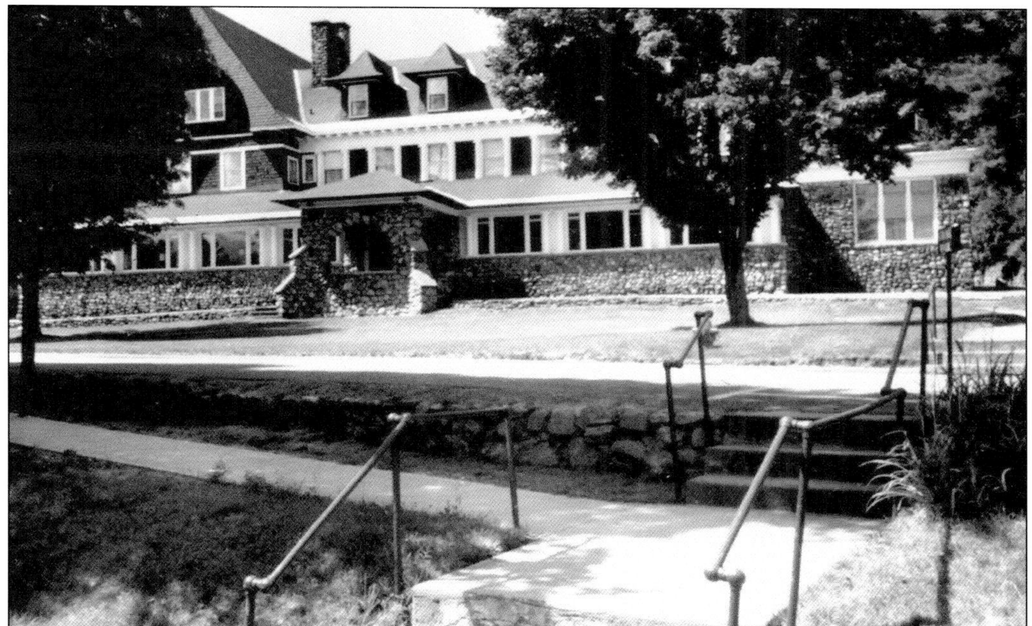

Dr. Edward Livingston Trudeau came to the Adirondacks in 1873 to die of tuberculosis, but he survived and created the world-renowned sanatorium and today's Trudeau Research Institute. His research and the healthy Adirondack climate contributed to new findings and new treatments for tuberculosis patients. The original sanatorium buildings are in use today by private groups.

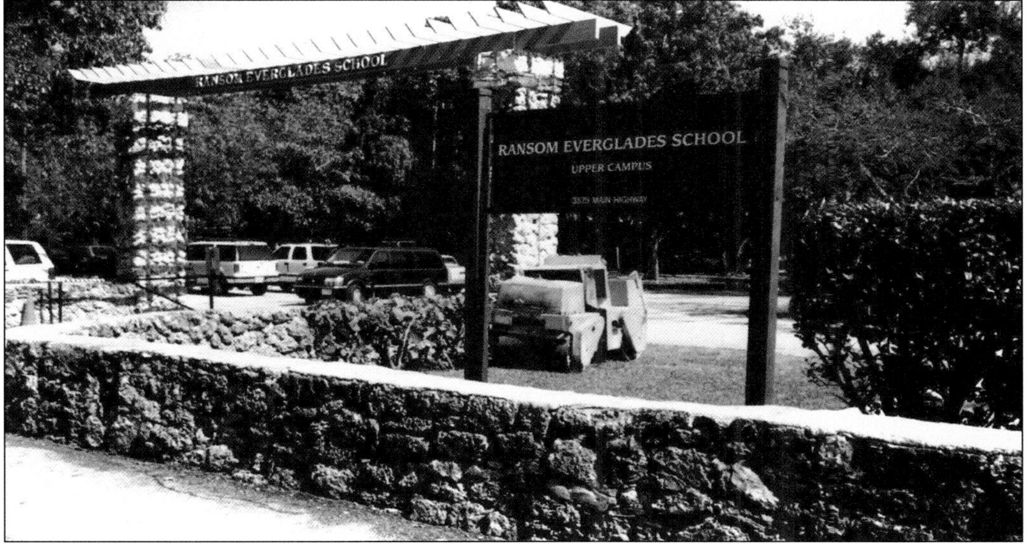

The Ransom Everglades School stands in Florida today, an offspring of the Adirondack-Florida School. Paul Ransom opened the Pine Knot School at Coconut Grove, Florida, in 1896 and, in 1903, added a fall and spring term at Meenahga Lodge near Rainbow Lake in the Adirondacks. He moved students back and forth because of his belief that better daylight conditions contributed to better learning. The Adirondack campus closed during World War II because of the lack of teachers, and it never recovered.

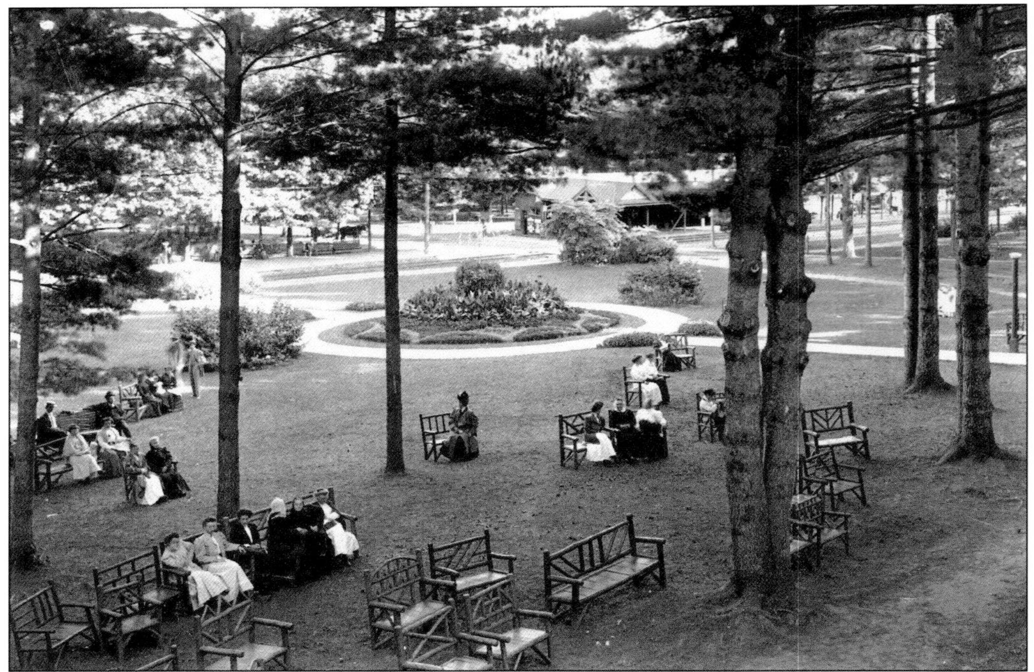

The Sacandaga Park, which began as a Methodist campground, evolved into a resort with a midway, hotels, and a railroad station. Rustic bridges, signs, fences, and furniture were featured around the well-kept grounds of the park. This is the scene in front of the Adirondack Inn.

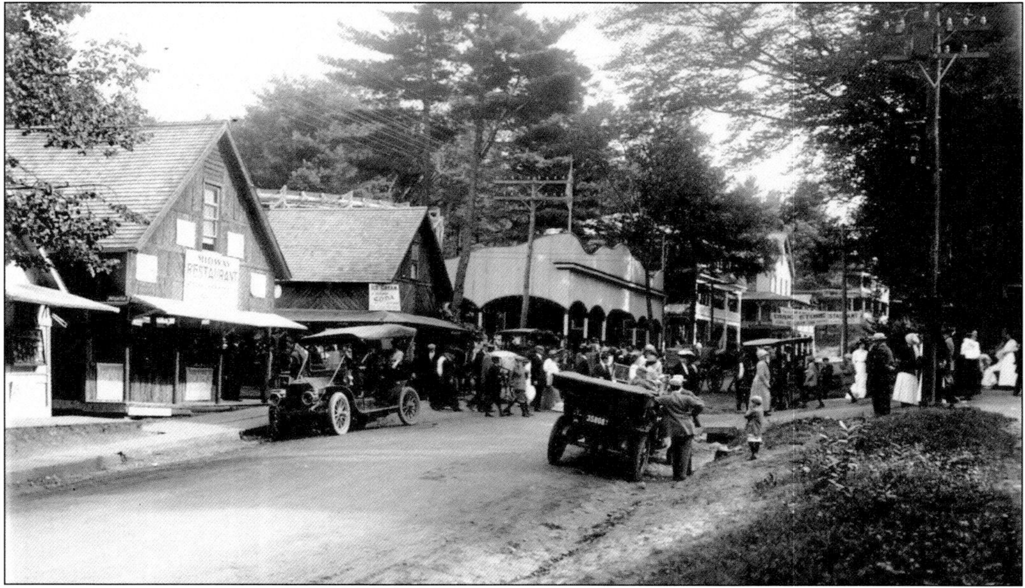

The midway at Sacandaga Park provided recreation for thousands in the southern Adirondacks who came by train or car to the "Gem of the Adirondacks" at the beginning of the 20th century. When the Great Sacandaga Lake (reservoir) was dammed in 1930, the popular park was torn down and closed. Note the roller coaster towering over the other buildings. Nothing remains today of the amusement park except the skating rink, which is privately owned.